IMAGES
of America

KNITTERS OF NEEDHAM

On the Cover: The staff of Moseley and Company pose on September 19, 1911, in front of the mill with a horse-drawn float advertising the company's Tiny-Wear products during a celebration of Needham's 200th birthday. (Needham Historical Society.)

IMAGES
of America

KNITTERS OF NEEDHAM

Chaim M. Rosenberg and
the Needham Historical Society

ARCADIA
PUBLISHING

ISBN 978-0-7385-9109-4

Published by Arcadia Publishing
Charleston, South Carolina

Printed in the United States of America

Library of Congress Control Number: 2011932836

For all general information, please contact Arcadia Publishing:
Telephone 843-853-2070
Fax 843-853-0044
E-mail sales@arcadiapublishing.com
For customer service and orders:
Toll-Free 1-888-313-2665

Visit us on the Internet at www.arcadiapublishing.com

CONTENTS

ACKNOWLEDGMENTS

The Needham Historical Society has, for many years, assembled the stories, documents, and images of our town, which celebrated its 300th birthday in 2011. Gloria Greis, the executive director of the Needham Historical Society, has shared with me her vast knowledge and helped me select images from the society's large collection that best tell the story of the knitters of Needham. Thanks also to Mark Gluesing, president of the society, for supporting my wish to tell the story of the English knitters who settled in Highlandville, now called Needham Heights. Unless otherwise noted, images are from the collection of the Needham Historical Society.

The Leonard Dawson Collection of the Needham Free Public Library comprises some 700 photographs and images of Needham. I am most grateful to Ann MacFate, director of the library, for obtaining permission for me to use a large number of these photographs in the book. The library archivist, Danielle Tawa, simplified my search to select the most suitable images from the Leonard Dawson Collection.

Many of the historical details recorded in this book come from the *History of Needham, Massachusetts, 1711–1911*, by George Kuhn Clarke, published by the University Press in Cambridge, Massachusetts.

My thanks go to Linda, John, and Colin Reed, as well as to Adrienne Rosenberg and David Rosenberg for their technical help. Most of all, my thanks and love to my wife, Dawn, who has read and corrected my prose and supported my efforts to tell stories.

I am proud to live in Needham and am delighted for this opportunity to write the history of the English knitters who settled in the town during the 19th century. They came poor, worked hard, and brought prosperity to themselves and to Needham, their adopted town.

INTRODUCTION

Arriving in 1833, John Turner was the first of the English knitters to settle in the village of Needham, Massachusetts. He set the example for many of his countrymen by using the hand and foot operated knitting machines they brought with them. The Civil War gave a great boost to the American knitting industry as the government bought huge quantities of underwear, gloves, shirts, and socks. With the coming of peace and a fast-growing population, the American knitwear industry expanded. The most successful of the English knitters moved from their knitting frames to mills and power machinery. The knitters brought with them their Midland accents, manner of dress, religious practices, love of cricket, and above all, their desire to succeed in the New World.

By 1890, the town of Needham had 32 knitting companies, both large and small, employing hundreds of workers. The knitting mill owners became prominent men of the town, contributing greatly to its growth and progress. They served as selectmen and on the school committee, helped build the town library, and developed land for commercial and residential use. Their mills provided employment for hundreds of immigrants coming from Ireland, Italy, and Canada. Many of these mill workers made Needham their home.

William Carter, born in Alfreton, Derbyshire, England, was by far the most successful of the Needham knitters. His company continued to expand and absorb workers from other mills. In the mid-20th century, Carter's began to move its manufacturing from Needham to mills in the South. Carter's kept its administrative offices in the town until 1989, but the local manufacture of knitwear had long since come to an end. With the opening of Route 128, Needham has largely changed from a manufacturing to a dormitory town with easy access to Boston. *Knitters of Needham* tells how these poor but skilled and enterprising immigrants put their mark on a small Massachusetts town.

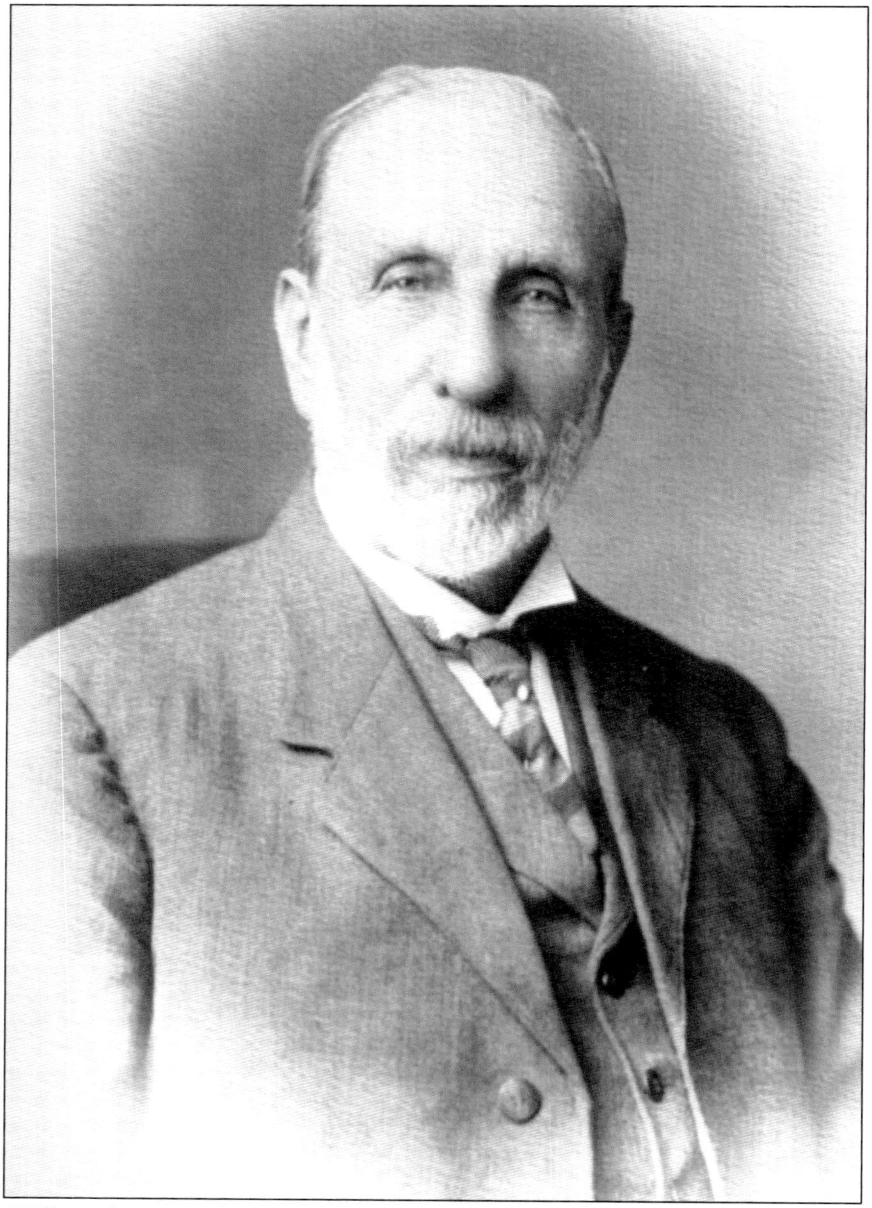

In 1830, William Carter was born in Alfreton, Derbyshire, where he apprenticed as a frame knitter. The industrial revolution in England destroyed home craft industries, driving the knitters to seek work in factories and leaving many unemployed. With 10 shillings remaining in his pocket after buying a ticket, Carter sailed for the United States, arriving on January 28, 1857. Helped by Alexander Lynes, William Moseley, and other friends from back home, he settled in Needham in 1860. With borrowed money, he bought a knitting frame and was ready to start work as an independent knitter. Later, he formed a partnership with John and Mark Lee as Lee, Carter, and Company. When the Lee brothers left, it became the William Carter Company, and Carter expanded production with power machinery. In 1910, William Carter provided the capital to establish the Needham Trust Company. He served as company president with William Moseley as vice president of the bank. William Carter became the best known and most successful of the knitters who came to Needham. He died in 1918 and was buried in the Needham cemetery.

One

The Knitting Industry Comes to America

Knitting is the process of intertwining a single thread into fabric through the use of needles. Hand knitted socks, mittens, underwear, and caps eased the chill of winter, and the practice developed into a major cottage industry in the Midlands of England. The industry was given a boost after 1589, when the Reverend William Lee of Calverton, Nottinghamshire, invented the framework knitting machine that imitated hand movements but worked much faster.

Some 15 miles away and over a century and a half later, Jedediah Strutt advanced the knitting frame to a higher level. Strutt formed a partnership with Sir Richard Arkwright to build a water-powered spinning mill to meet growing demand by the knitters for cotton yarn. The Midlands towns of Leicester, Derby, Nottingham, and nearby small towns derived much of their wealth as the leading knitting region of England. By the start of the 19th century, 45,000 framework knitters worked from home or in small workshops, with an additional 100,000 employed in sewing, mending, and finishing the garments. Using silk, cotton, or wool, they made socks, mittens, gloves, and underwear, earning barely 15 shillings for 60 hours of work a week.

The power machinery of the British industrial revolution took knitting out of the hands of the home knitters and into the mills, leading to overproduction, falling prices, widespread unemployment, and social unrest. Many thousands of people in the Midlands migrated to the United States for opportunities to practice their home craft and make a living. These Englishmen provided America with knitting skills, most of them settling in Pennsylvania and New York, with Massachusetts as the third leading state in the knitting trade.

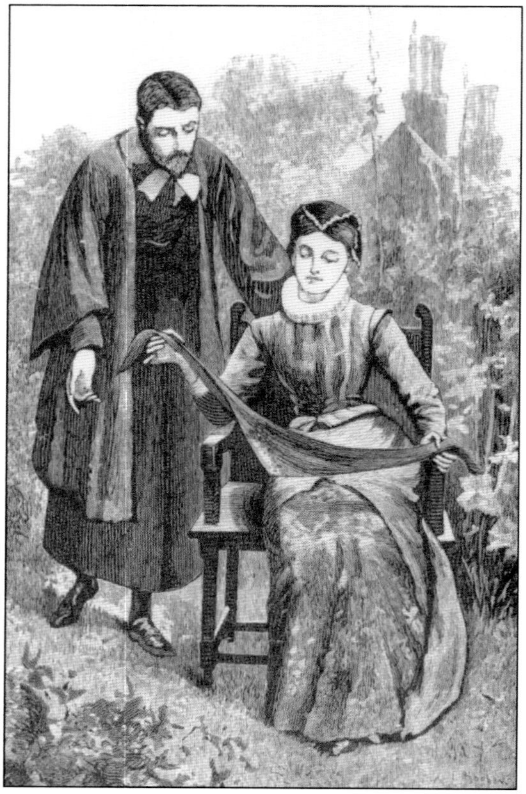

William Lee (1554–1614) of Calverton, Nottinghamshire, graduated from Christ College, Cambridge. After watching his wife doing her hand knitting, he invented the hand and foot operated framework machine to knit stockings in 1589. William Lee's machine was the foundation of the knitting industry in the Midlands of England.

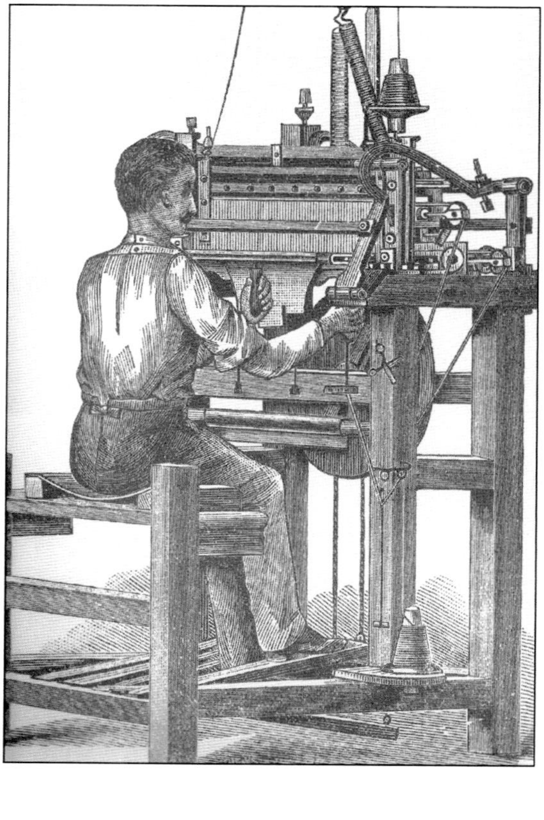

Pictured is William Lee's stocking frame. With 20 needles to the inch, Lee's machine worked far more quickly than knitting by hand. Seated for hours at the hand-and-foot-operated knitting frame, a worker eked out a paltry living making socks, leggings, gloves, and underwear.

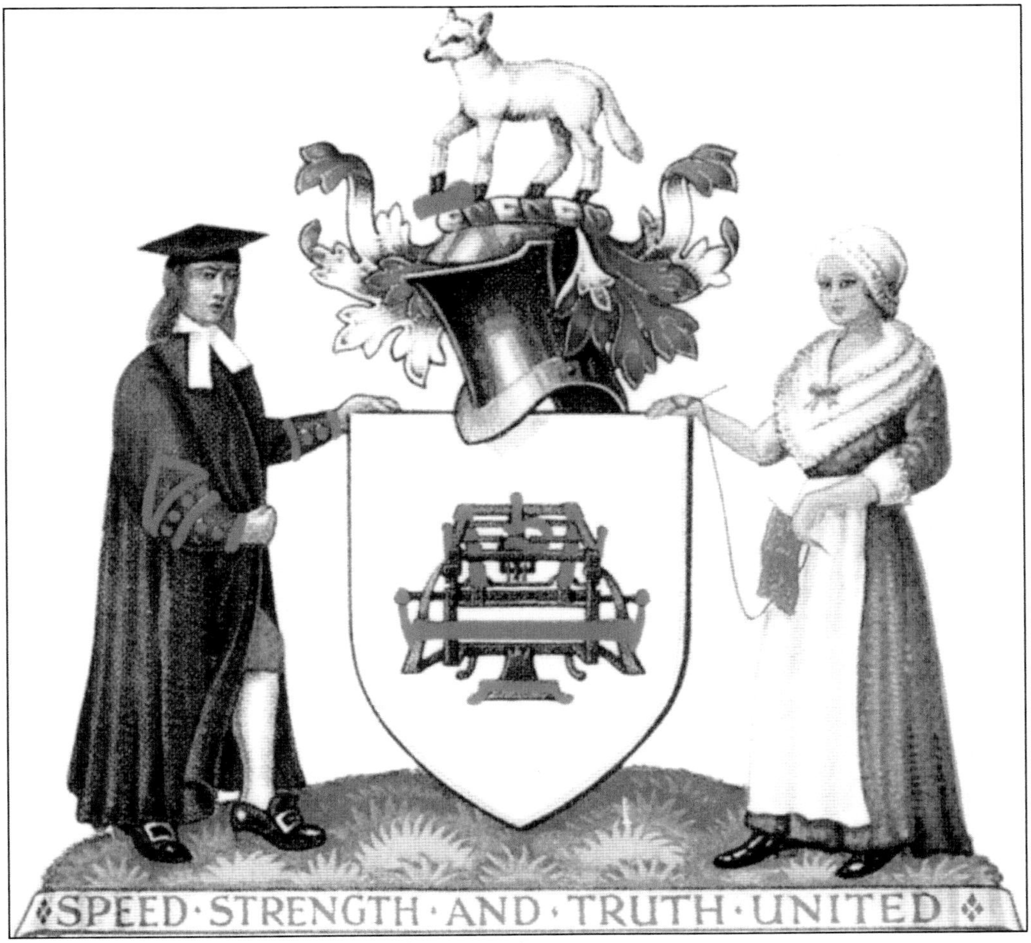

Shown are the arms of the Society of Framework Knitters. The fraternity traces its origins to 1589, when William Lee invented a method of knitting by machine. Charles II incorporated the society in 1663, and its motto reads, "Speed Strength and Truth United." The society sought to control the knitting trade, protect the interests of its members, and train the next generations of knitters.

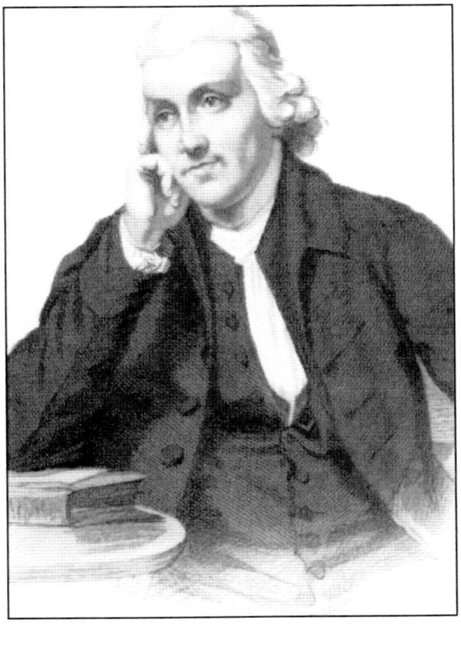

Born near Alfreton, Derbyshire, Jedediah Strutt (1728–1797) improved on the stocking frame in 1758 with an attachment known as the Derby Rib. This advance greatly increased the number of knitters competing for work. With Richard Arkwright as his partner, Strutt built a water-powered cotton-spinning mill to meet the fast growing demand for spun cotton. Several of the knitters who settled in Needham, such as William Carter, came from the same part of the Midlands as Jedediah Strutt and had used his machine.

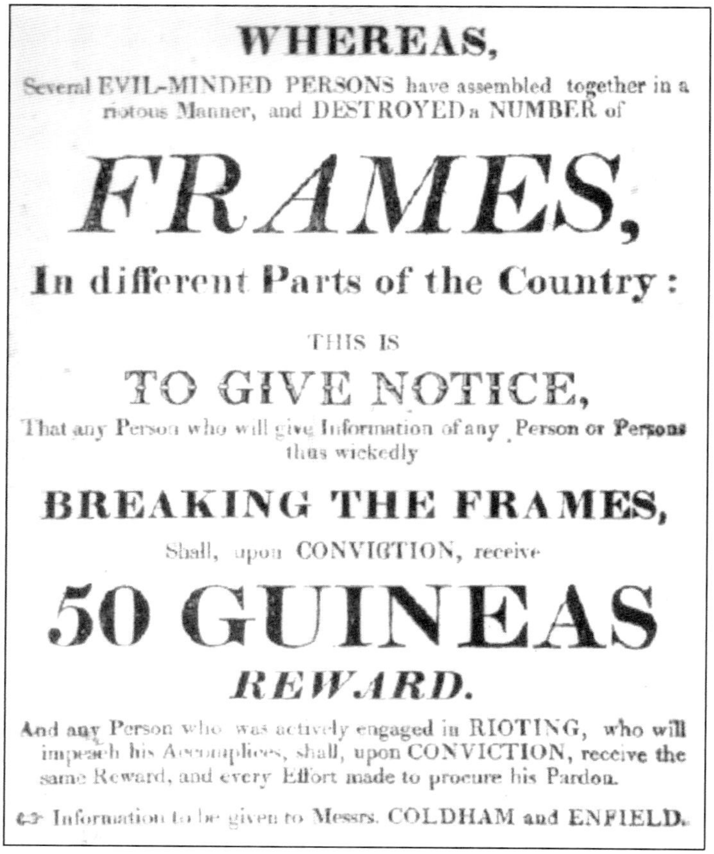

WHEREAS,

Several EVIL-MINDED PERSONS have assembled together in a riotous Manner, and DESTROYED a NUMBER of

FRAMES,

In different Parts of the Country:

THIS IS

TO GIVE NOTICE,

That any Person who will give Information of any Person or Persons thus wickedly

BREAKING THE FRAMES,

Shall, upon CONVICTION, receive

50 GUINEAS

REWARD.

And any Person who was actively engaged in RIOTING, who will impeach his Accomplices, shall, upon CONVICTION, receive the same Reward, and every Effort made to procure his Pardon.

☞ Information to be given to Messrs. COLDHAM and ENFIELD.

Reacting to the great expansion of knitting by machine, the Luddite movement destroyed knitting frames in factories. The British government responded by enforcing steep fines, imprisonment, deportation, and even death by hanging. The industrial revolution and the use of machines powered by water or steam further eroded the livelihood of the home knitters, forcing many to emigrate. This notice of reward dates to 1811.

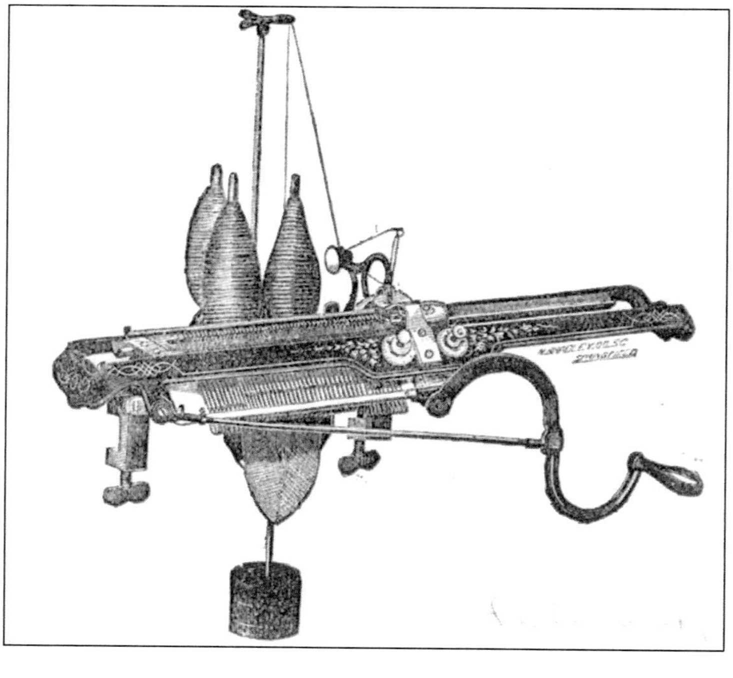

Until the 1850s, hand-operated knitting frames were the tools of the trade. In 1867, Isaac W. Lamb of Michigan designed a small knitting machine for home use. The Lamb knitting machine, which was 26 inches long and nine inches high, could not stop the transfer of work to the factories. By 1870, large machines powered by steam could yield 320 dozen pairs of socks in a week.

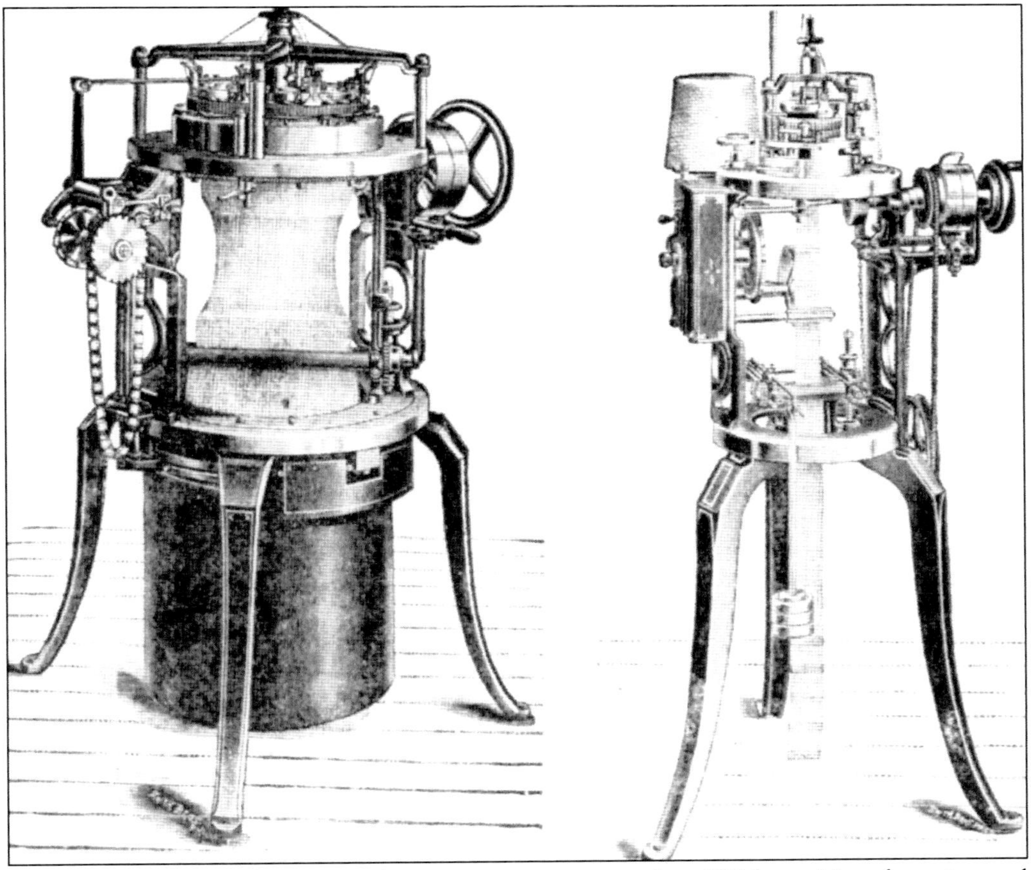

By the start of the 20th century, American companies, such as Wildman Manufacturing and the Branson Machine Company, were making efficient knitting machines like those used in the Needham knitting mills. At left is an automatic body machine, and at right is a hosiery ribber. These knitting machines could be adjusted to create different and complicated patterns. Their introduction greatly increased the output of the mills. These knitting machines demonstrated the shift from steam to electric power.

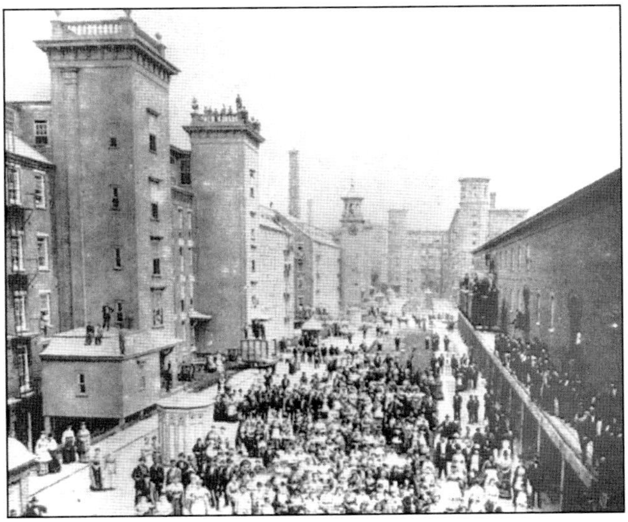

In 1815, the industrial revolution arrived in the United States when Francis Cabot Lowell opened the Boston Manufacturing Company in Waltham, Massachusetts. The company was built to spin cotton into thread and weave it into textiles using machines powered by the flow of the Charles River. In Lowell, the quickly flowing Merrimack River powered many mills.

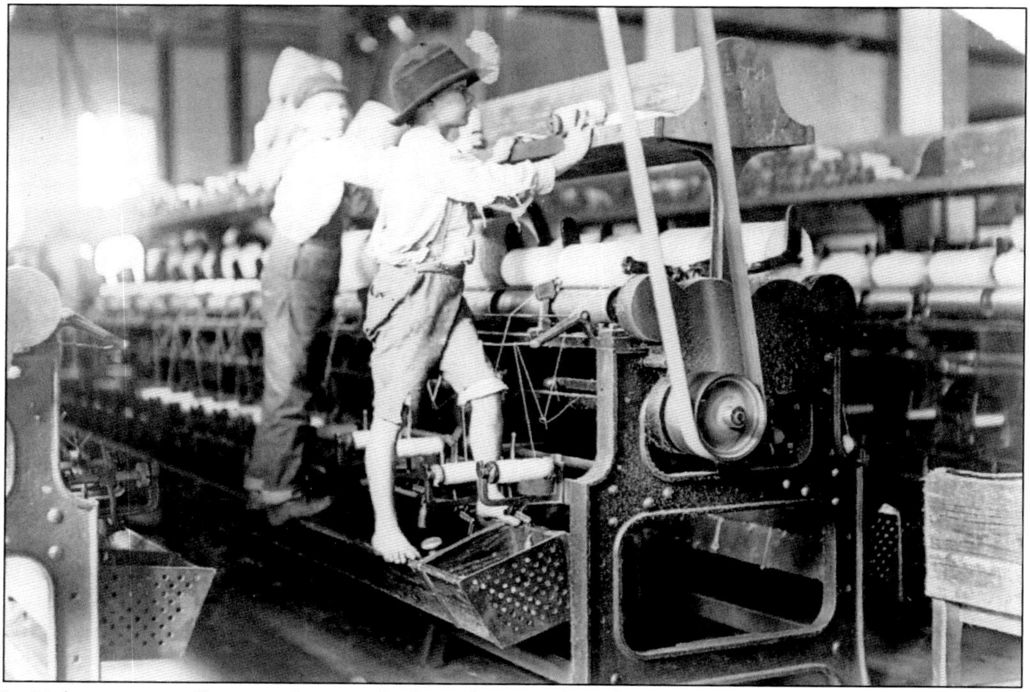

In 19th-century mills, young boys worked a 60-hour week for $1 collecting full bobbins of spun cotton. Scottish-born Andrew Carnegie started work as a bobbin boy and went on to become America's great steel tycoon. In 1904, Carnegie funded the Needham Public Library at Highlandville.

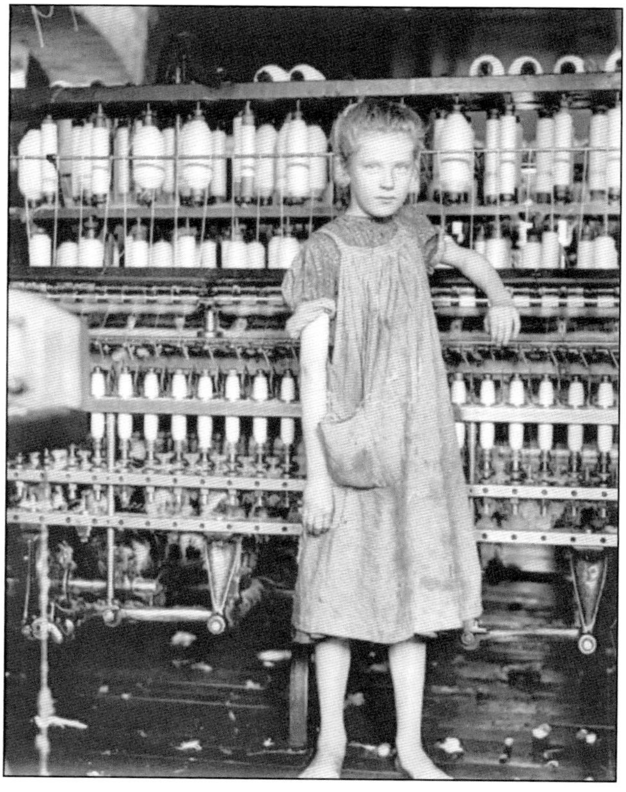

Young children with nimble fingers were much desired in the early mills. The employment of children in factories continued well into the 20th century, ending in 1938 with the Fair Labor Standards Act. The early American spinning and weaving mills were built along rivers to use the waterpower. Knitting mills were established later and from the start used steam power. Knitting mills were built largely in the center of towns, near the railroad stations.

The mill workers, mostly young women, worked 10 to 12 hours a day with the constant clanging and whirling of power machinery. Despite the monotony of their work, many remained intellectually curious and eager to find expression through literature and art.

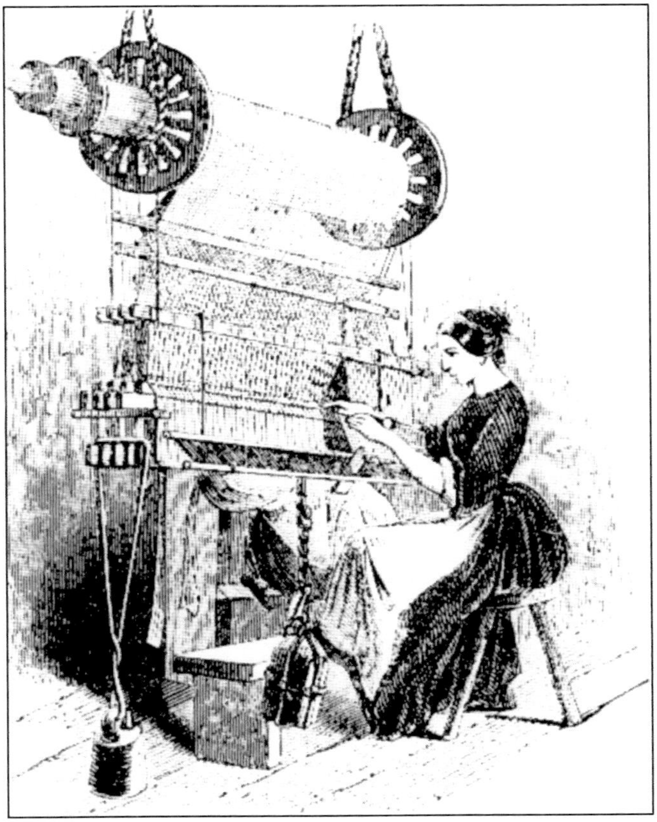

Each of the great mills in Lowell and in other textile cities contained hundreds of power looms. The mill workers supervised the heavy machines under conditions of dim light, poor air circulation, and the constant clanging of the machinery. Knitting was the last section of the textile industry to move from handwork to mechanical power. Knitting mills were built close to the railroads, which carried the coal needed to generate steam power.

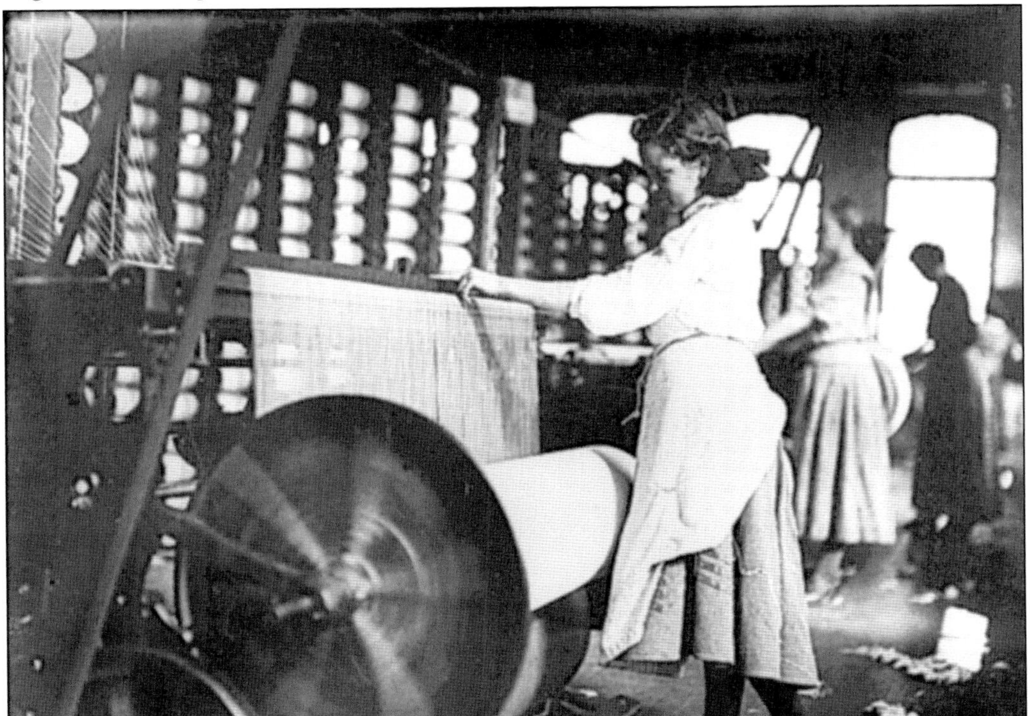

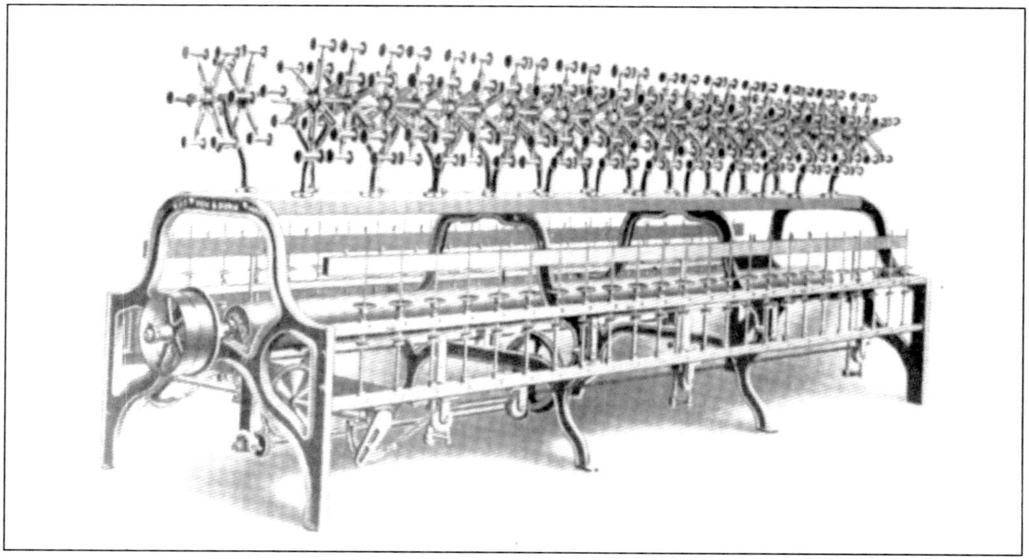

By 1880, the framework knitter who worked at home was fast disappearing as the knitwear industry moved into factories, which were using power machinery. These are examples of the heavy machinery made for American knitting mills in the late 19th century. Draper Corporation of Hopedale, Massachusetts; Saco and Pettee of Saco, Maine; Crompton and Knowles of Worcester, Massachusetts; Easton and Burnham of Pawtucket, Rhode Island; Lowell Machine Shop of Lowell, Massachusetts; and many other machine shops were making looms and knitting machines for mills in Needham and across the nation. Machinery greatly increased the efficiency of the knitting mills, leading to overproduction and intense competition.

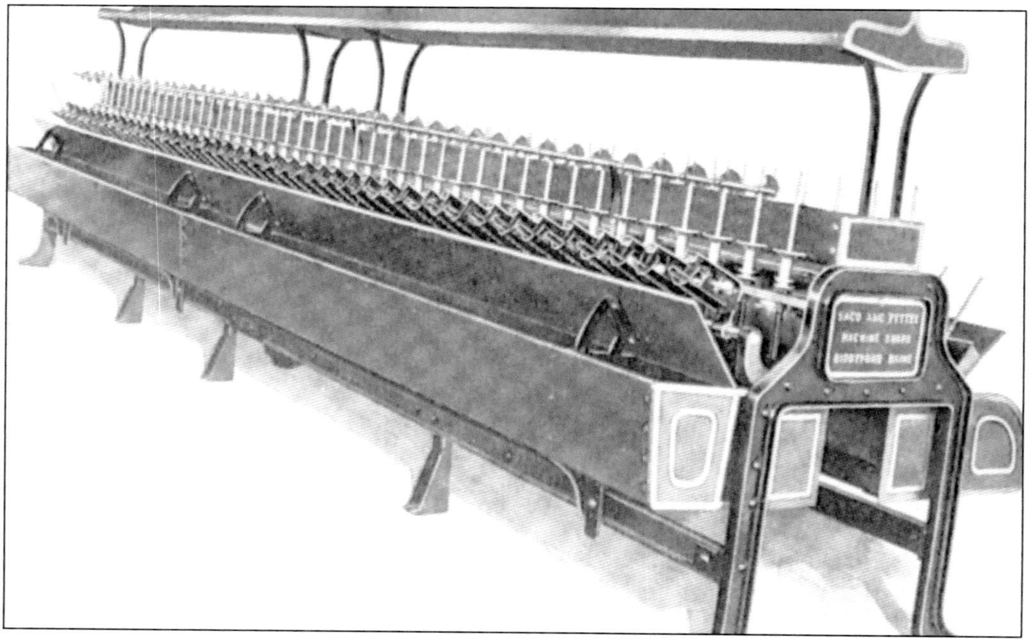

Two

Old Needham

On November 5, 1711, a total of 250 residents split off from Dedham, Massachusetts, to establish a separate town called Needham, named after Needham Market in Suffolk, England. Needham was then split up into two villages: East Needham, which was centered where Central Avenue meets Nehoiden Street; and West Needham, which, in 1881, separated to become the town of Wellesley. The early residents raised cattle, engaged in farming, and took advantage of water from the Charles River, which bordered the town on three sides.

During the Revolutionary War, Col. William McIntosh served with distinction, but sadly, five other Needham men lost their lives. With the coming of independence, the town settled back to farming and, by 1800, Needham had 247 mostly small farms. Few in the town were wealthy and most were self-employed but able to make a decent living. As everywhere else in Massachusetts, industry arrived in Needham in the early 19th century. In 1815, Rufus Ellis built a cotton mill powered by the waters of the Charles River at Upper Falls. Needham had several factories making hats, window sashes, hinges, paper, and nails.

The Civil War disrupted the calm of the 2,700 inhabitants of Needham. During the war, 282 of the town's menfolk enlisted to do battle to keep the Union whole. A number of them, like private Ezra Newell Fuller, paid with their lives.

The coming of the railroad linking Needham to Boston brought profound changes. The town center moved to Great Plain Avenue, which was close to the railroad station. Electric streetlights came in 1893, soon to be followed by electric-powered street trolleys. One trolley line ran from Wellesley along Great Plain Avenue to end at the railroad tracks. A second line started on the southern side of the railroad tracks and ran along Dedham Avenue to Dedham. A third line started in Natick via Chestnut Street, ran along Highland Avenue into Newton, and all the way to Watertown Square to link up with trolleys heading for Boston. By the 1920s, the streetcars were gone, replaced by automobiles and buses that were powered by gasoline.

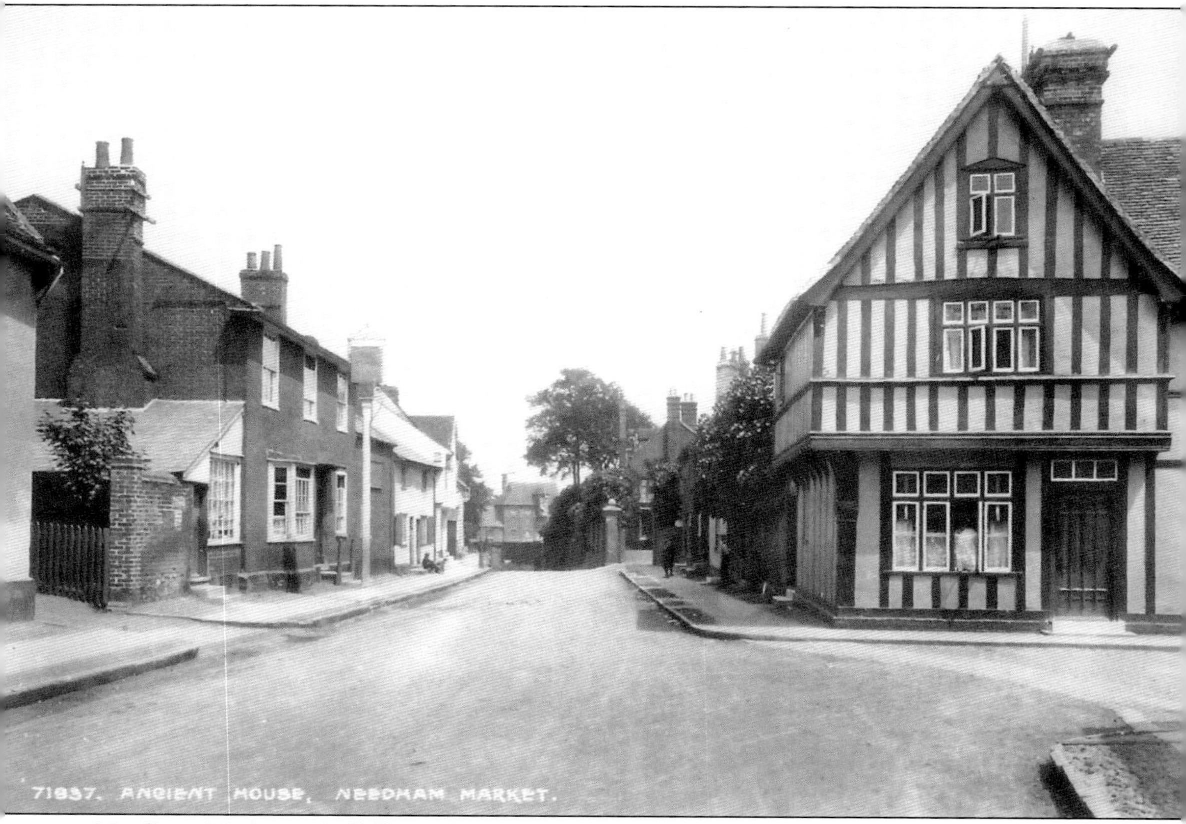

Needham Market in Suffolk, England, was established as early as the 13th century. Its prosperity depended on weaving and wool combing. From 1663 to 1685, the plague isolated the town and killed two thirds of its people, but the coming of the railroad in 1846 connected Needham Market to Cambridge and beyond, restoring its vitality. The town is known for its 15th-century parish church. In 1711, Joseph Dudley, the royal governor of Massachusetts, agreed to allow the residents of North Dedham to form a separate town and named it Needham, after the English town. Dudley was born in Roxbury, Massachusetts, and attended Harvard College. There is also a Needham in Norfolk, England.

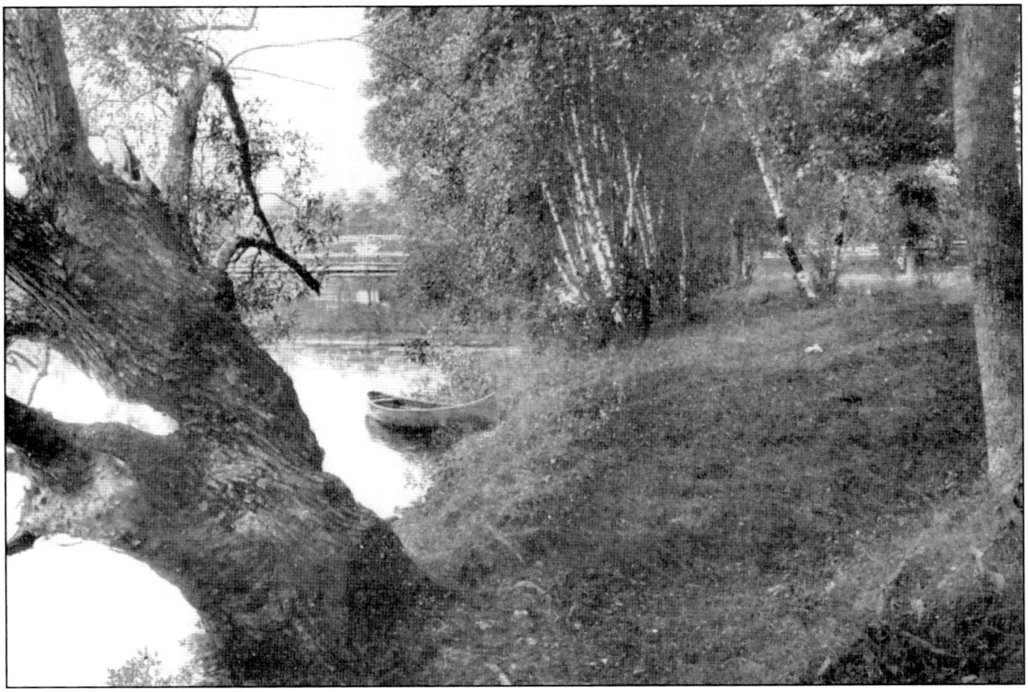

The town of Needham, Massachusetts, is largely surrounded by the Charles River. The river flows gently, except at Upper Falls and at Charles River Village, where the falls were harnessed to provide power for early industries in the town, such as gristmills, paper mills, and cotton mills.

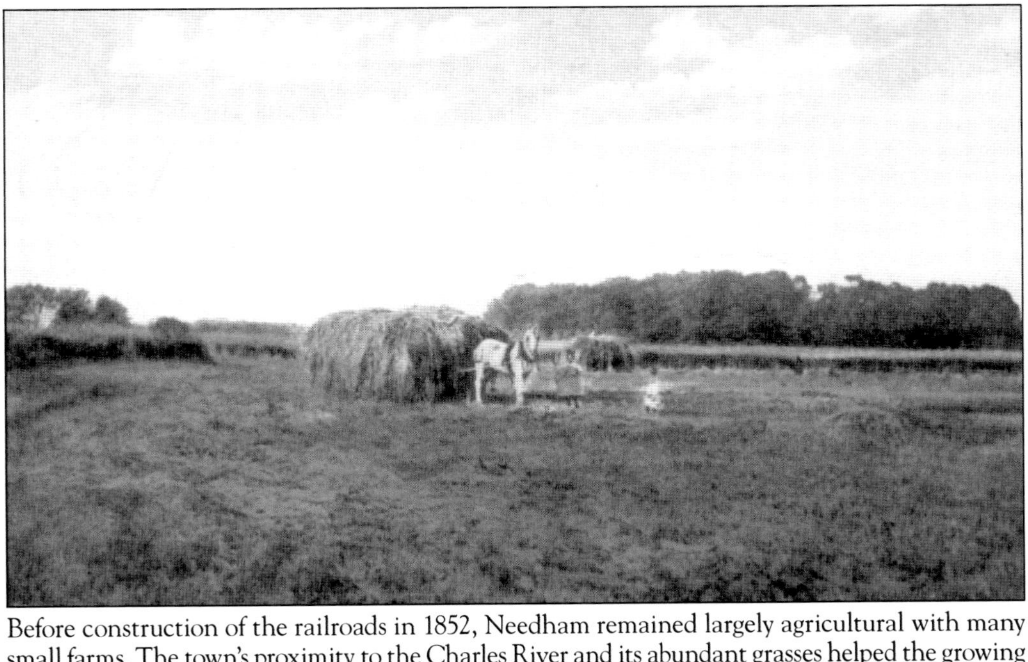

Before construction of the railroads in 1852, Needham remained largely agricultural with many small farms. The town's proximity to the Charles River and its abundant grasses helped the growing of crops and raising of cattle. This image shows haying in the meadows of the Great Plain.

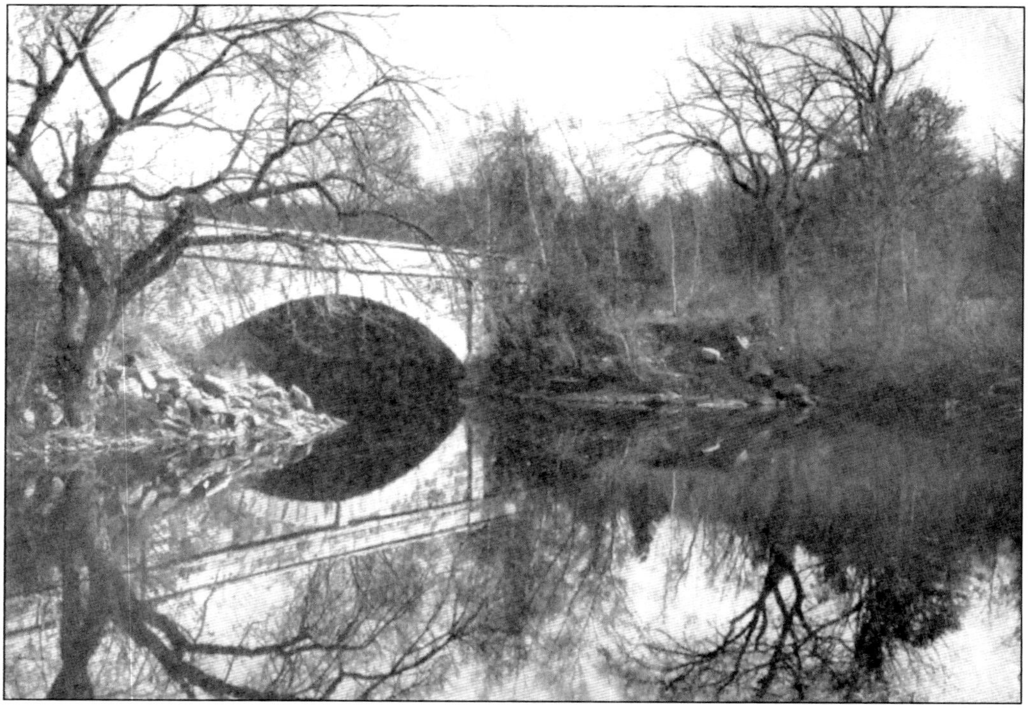

Built in 1877, the single-arch Lyon's Bridge gracefully spans the Charles River and connects Needham to Dedham at Greendale Avenue. The Lyon family owned much of the abutting land. The bridge cost $10,000 and was built by contractor William H. Ward.

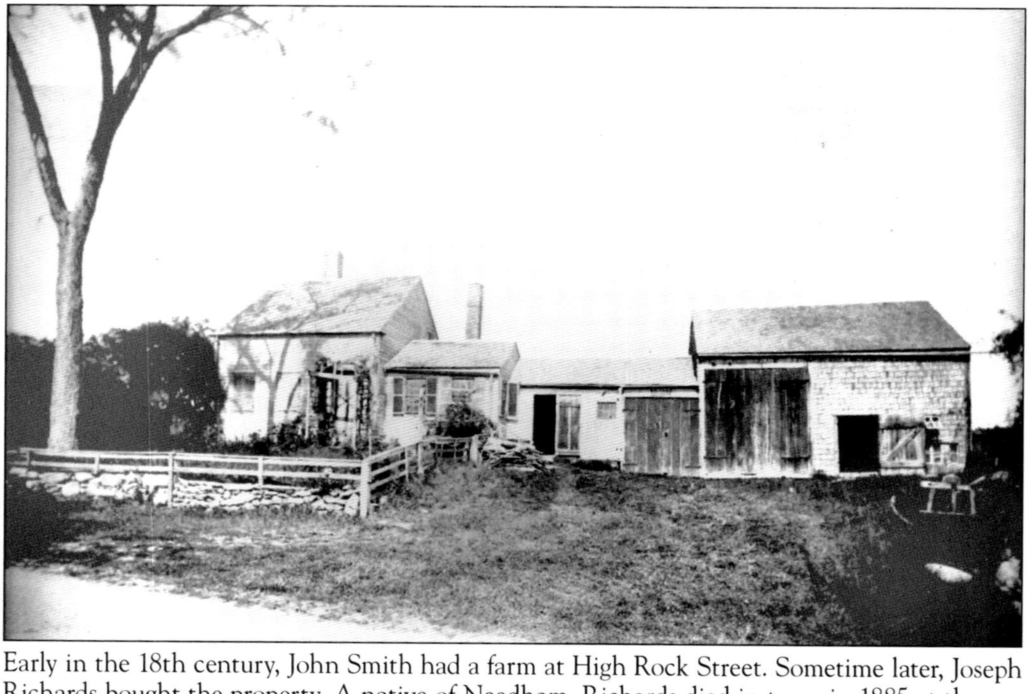

Early in the 18th century, John Smith had a farm at High Rock Street. Sometime later, Joseph Richards bought the property. A native of Needham, Richards died in town in 1885 at the age of 87. This photograph shows the Richards house and stable on High Rock Street around 1880. (Leonard Dawson Collection of the Needham Free Public Library.)

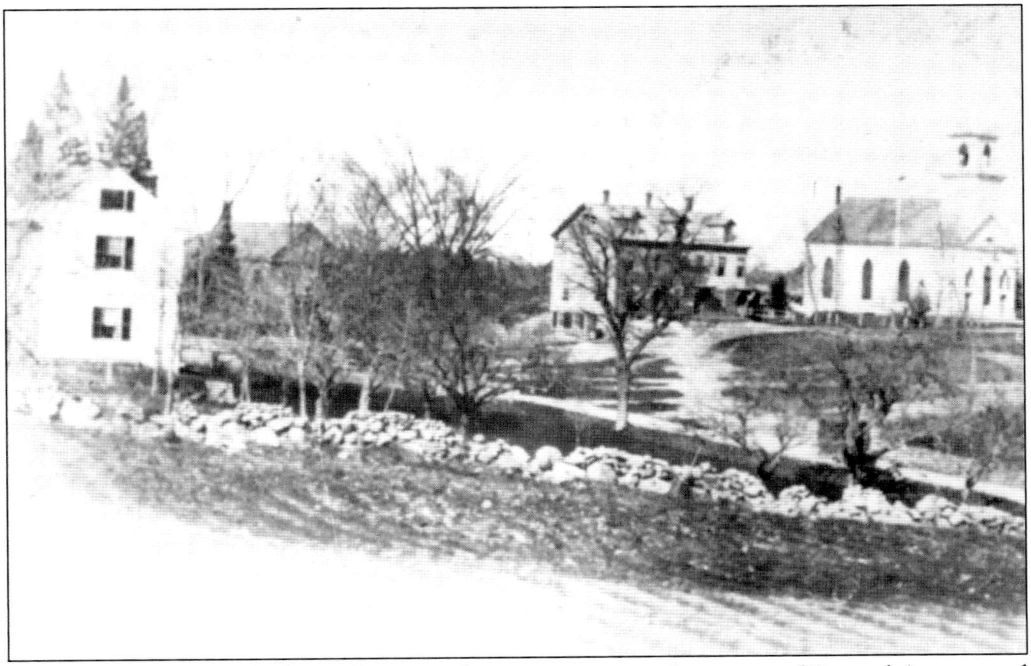

This c. 1870 photograph shows the original town center near the corner of Central Avenue and Nehoiden Street. This area lost its importance when the new town center, with shops and town offices, was established around the Needham railroad station.

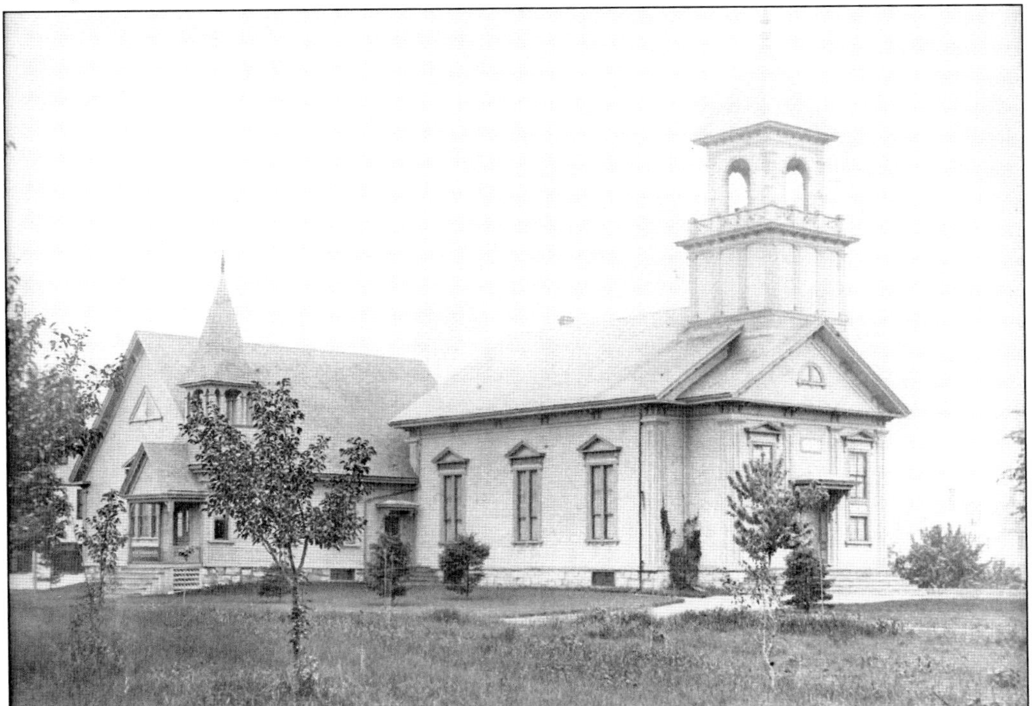

With the shift of the town center, the First Parish Church was moved in 1879 from its original site at the corner of Central Avenue and Nehoiden Street to its present site on Dedham Avenue off Great Plain Avenue. (Leonard Dawson Collection of the Needham Free Public Library.)

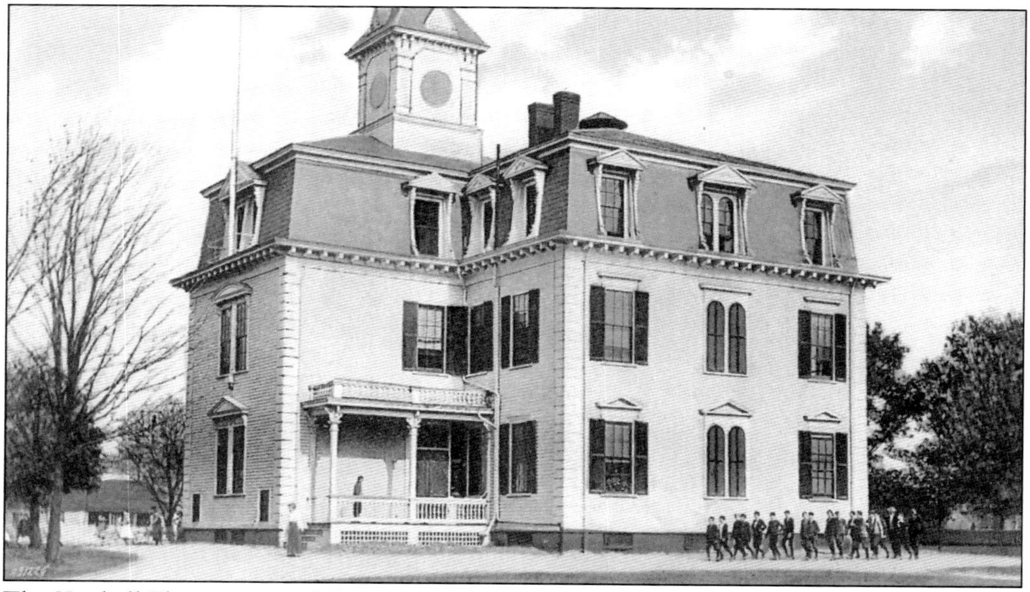

The Kimball Elementary and Grammar School, built in 1871, stood at the corner of Chestnut and School Streets. It was named for the Reverend Daniel Kimball, an 1837 graduate of Harvard University and a leading educator of his time. The Kimball school shares the architectural design of the first Avery school in Highlandville, built in 1869. (Leonard Dawson Collection of the Needham Free Public Library.)

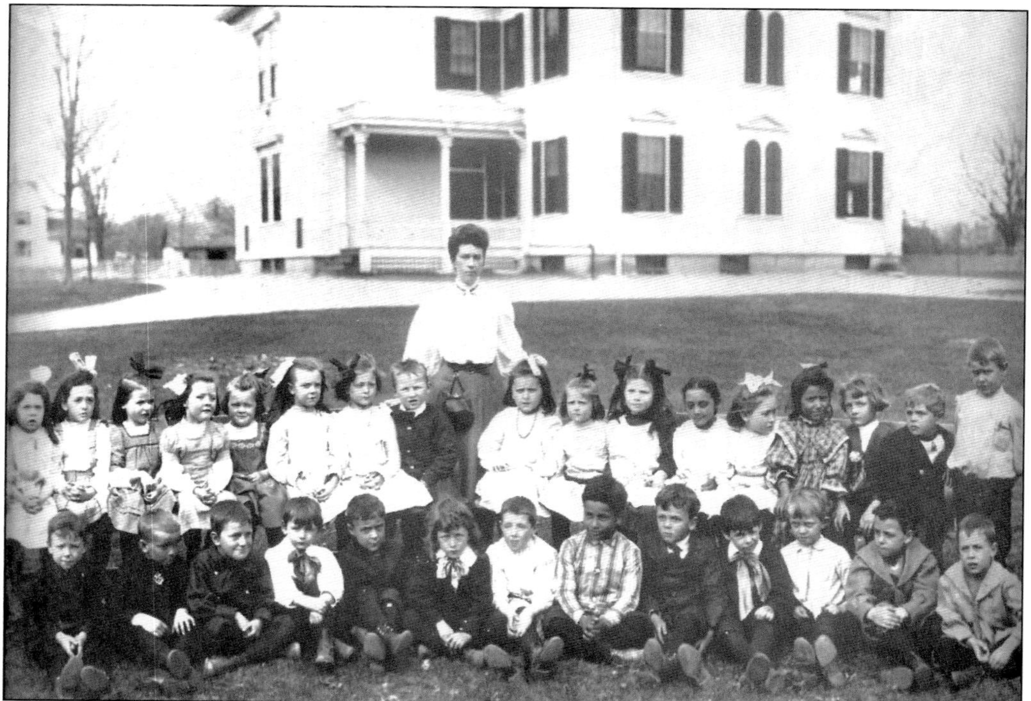

The Kimball Elementary and Grammar School class is pictured around 1910. At this time, a total of 896 children between the ages of five and 15, including 468 boys and 428 girls, attended Needham schools. There were 34 female teachers and only three male. (Leonard Dawson Collection of the Needham Free Public Library.)

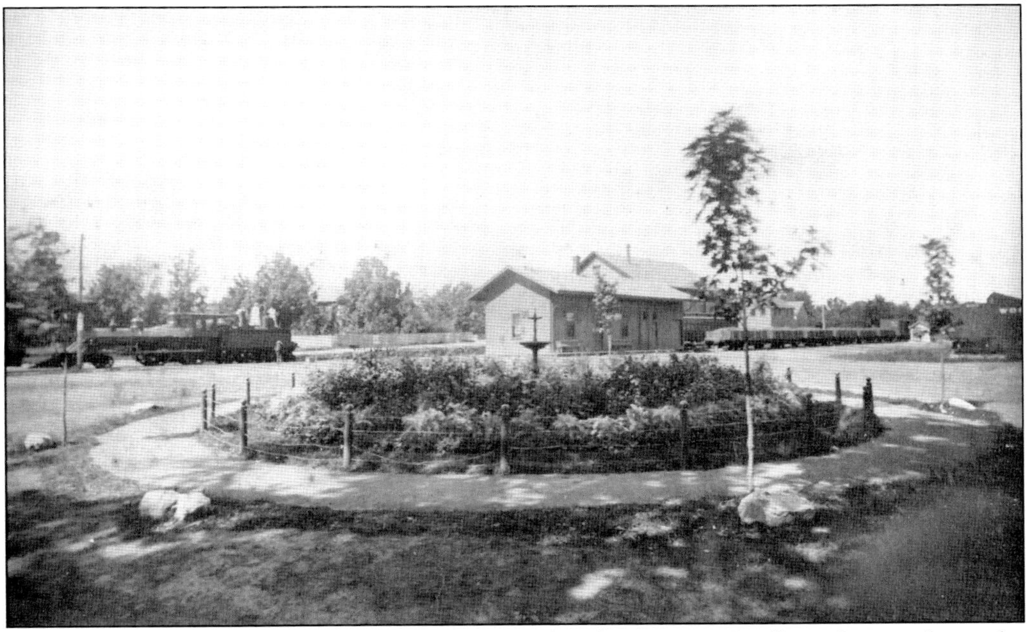

This c. 1885 photograph of the Old Depot, the railroad station at Needham Center, shows the fountain in front and a freight train on the railroad tracks. The small wooden building was replaced in 1887 by a more imposing structure built of granite blocks. (Leonard Dawson Collection of the Needham Free Public Library.)

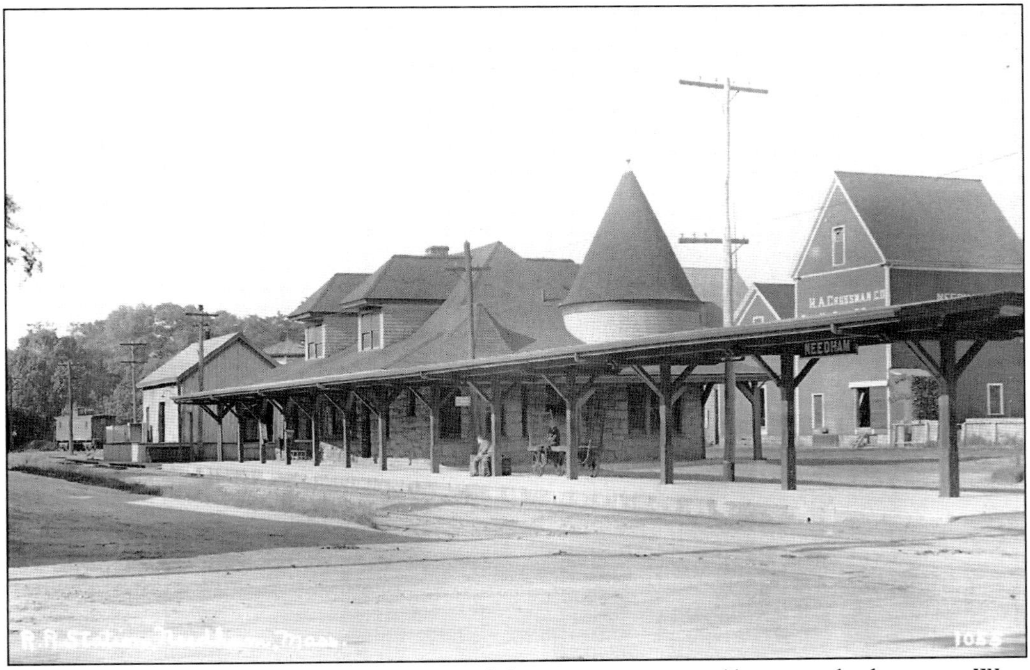

In 1834, the Boston & Worcester Railway, with locomotives powered by steam, had a stop at West Needham (now Wellesley). In the 1850s, efforts to build a railroad alongside Central Avenue failed. Instead, the New York & New England Railroad Company routed the Woonsocket to Boston line further south. This c. 1900 photograph shows the Needham station near the corner of Great Plain Avenue and Chapel Street.

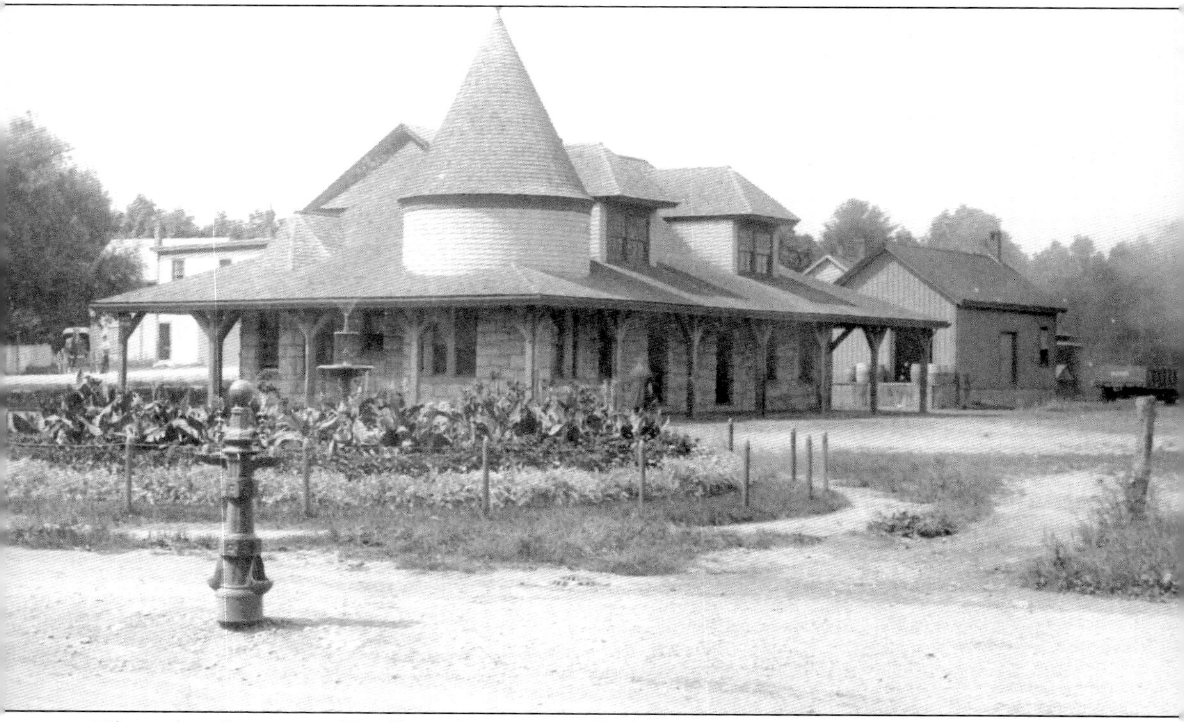

The railroad station at Needham Square was rebuilt in 1887. In 1873, the Woonsocket & Boston Railroad was acquired by the New York & New England Railroad Company. The train stopped at Needham Square, traveled on to Highlandville, and continued northeast to Newton and Brookline before reaching Boston. In 1875, the travel time from Needham to Boston was 46 minutes. The schedule for 1888 showed that 10 trains a day each way linked Boston and Needham. Myron A. Munson, a Needham resident, served as conductor on the line from 1861 until 1911. Isaiah Heath and Daniel Barnes, both of Needham, served for many years as engineers on the Woonsocket to Boston line. In the 1860s, an extension of the line was built to transport gravel from Needham to fill Back Bay in Boston. (Leonard Dawson Collection of the Needham Free Public Library.)

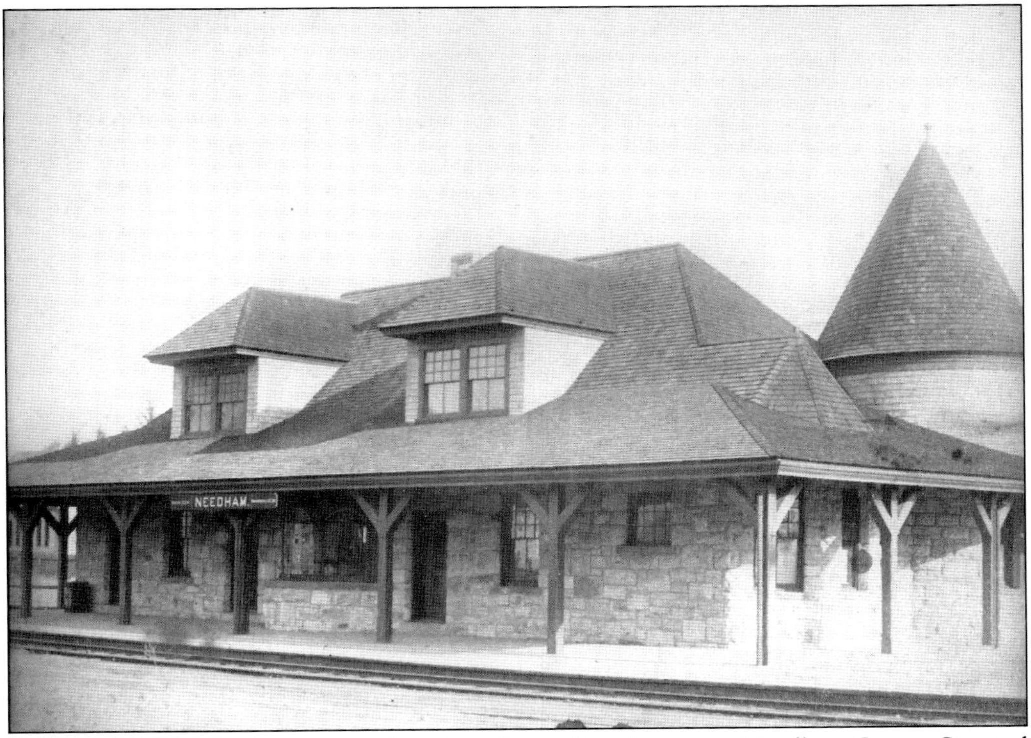

This c. 1900 photograph shows another view of the railroad station at Needham Center. Situated at the center of Needham, close to stores and town offices, this station was more imposing than the Highlandville and Needham Junction stations. (Leonard Dawson Collection of the Needham Free Public Library.)

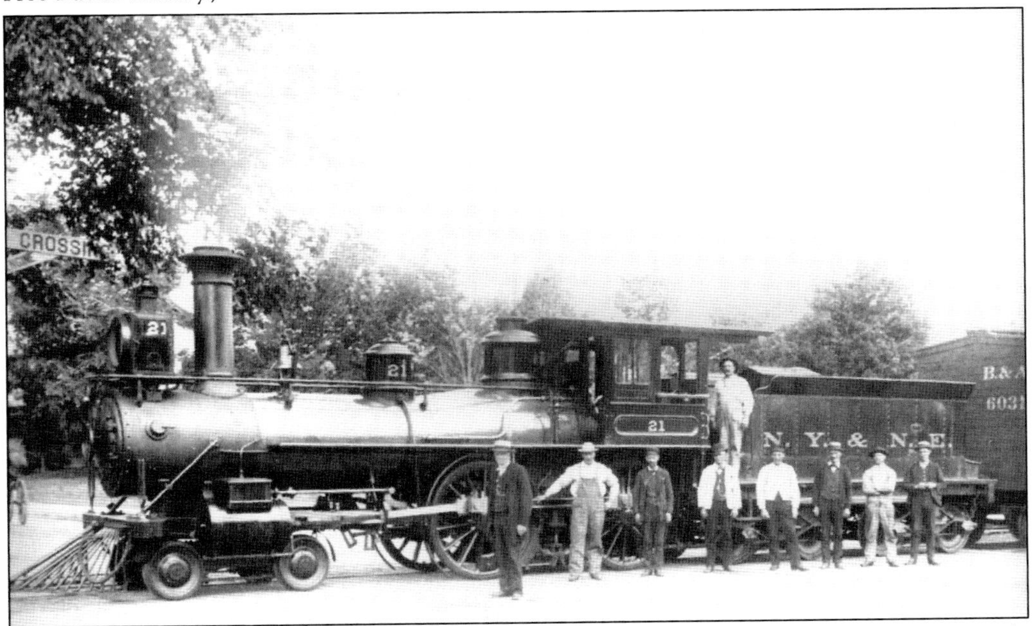

A locomotive of the New York & New England Railroad Company, its crew, and local people are seen at the crossing at Great Plain Avenue before entering Needham station. Passengers and freight passed daily through Needham to and from Boston.

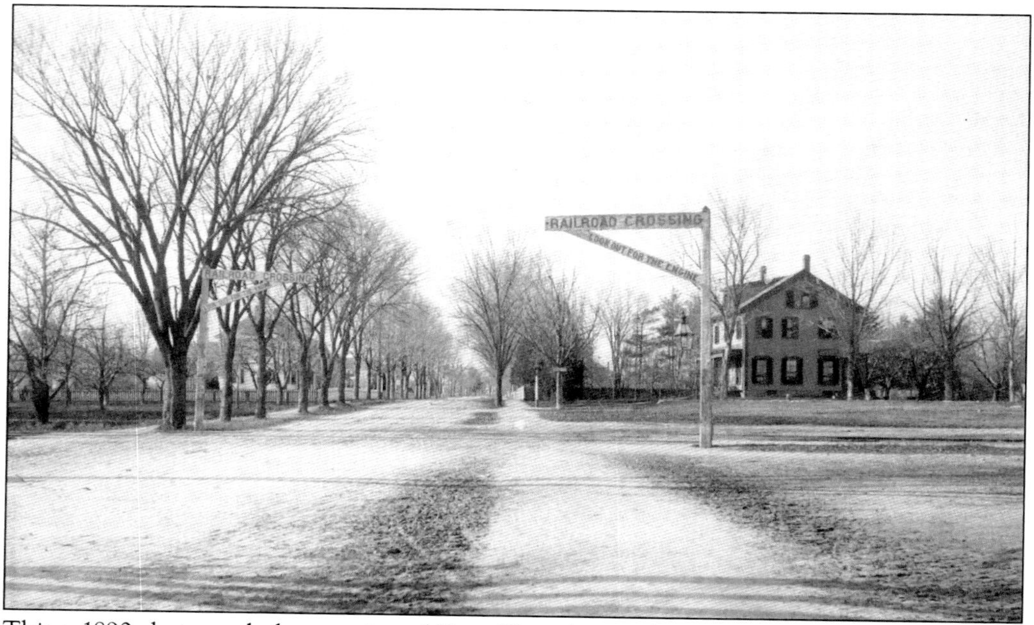

This c. 1890 photograph shows a view of Great Plain Avenue looking west toward Wellesley. The same railroad crossing can be seen but without people, animals, carts, or locomotives in sight. In 1906, the New England Railroad Company completed a line linking Needham with the Boston & Providence Railroad. Express trains on the new line carried passengers from Needham to South Station in Boston in 21 minutes.

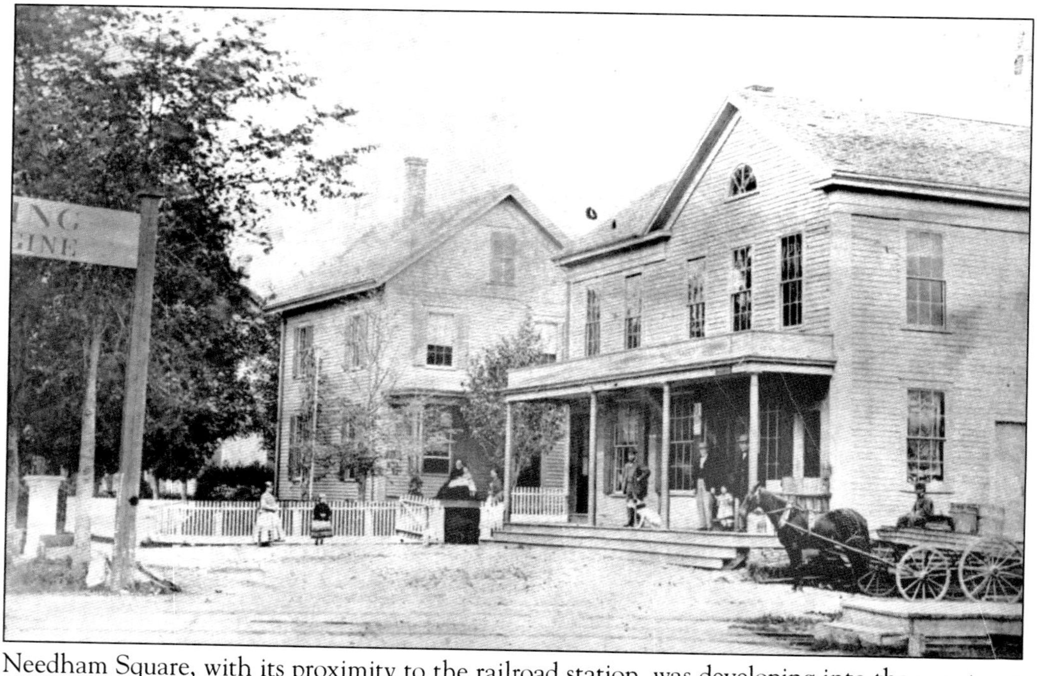

Needham Square, with its proximity to the railroad station, was developing into the new town center with shops and houses. This c. 1880 photograph shows formally dressed men wearing hats; in the age of corsets and petticoats, the women are heavily dressed. Within a decade, women's fashions would change radically with the introduction of one-piece underwear, called Union Suits, made by William Carter and other knitwear companies.

With buildings constructed of wood, fires were a frequent danger. In 1893, Needham was equipped with a fire department and the latest in horse-drawn firefighting equipment. The appropriation for the Needham Fire Department was $1,625 in 1890 and $2,075 in 1895. In 1900, the appropriation increased to $2,206. (Leonard Dawson Collection of the Needham Free Public Library.)

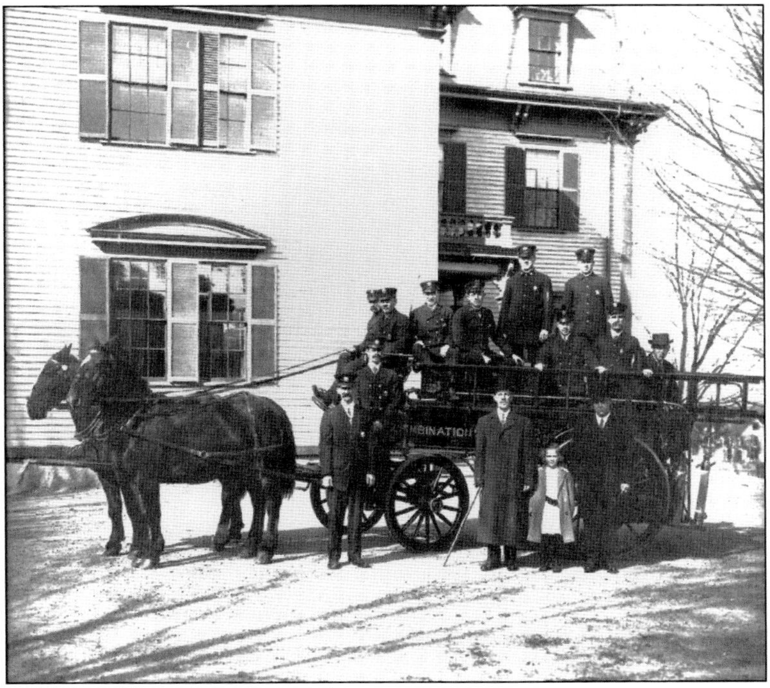

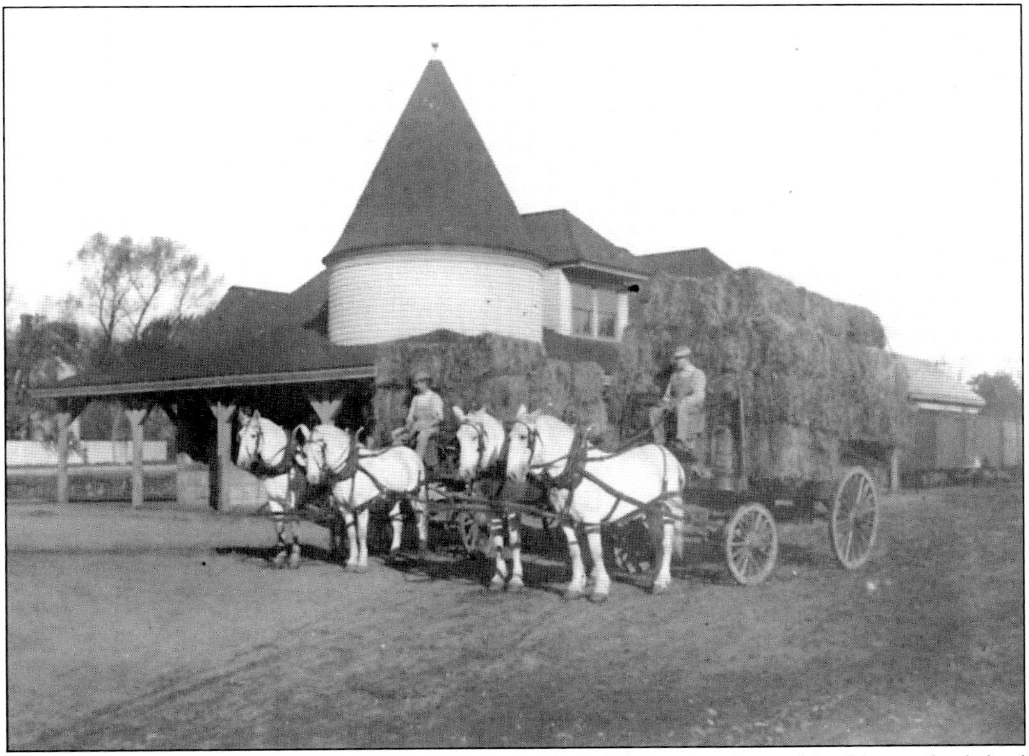

In 1887, the granite Needham Railroad Station replaced the original wood building, which had been damaged by fire. The railroad station attracted buildings and stores to the new town center. Here, the town's grain and hay merchant poses with his fine horses and wagons at the rear of the station.

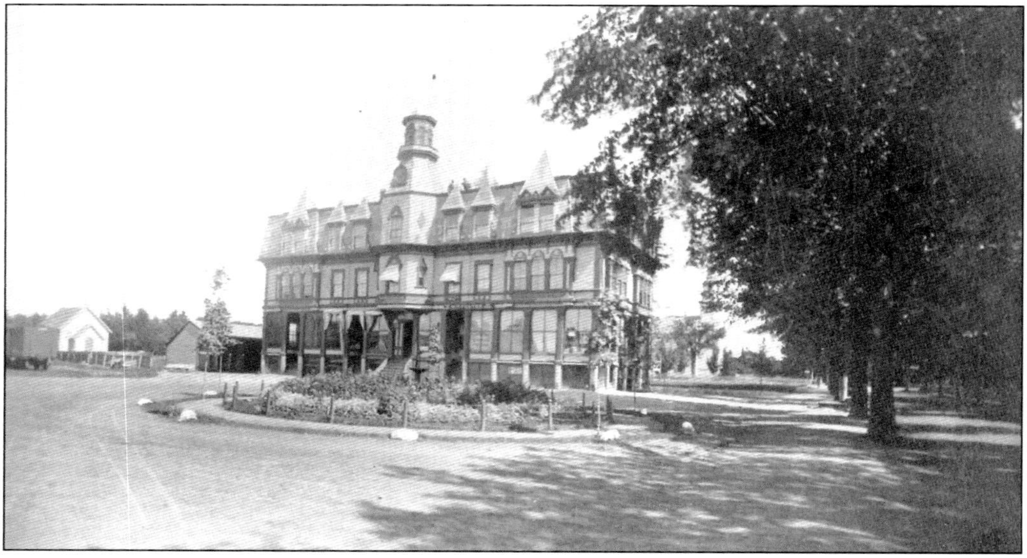

Once the grandest block in Needham, the Odd Fellows Building stood on the corner of Great Plain Avenue and Chapel Street. The building housed the town library, professional offices on the upper floors, and stores at street level. The Odd Fellows Building burnt to the ground during the night of May 12 and May 13, 1887. (Leonard Dawson Collection of the Needham Free Public Library.)

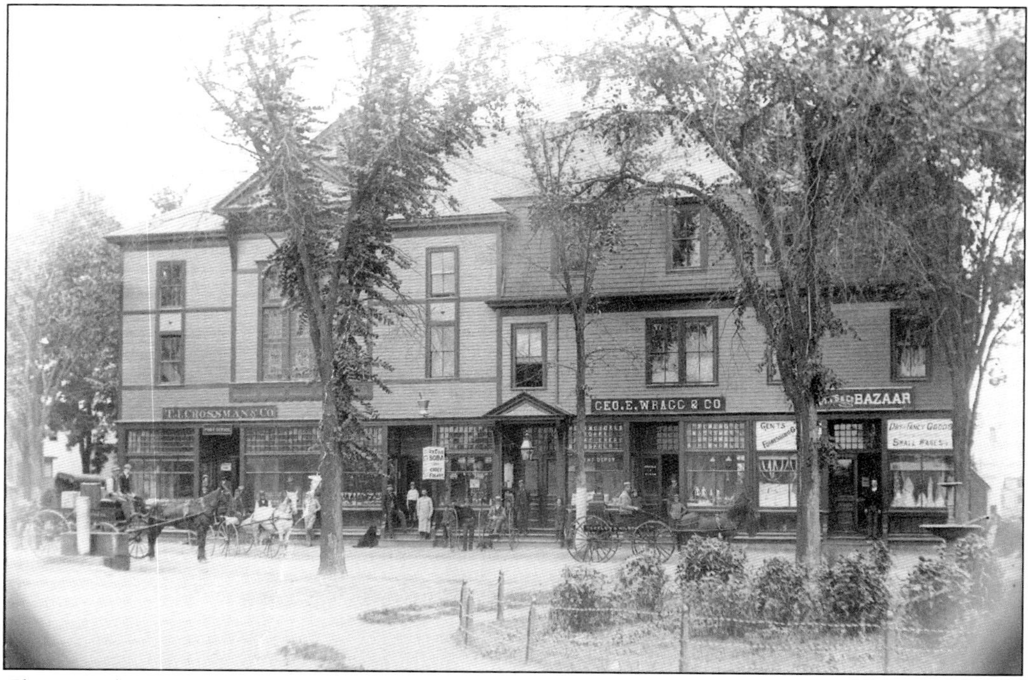

The Moseley Building was completed in 1884 and stood in Needham Square at the corner of Great Plain Avenue and Chestnut Street. One store was leased to George E. Wragg, who also served as the town's first night police officer. People got around mainly by horse and cart. One young man had a high wheeler, a bicycle with a large front wheel and a small back wheel. The man sitting in the contraption with two large wheels operated by hand was a local cobbler, who was crippled in one leg.

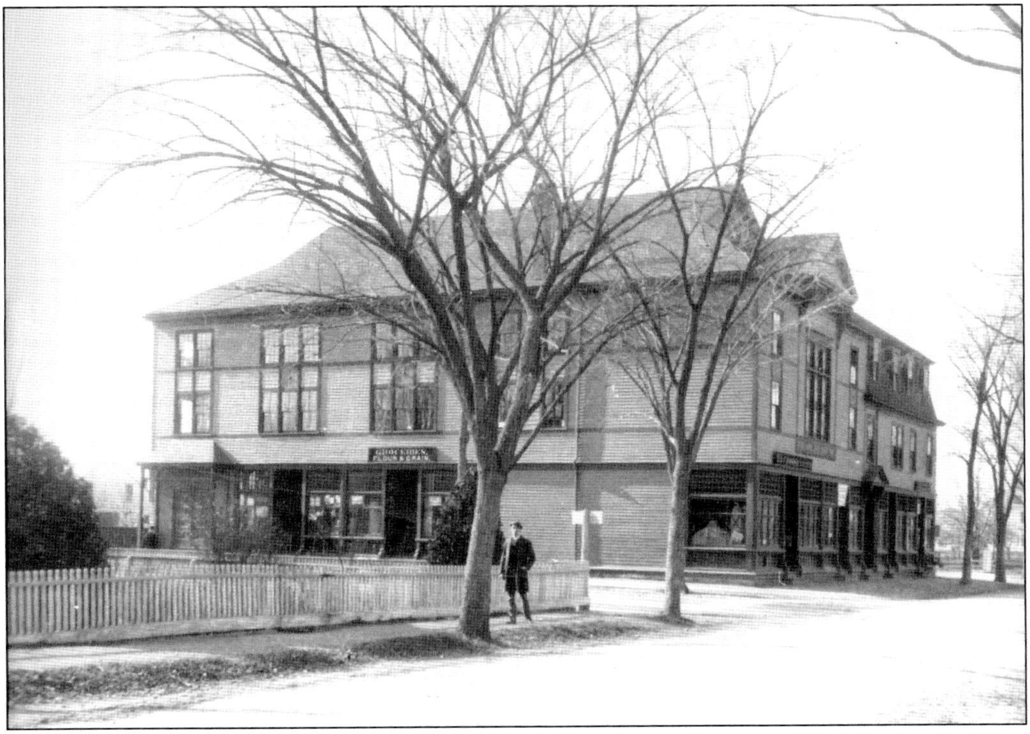

For several years, the town of Needham leased the hall and several rooms of the Moseley Building to serve as town offices at an annual cost of $650 a year. The building is pictured around 1887. (Leonard Dawson Collection at the Needham Free Public Library.)

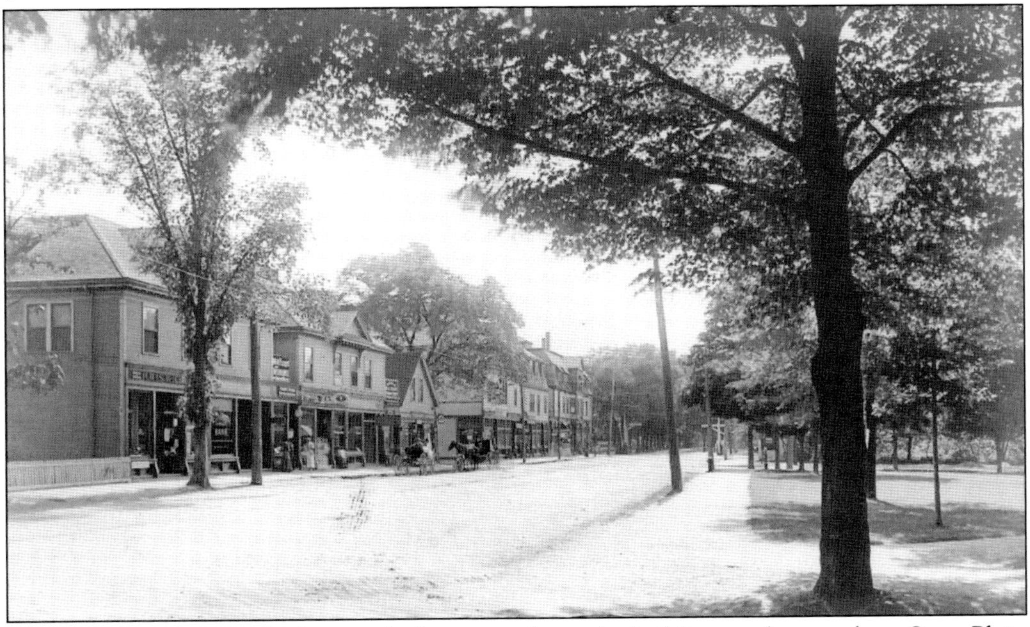

In this c. 1895 photograph, the view looking west shows the buildings and stores along Great Plain Avenue, close to the Needham railroad station. The Moseley building, built in 1874, also housed the post office and several stores at street level, such as Thomas Sutton's market and George E. Wragg and Company. The town's offices and meeting rooms were located above.

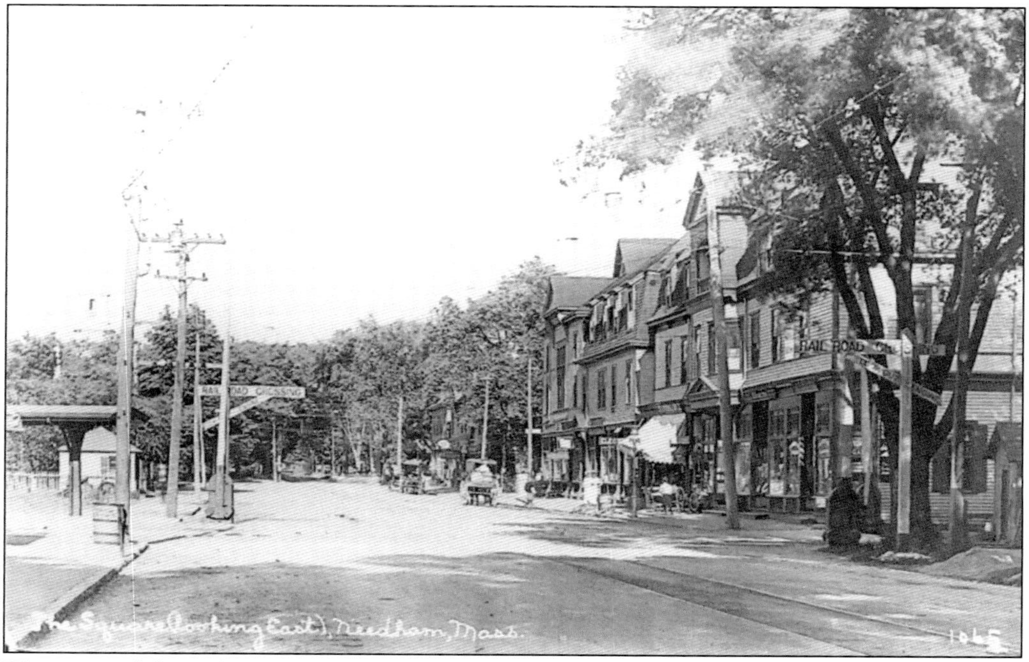

This view of the railroad crossing at Great Plain Avenue, looking east around 1905, shows the Moseley building. The tracks along Great Plain Avenue belonged to the Needham to Dedham electric street railway, built in 1897.

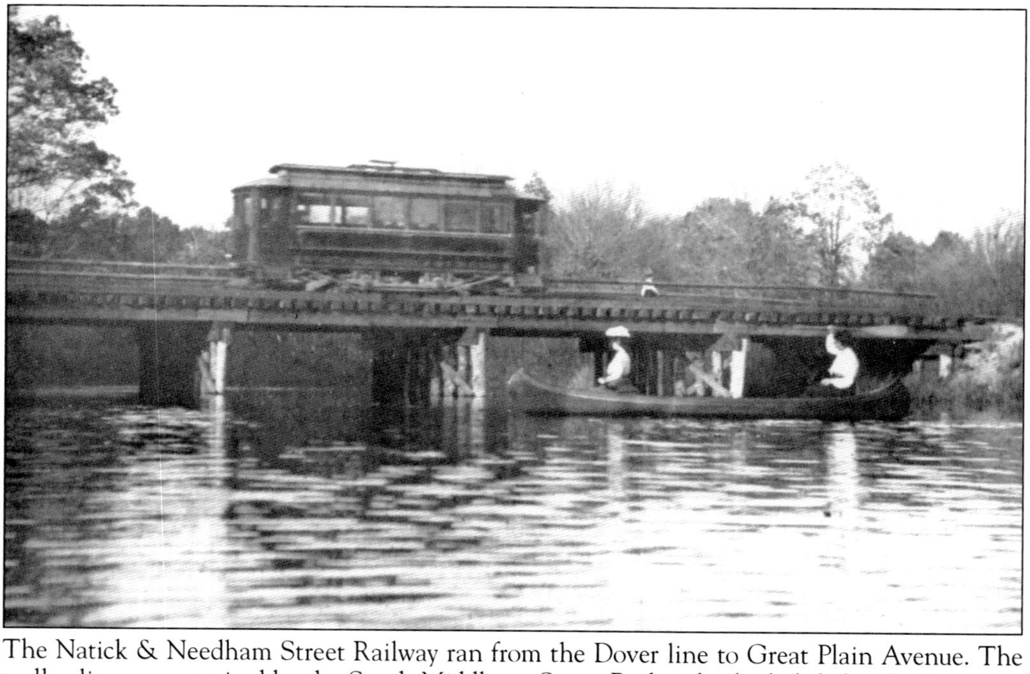

The Natick & Needham Street Railway ran from the Dover line to Great Plain Avenue. The trolley line was acquired by the South Middlesex Street Railroad, which failed in 1903. In this 1901 photograph, the trolley is seen crossing the trestle over the Charles River at the west end of Charles River Street. (Leonard Dawson Collection of the Needham Free Public Library.)

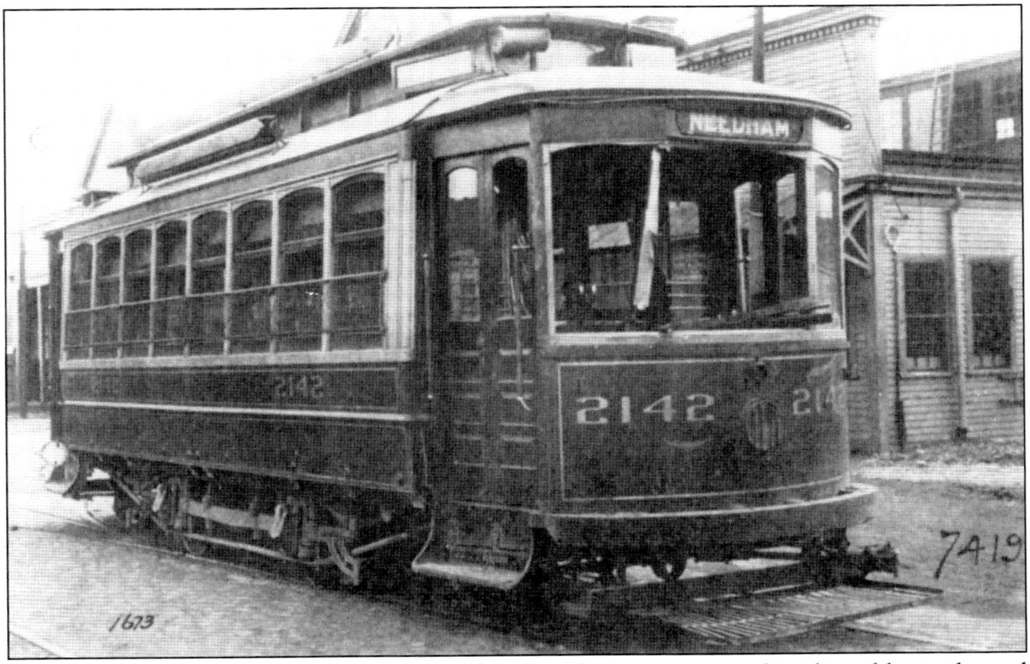

Pictured is Needham trolley car No. 2142. Closed trolley cars were used in the cold months and open cars were used in warmer weather. Electric trolley lines once linked Needham with Natick, Wellesley, Dedham, Newton, and Boston.

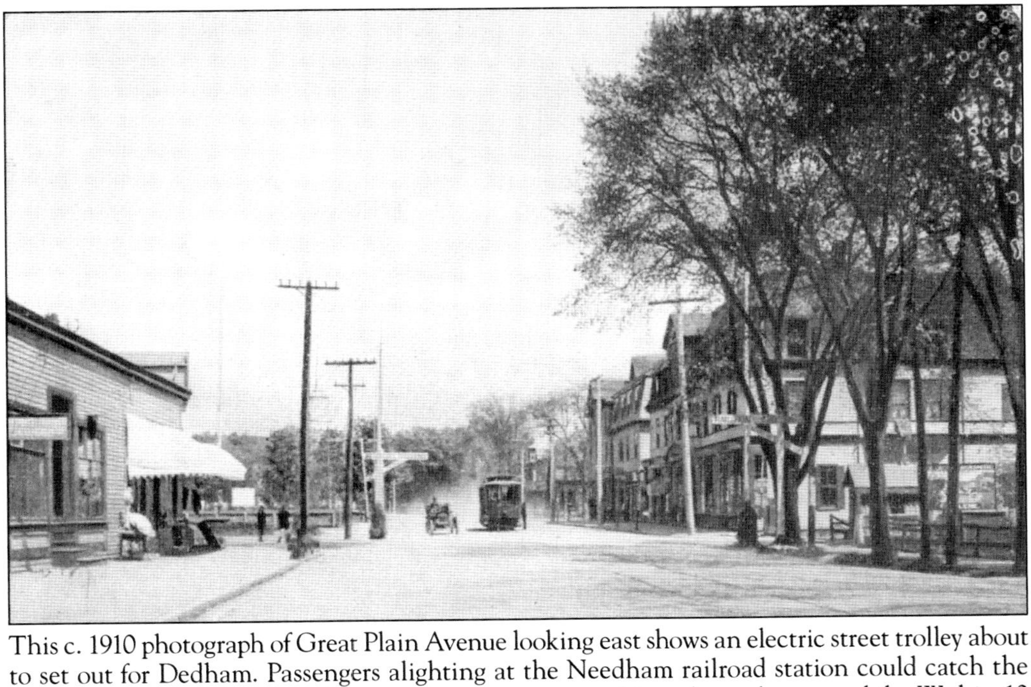

This c. 1910 photograph of Great Plain Avenue looking east shows an electric street trolley about to set out for Dedham. Passengers alighting at the Needham railroad station could catch the nearby streetcars headed north to south or east to west. Note the early automobile. Within 10 years, the automobile age would put an end to most suburban street trolley lines.

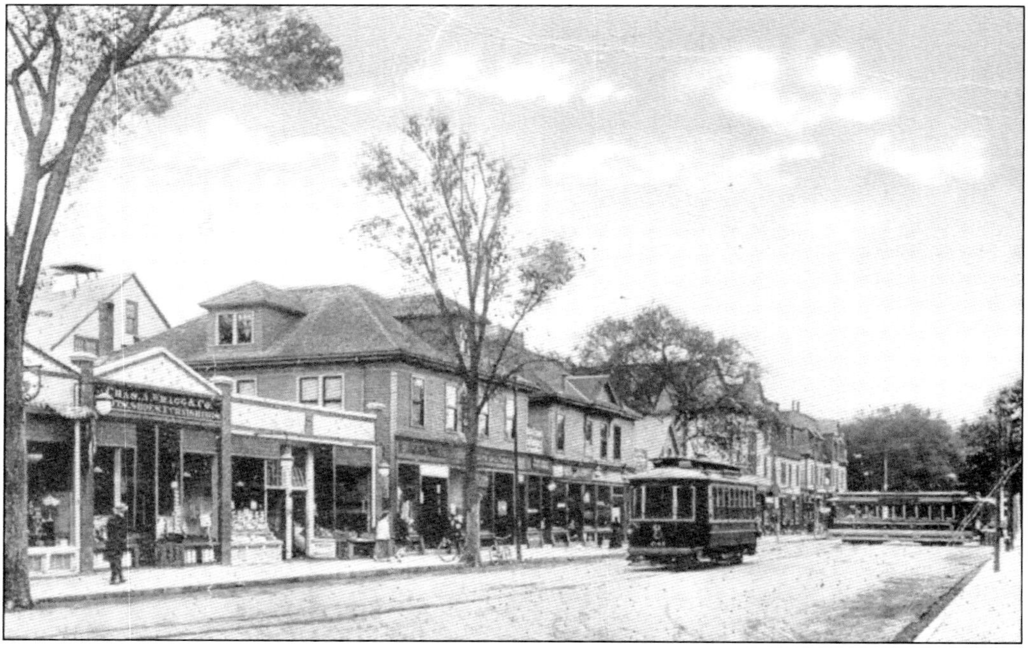

Another view of the Needham shopping section around 1910 shows a trolley crossing Great Plain Avenue along Chestnut Street headed toward Needham Heights and on to Newton. A second trolley is seen headed east along Great Plain Avenue and on to Dedham. The small trolley companies frequently fell into bankruptcy and were sold to larger systems.

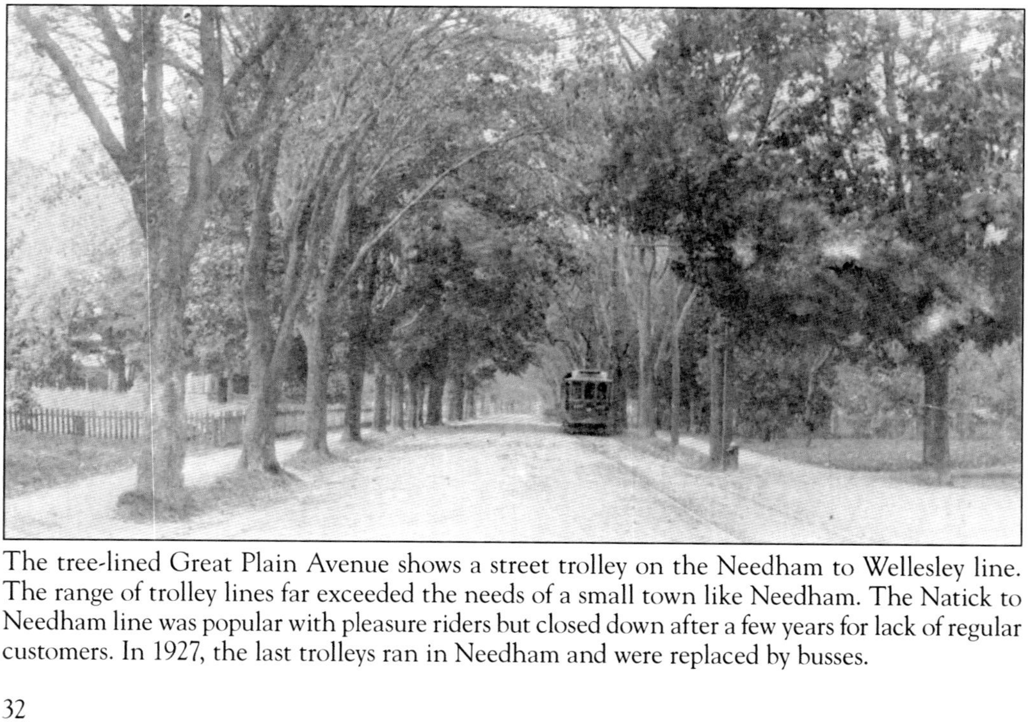

The tree-lined Great Plain Avenue shows a street trolley on the Needham to Wellesley line. The range of trolley lines far exceeded the needs of a small town like Needham. The Natick to Needham line was popular with pleasure riders but closed down after a few years for lack of regular customers. In 1927, the last trolleys ran in Needham and were replaced by busses.

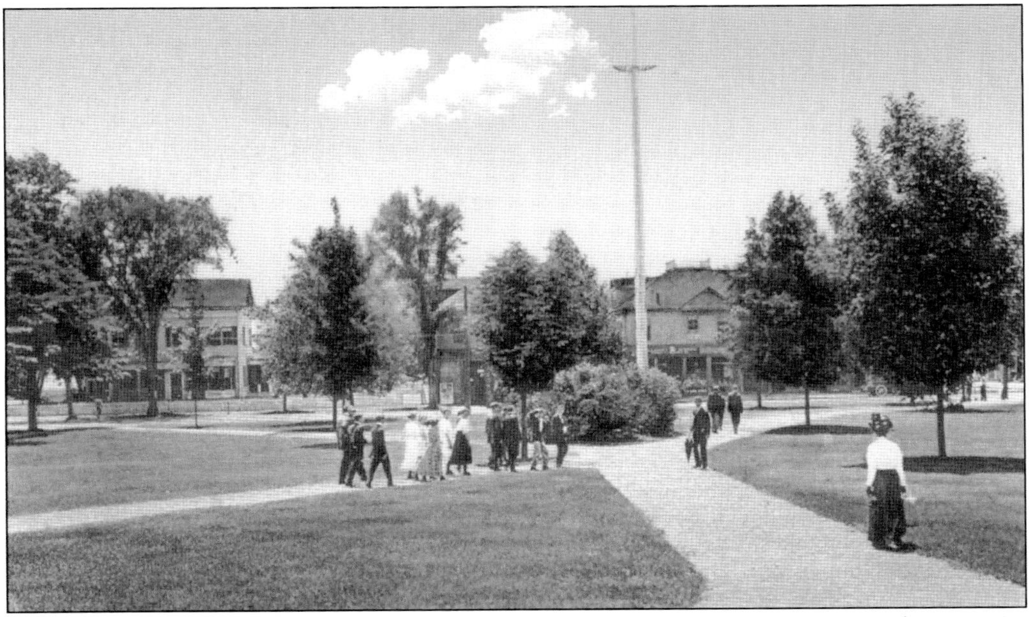

The land for Needham Common was purchased in 1884 from George P. Davis for $2,850. The area facing Great Plain Avenue remained a park while the back section was the site of the town hall, completed in 1903. In 1911, a bandstand was built on the common, where the Needham Military Band regularly entertained.

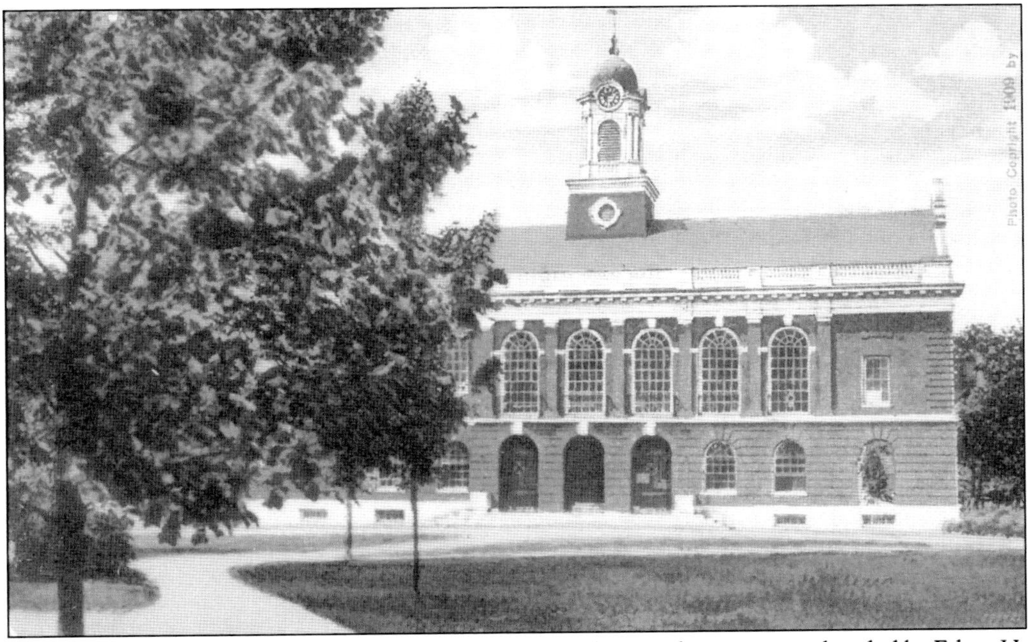

In 1902, the town of Needham accepted the recommendation of a committee headed by Edgar H. Bowers to build a town hall on the common. Bowers ran a factory making hinges and fasteners and for years was active in the town's management. The town hall building was completed in December 1903 at a cost of $57,500, including furnishings.

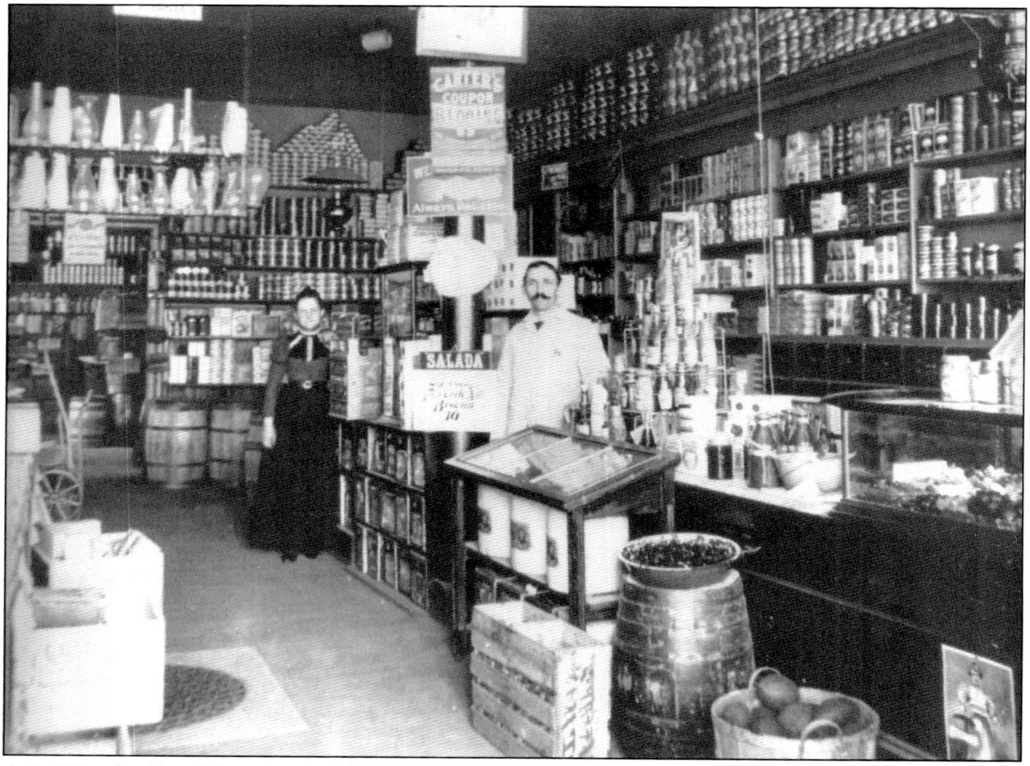

A.L. Woodruff and Sons' general store opened in 1888 on the corner of Great Plain Avenue and Chestnut Street. This c. 1900 photograph shows Charles Woodruff with his clerk Nellie Burhill. The goods for sale are piled high on shelves and reached by ladders.

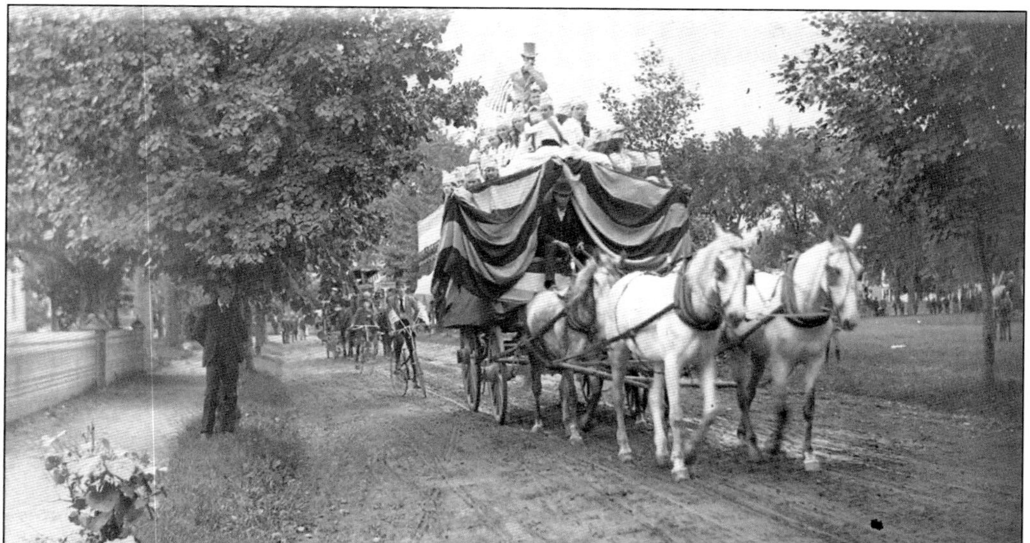

This c. 1900 photograph shows a float in the Fourth of July celebration. Uncle Sam is accompanied by children of the town and pulled by two white horses, moving along the unpaved Highland Avenue close to Needham Common. The bicycles following the float may well have been made by the Union Cycle Company, which functioned in Needham from 1888 to 1900. Needham then had two cycle clubs, the Needham Cycle Club and the Union Rovers.

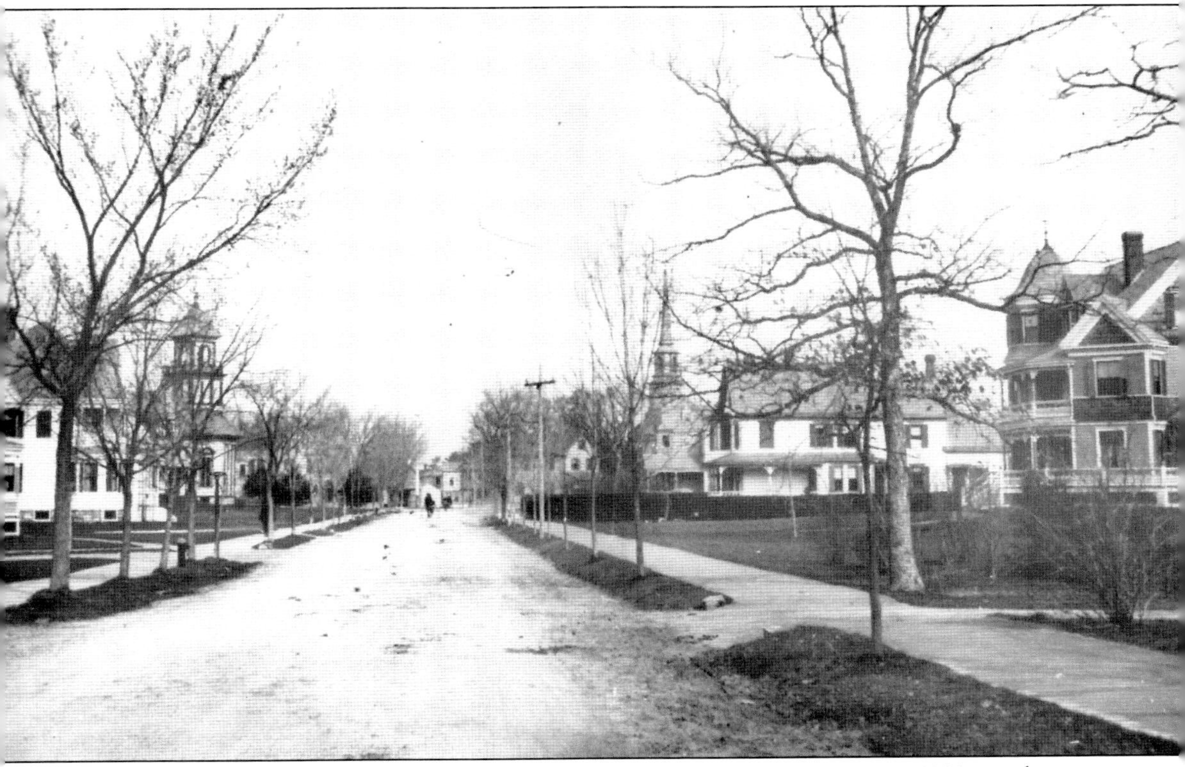

Pictured around 1900 are the grand homes along Dedham Avenue. Starting in 1899, an electric street trolley ran from Great Plain Avenue along Dedham Avenue, crossed the Charles River over the Dedham Avenue Bridge, and into Dedham. The Dedham Avenue Bridge was originally completed in 1873 to link the towns across the Charles River. Dedham Avenue, now part of Route 135, links Needham to the older town of Dedham. George E. Wye built his knitting mill at the corner of Pleasant Street and Dedham Avenue. (Leonard Dawson Collection of the Needham Free Public Library.)

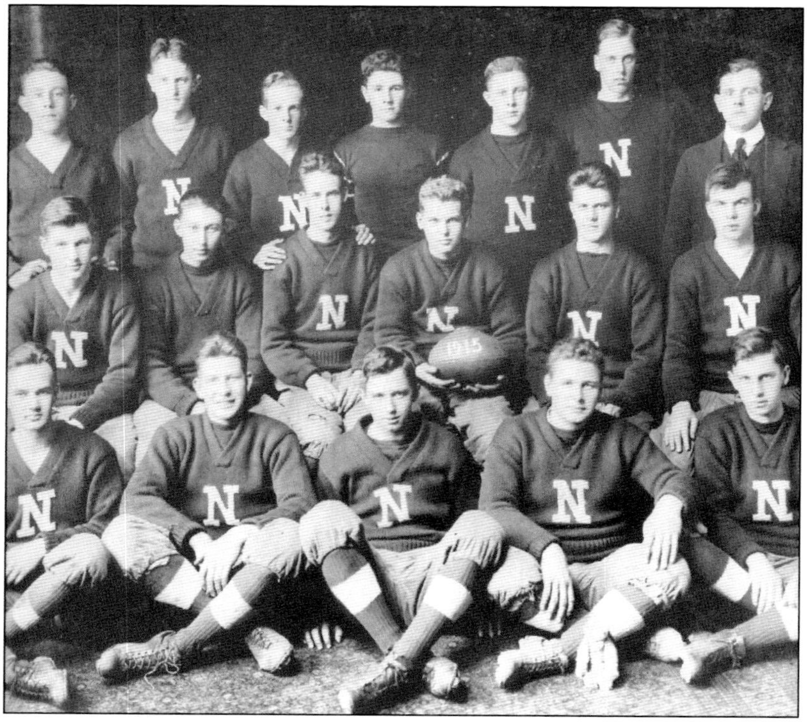

Pictured is the 1915 Needham High School football team. Needham and Wellesley have kept a high school football rivalry since 1882. With many children leaving school at age 15, Needham High School had but a small pool of male students from which to choose a football team. (Leonard Dawson Collection of the Needham Free Public Library.)

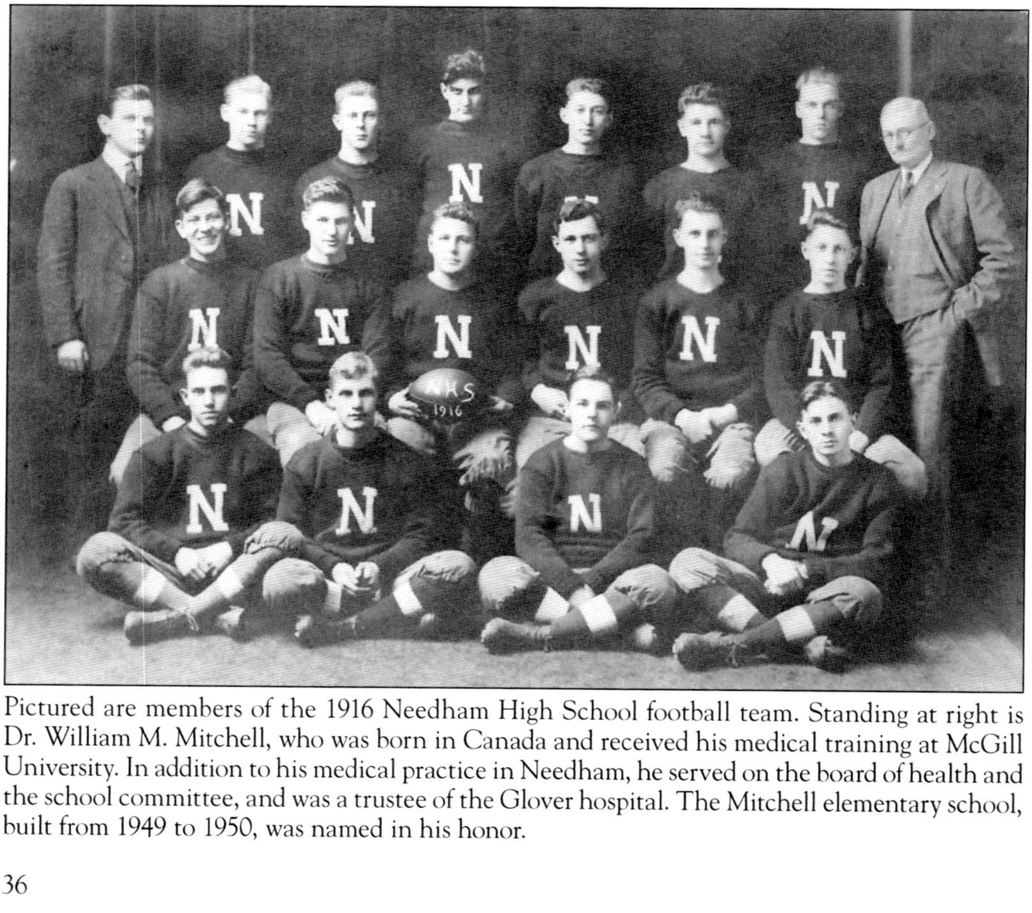

Pictured are members of the 1916 Needham High School football team. Standing at right is Dr. William M. Mitchell, who was born in Canada and received his medical training at McGill University. In addition to his medical practice in Needham, he served on the board of health and the school committee, and was a trustee of the Glover hospital. The Mitchell elementary school, built from 1949 to 1950, was named in his honor.

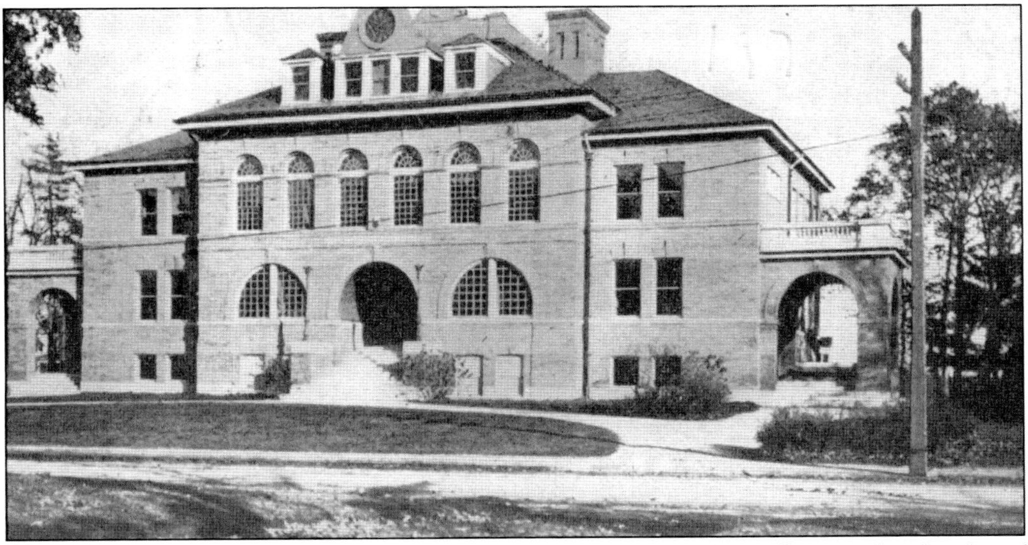

In 1897, knitting mill owner John Moseley presented the Town of Needham with a fine lot of land on Highland Avenue on which to build the high school. The high school was dedicated on September 1, 1898, built at a cost of $33,000. By 1911, 138 students were attending the school.

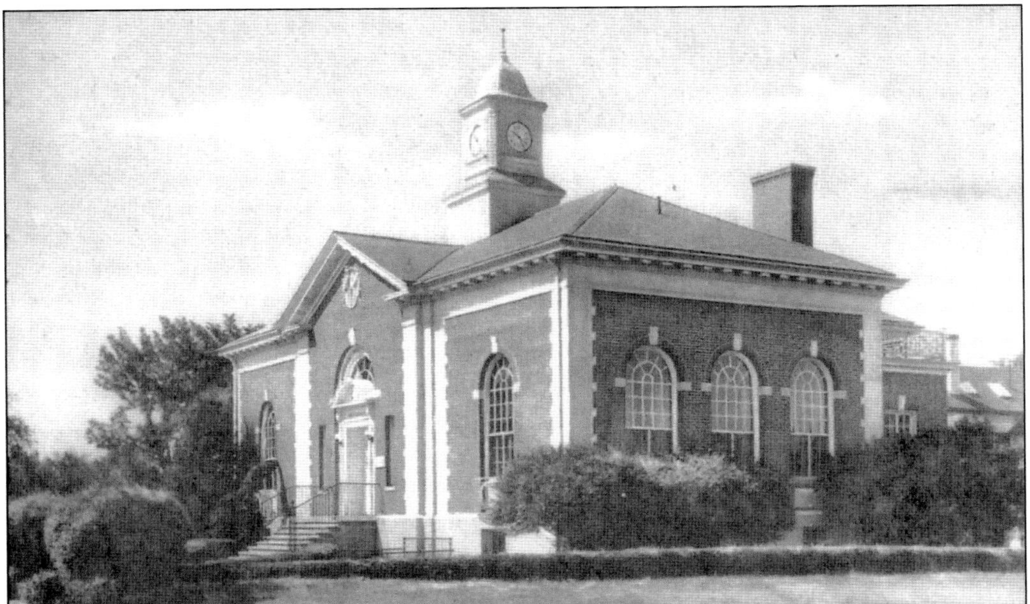

Needham's first public library was founded in 1796. In 1888, almost all of the Needham Library Association's books were destroyed in a fire. A new library was built in 1903 on land donated by William Carter and with $10,000 donated by Andrew Carnegie. Located in Highlandville, it was not popular with the residents of "old" Needham. In 1915, a new library was built at the corner of Highland Avenue and Rosemary Street, halfway between the two villages. William Carter was the chairman of the building committee. In recent years, the Needham Public Library has been greatly enlarged, but the original entrance has been retained.

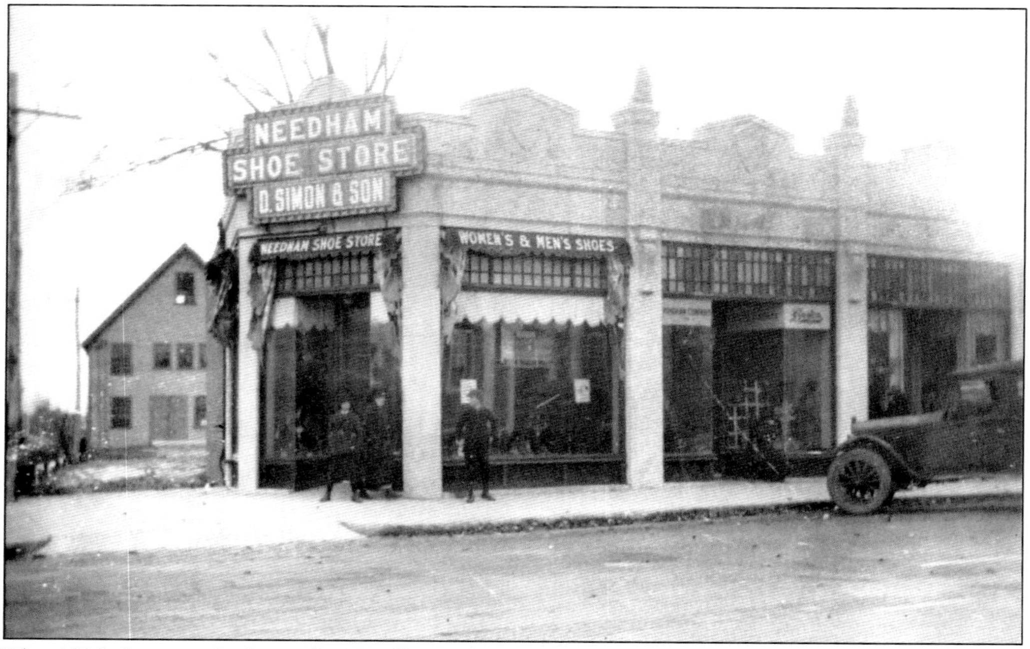

This 1920 photograph shows the Needham Shoe Store and Windham Company Real Estate office, which were located on Great Plain Avenue at Needham Square. In the 1920s, a wide range of stores served Needham. (Leonard Dawson Collection of the Needham Free Public Library.)

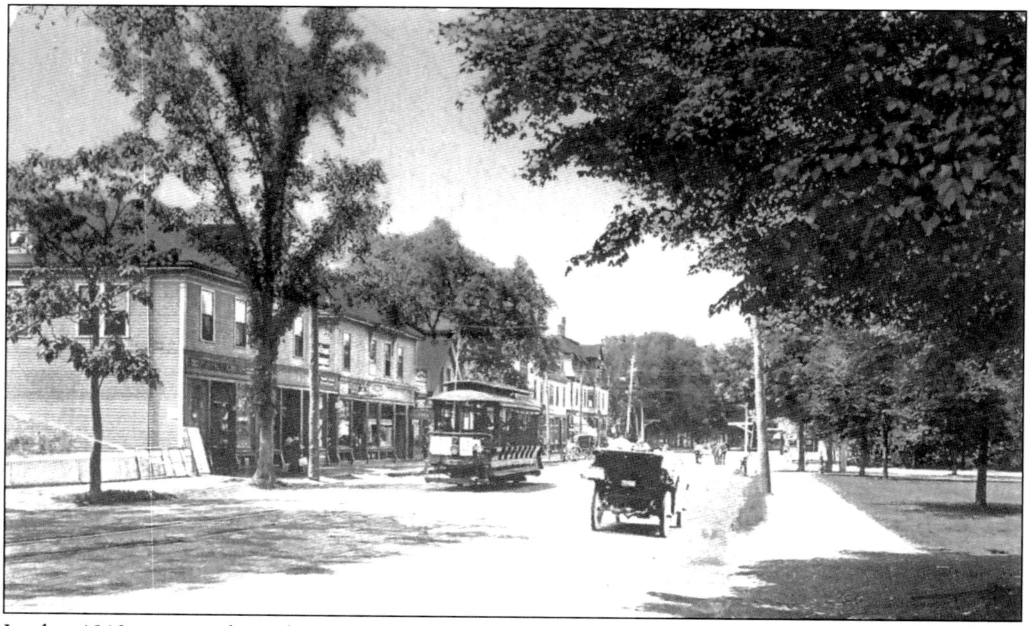

In this 1910 image, a horseless carriage passes the Needham to Dedham electric street trolley on Great Plain Avenue. A decade later, the trolley tracks were paved over as gasoline-powered cars and buses became the preferred modes of transportation.

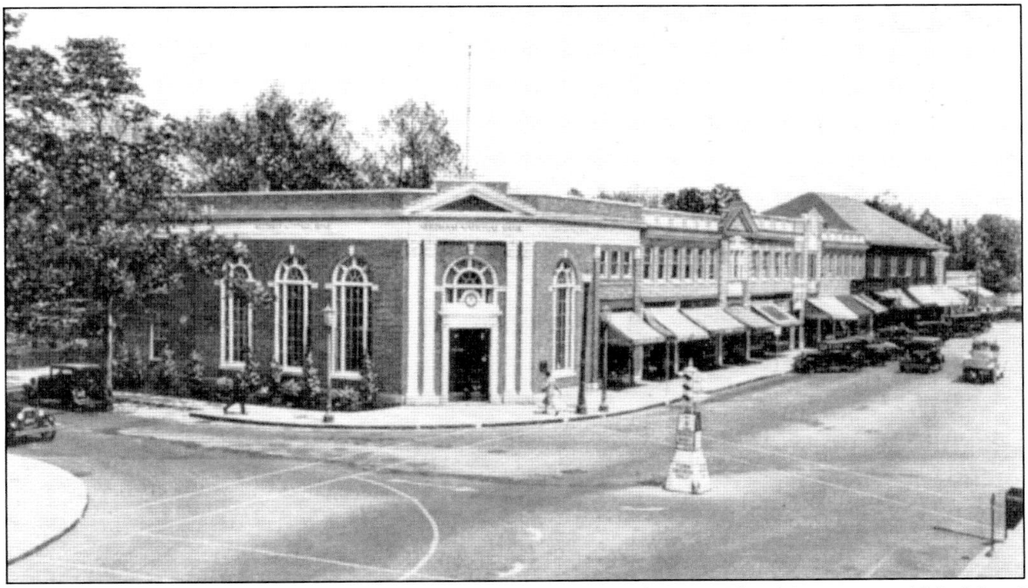

The Needham National Bank building was at the corner of Great Plain Avenue and Highland Avenue. Dedham Avenue (unseen) is to the right. This late 1920s photograph shows one of Needham's first traffic lights, placed in the middle of the intersection.

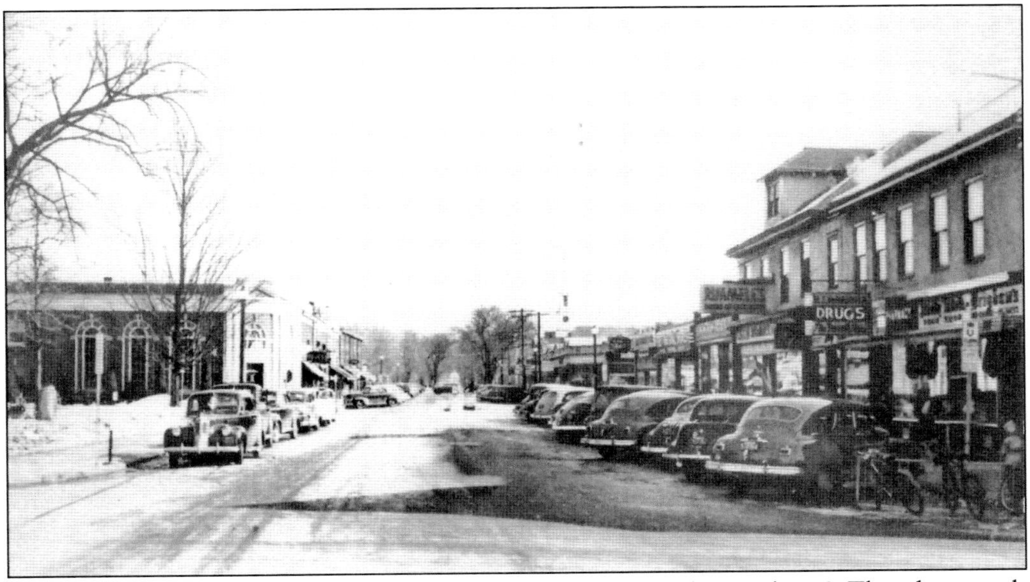

Great Plain Avenue with Dedham Street on the right is pictured around 1940. This photograph was taken some 20 years after the previous image and shows how the private automobile had become the dominant mode of transportation in Needham, as elsewhere in the United States. This section of Needham contained a bank, the Baptist church, several drugstores, and other shops.

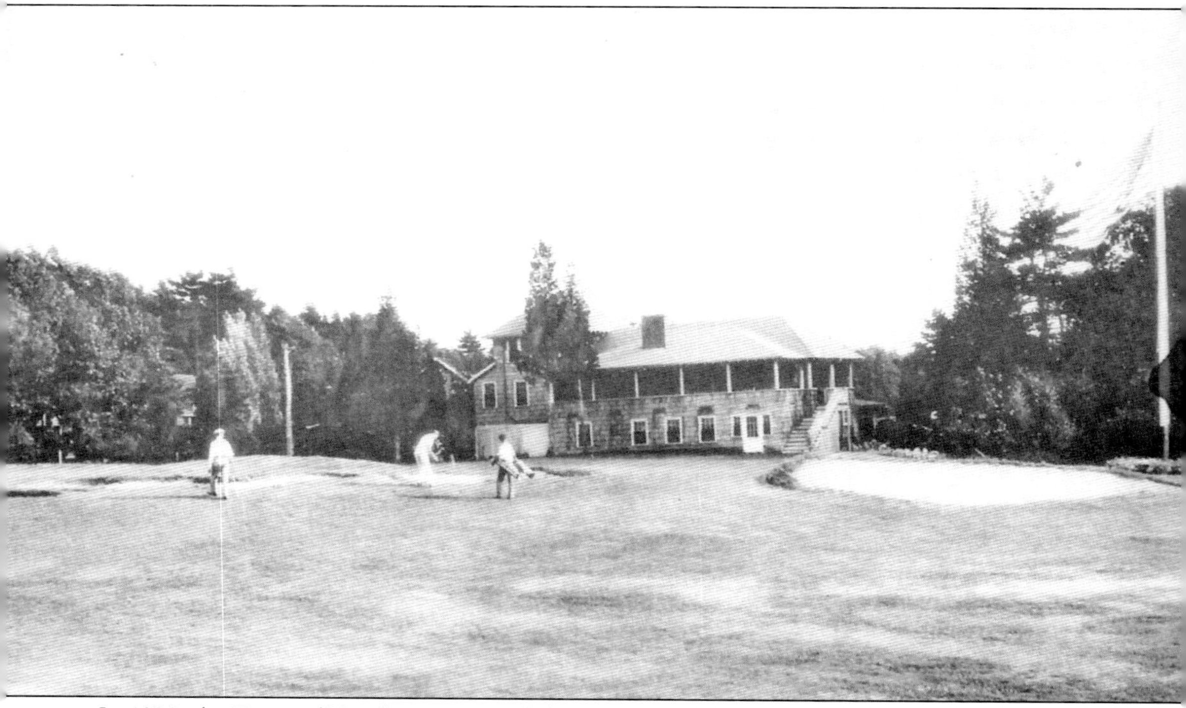

In 1898, the Town of Needham acquired the land on which the golf course was eventually built. The land was initially intended as a watershed area for the town's water supply, but in 1901, the town agreed to build a golf course on it. Wayne Stiles, the famed Massachusetts-based golf course architect, designed the nine-hole course that measured 3,109 yards from the longest tees. The old clubhouse, pictured around 1930, was replaced in 2011 by a grand 14,000-square-foot structure costing $3 million.

Three

HIGHLANDVILLE

Jonathan Avery (1806–1875) was the founder of Highlandville, an area lying one mile east of the center of Needham. Until 1866, only a cart path linked Highlandville to Needham Center. Highland Avenue, running parallel to the railroad tracks, was then built to join the villages. Later, the road was lengthened to cross the Charles River to Newton. Where Highland Avenue intersected Hunnewell Street became the center of the village of Highlandville.

Avery served as the first postmaster of the new village. He bought property near the Highlandville railroad station, divided the land into lots, and encouraged knitters coming from England to settle there and pursue their craft. Highlandville became the center of industry in contrast to the farms and fields of "old" Needham. In 1874, Jonathan Avery sold a parcel of land to the Methodist Episcopal community to build a church. Knitters William Carter, Alexander Lynes, Joseph B. Thorpe, and William Gorse were members of the building committee that raised the money to buy the land and build the church.

Jonathan Avery's daughter Jane Greenough Avery became the third wife of William Carter and mother to three of his children. Avery School, Avery Street, Avery Square, and Avery Manor, all in Highlandville, honor Jonathan Avery.

With many English knitters and a focus on industry, Highlandville developed a different character from the farming economy that dominated the rest of the town. Strict churchgoers and abstemious, they built their churches, established a temperance society, founded a fraternal society of the knitters, and funded the Anglo-American Lodge, which was a mutual benefit association. The knitters formed the Highlandville cornet band, a poultry and pigeon club, and a cricket club, established in 1867. Their accents, manners, and dress hailed from Nottinghamshire and Leicestershire in England.

Entering the 20th century, the town of Needham, with a population of 8,000, remained divided into the residential Needham Center and Highlandville, dominated by knitting mills. The rise of the American-born children of the knitters, coupled with the closing of the mills, gradually reduced the differences between the two villages of Needham. In 1907, Highlandville changed its name to Needham Heights. In 1921, thirty acres of land were purchased on Highland Avenue, midway between the two villages, for the Memorial Park. April 19 was declared Community Day with one parade of hundreds of townsfolk coming from Needham Heights and the other from old Needham. Needham had become a united town.

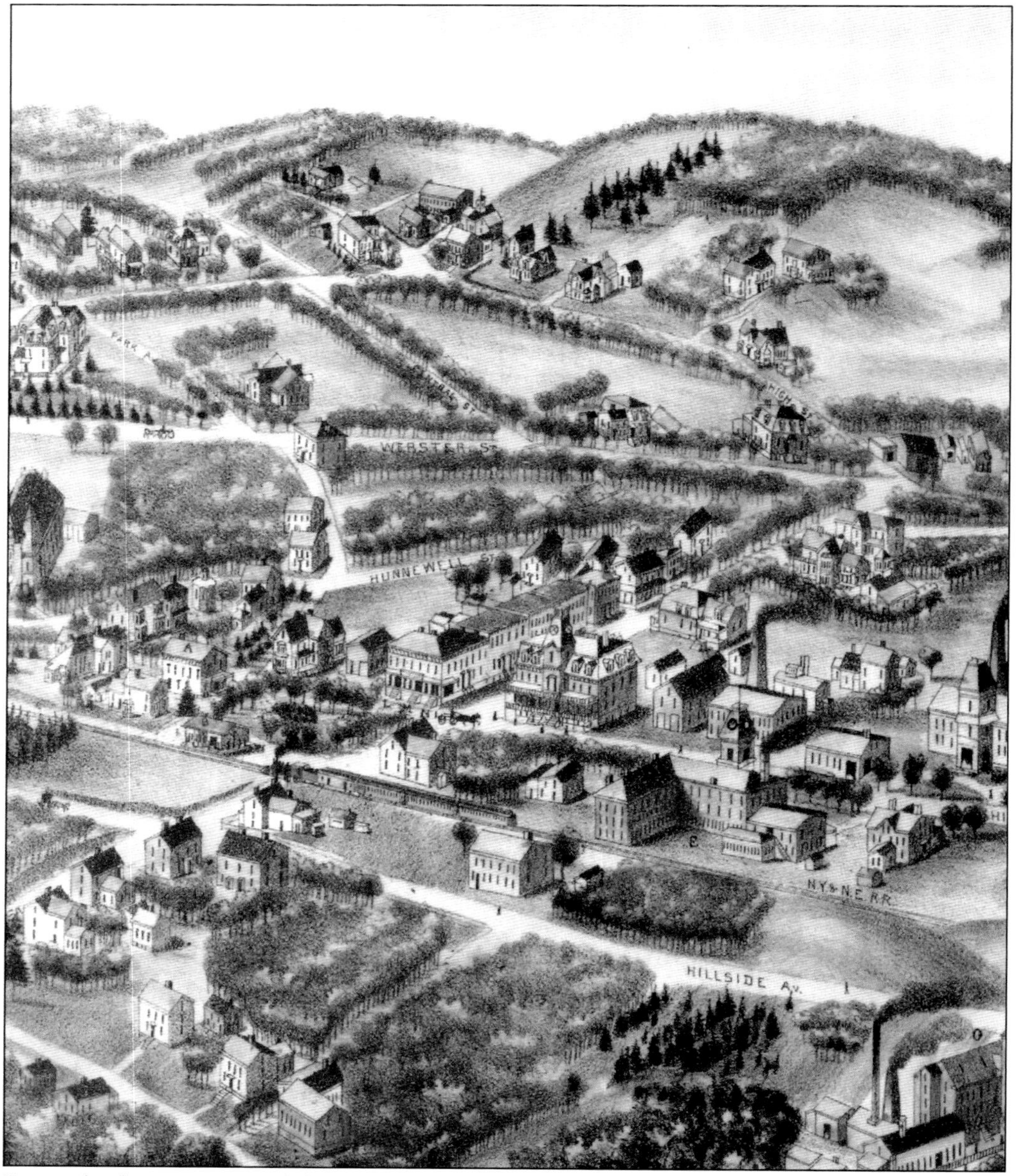

During his long career as a lithographer, Oakley Hoopes Bailey completed 325 views of American cities and towns, 130 of which were in Massachusetts. This town view of Highlandville was prepared in 1887 and gives pride of place to the knitting mills and the stores that served the mill workers. The William Carter hosiery mill, William Roper athletic knit goods mill, Alexander Lynes hosiery mill, and the Moseley hosiery mill are prominently displayed. Also shown are the homes of the knitters William Carter, Alexander Lynes, and Mark Lee, and the home of grocer J.J. Whetton. By the close of the 19th century, the knitting mills shifted production from socks and gloves to underwear. The New York & New England railroad runs in the middle of the image.

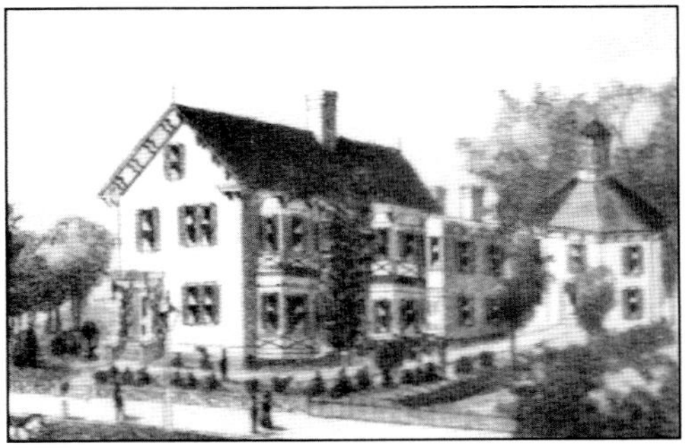 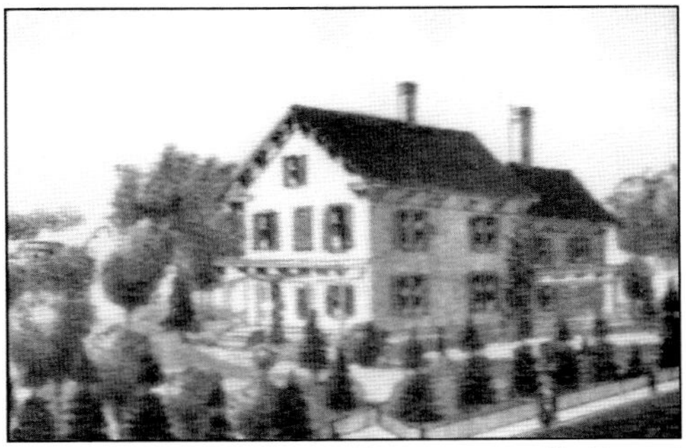

These details of the Highlandville town view show the large homes of William Carter (left) and Alexander Lynes (right.) Born in Leicester, England, Lynes arrived in Needham during the Civil War. He built the Leicester Hosiery Company on Hunnewell Street and employed 70 workers making woolen socks, mittens, and children's underwear. Alexander Lynes died in 1897 and was buried in the Needham town cemetery.

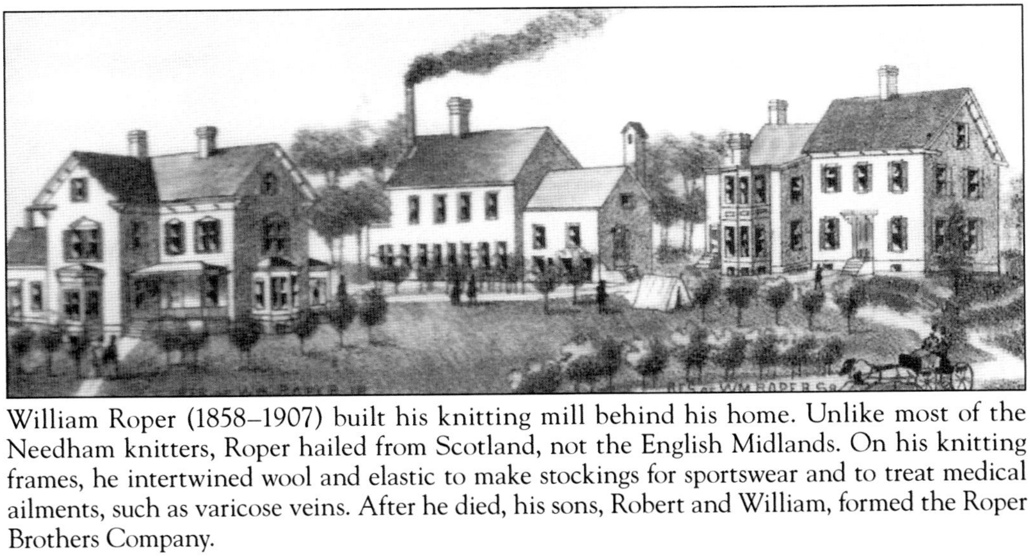

William Roper (1858–1907) built his knitting mill behind his home. Unlike most of the Needham knitters, Roper hailed from Scotland, not the English Midlands. On his knitting frames, he intertwined wool and elastic to make stockings for sportswear and to treat medical ailments, such as varicose veins. After he died, his sons, Robert and William, formed the Roper Brothers Company.

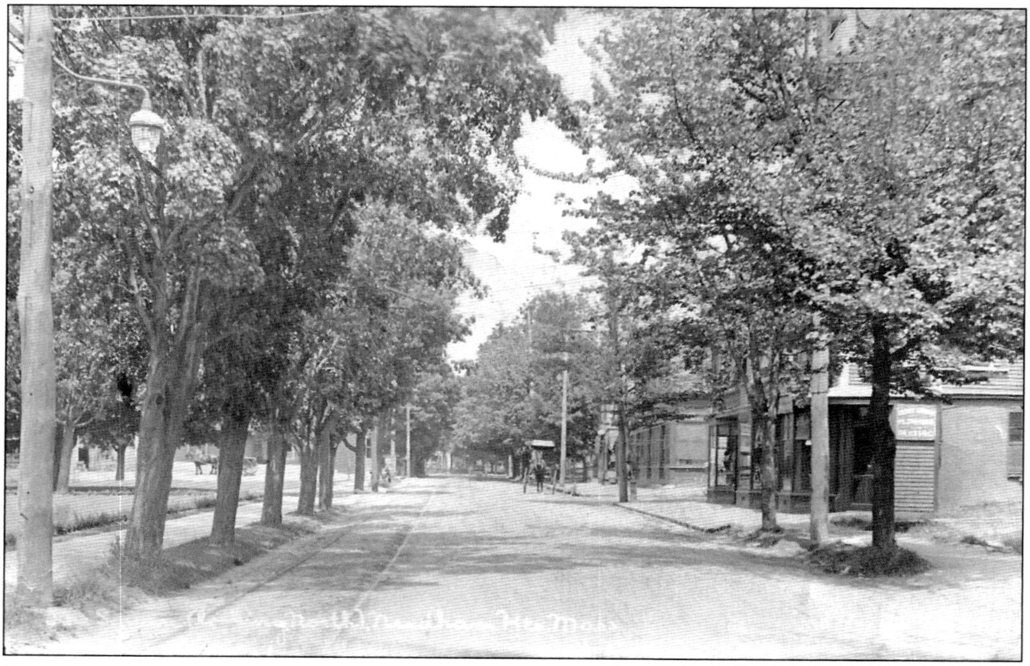

This photograph of Highland Avenue was taken facing northeast around the summer of 1905. The trolley tracks of the Needham to Newton line are running along the left side of Highland Avenue. The stores and offices at right, which are partly obscured by the leaves of the tress, served Carter's Mill No. 1 across the street.

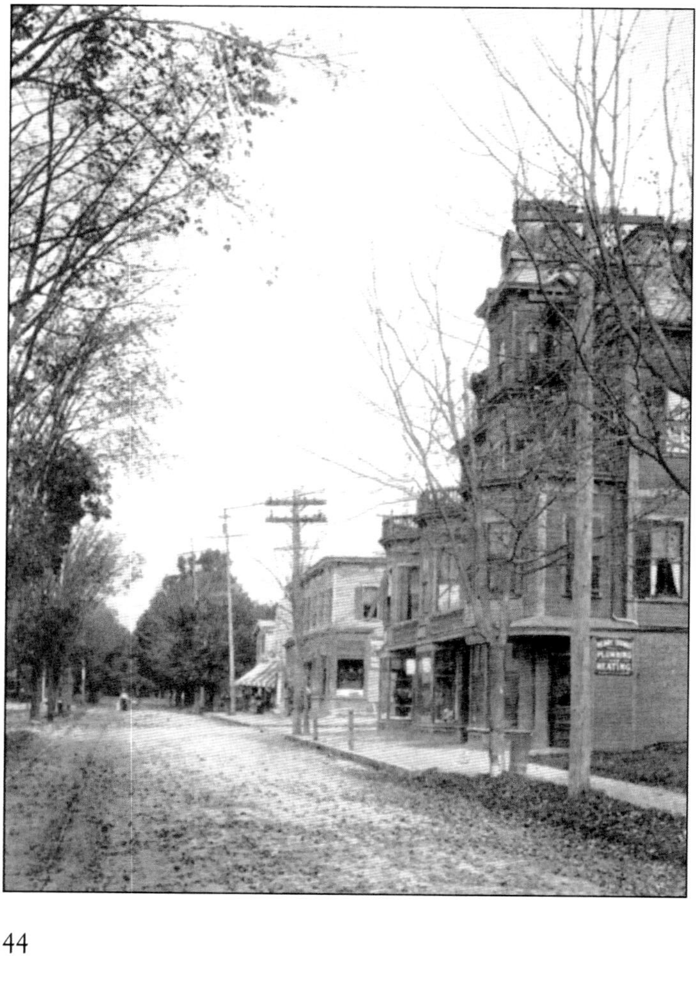

This similar view of Highland Avenue, taken in the fall, shows the Low's Block at the corner of Highland Avenue and West Street. At street level, Virgil A. Rowe's drugstore sold beauty and health aids. Rowe's Drug also had a soda fountain. The building across West Street was Oliver Crisp's Market.

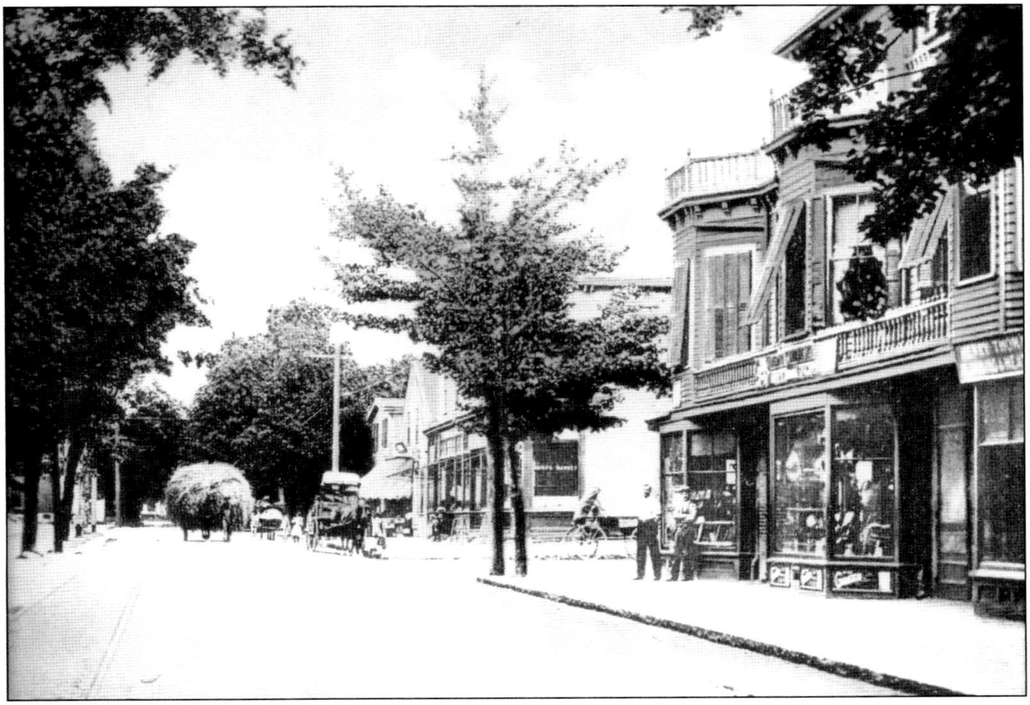

Another photograph of Highland Avenue at its intersection with West Street shows various modes of transport, including a hay wagon, carriages, bicycles, and the trolley tracks across the street from the William Carter Company. (Leonard Dawson Collection of the Needham Free Public Library.)

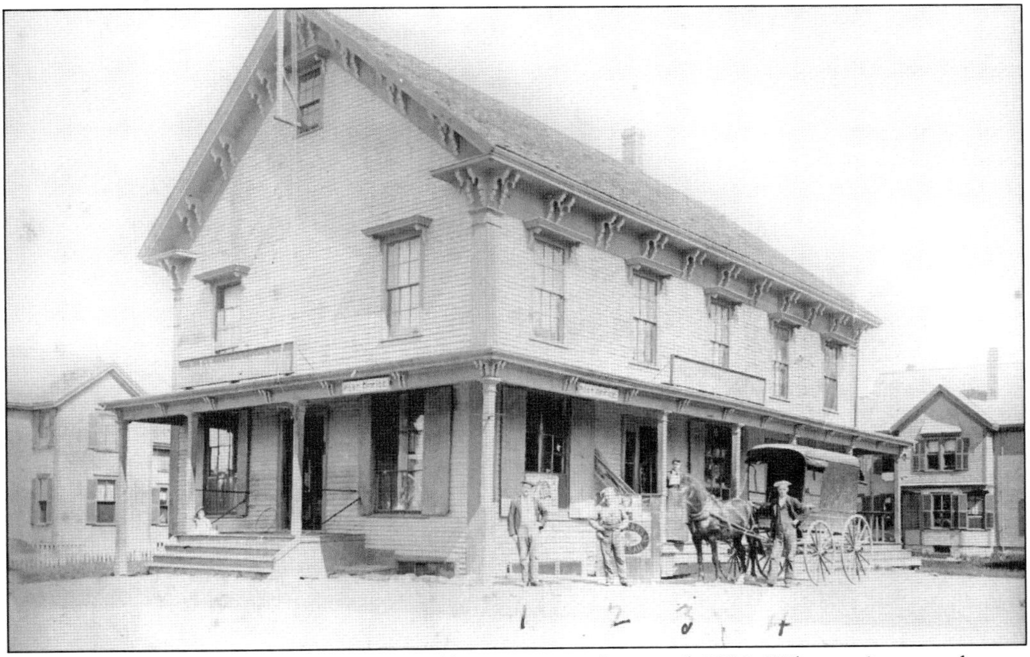

John James Whetton's store and post office is pictured around 1890. Whetton's general store offered foodstuffs and other goods to the workers of the nearby knitting mills. (Leonard Dawson Collection of the Needham Free Public Library.)

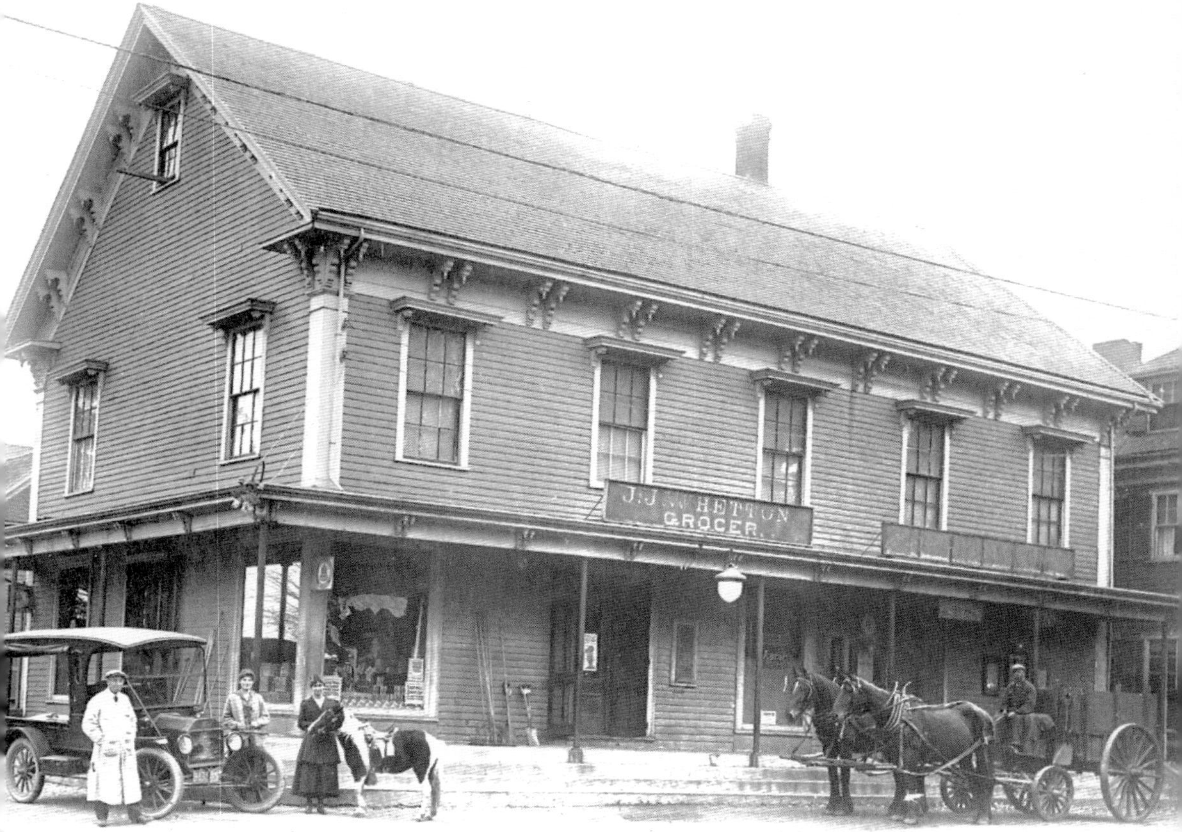

Pictured in 1915 is the building of J.J. Whetton, grocer. In front of his store are horses and cart, a pony, and an automobile. In addition to running the grocery shop, Whetton represented the Cunard, Dominion, and Allan steamship lines. The floor above the grocery was known as Highland Hall and was the meeting place for the Sons of Temperance, Odd Fellows, and the Sons of St. George, which was a fraternal organization of the knitters. The Highlandville Cornet Band also practiced in Highland Hall. The building stood close to the Needham Heights Common.

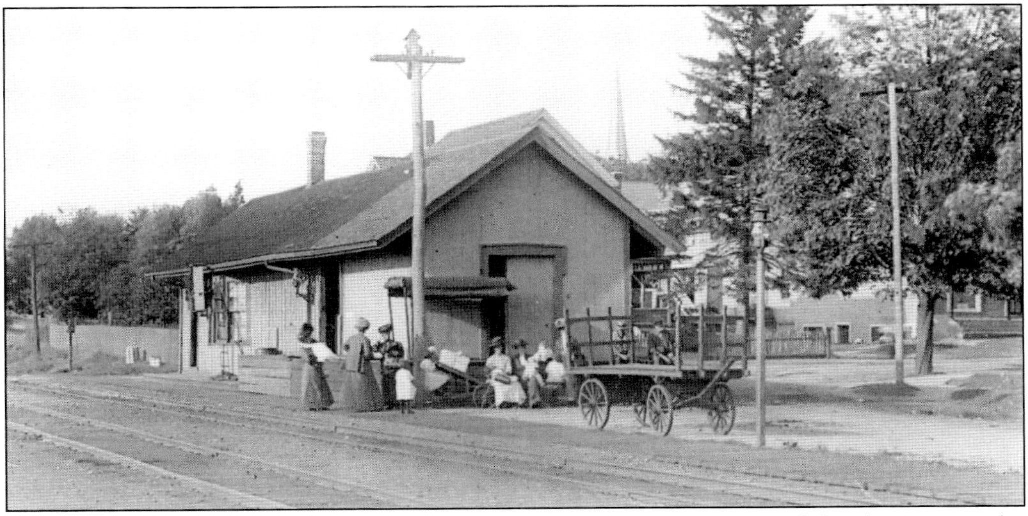

The Highlandville railroad station was built in the 1850s and encouraged development in the area. The Carter, Moseley, Thorpe, Saxony, and other knitting mills were clustered close by, as were stores to serve the workers. The railroads carried the coal to power the steam engines of the mills, brought in the raw materials, and took out the completed garments. This c. 1890 photograph shows the Highlandville railroad station.

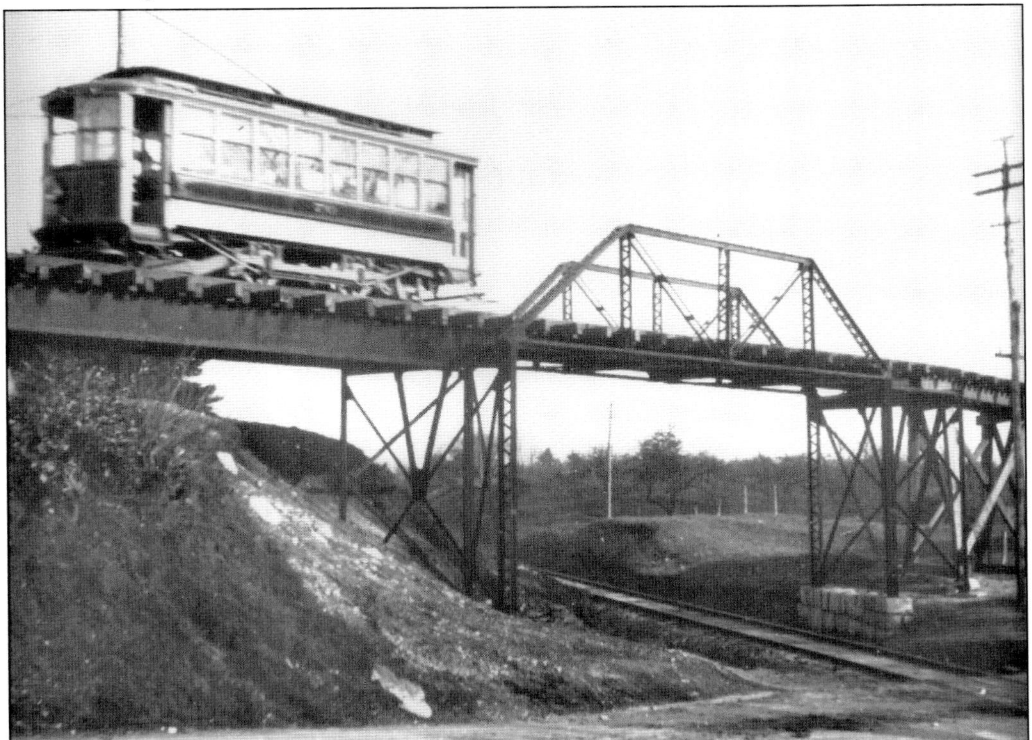

Trolley car No. 70 is on a bridge crossing the railroad line, heading northeast from Highlandville in 1900. The trolley continued into Newton and then Watertown for connections to Boston and other towns. The Needham electric trolleys were part of a vast network, linking towns to each other and to Boston.

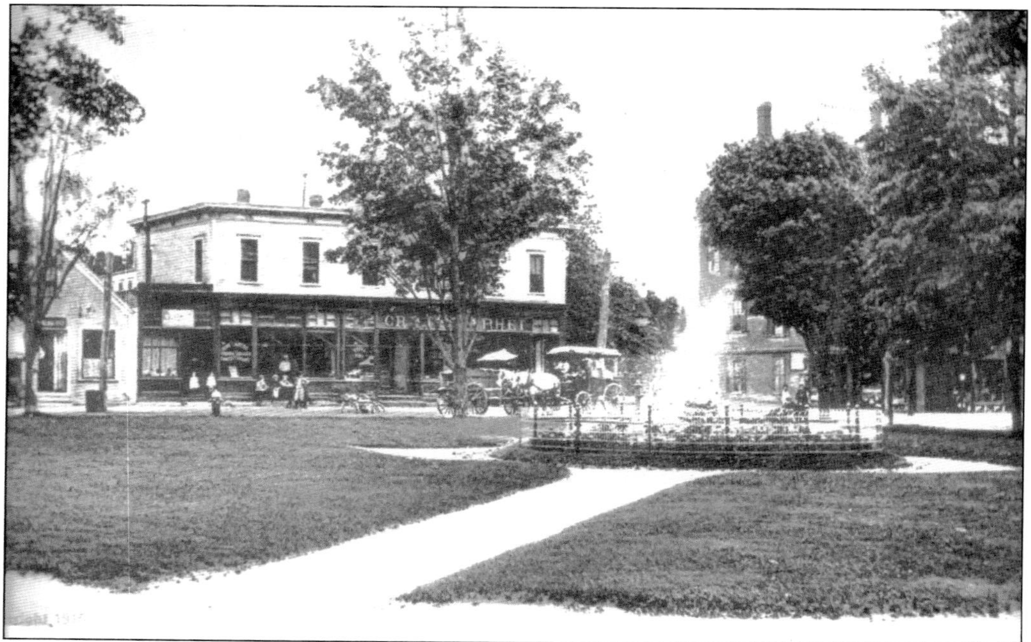

The Common at Needham Heights, pictured around 1910, shows horse-drawn traffic on Highland Avenue. The large Victorian building at the corner of Highland Avenue and West Street was the Low's Block, which was demolished in the 1930s. Situated across West Street was Oliver Crisp's Market, one of several grocery stores that served the mill workers.

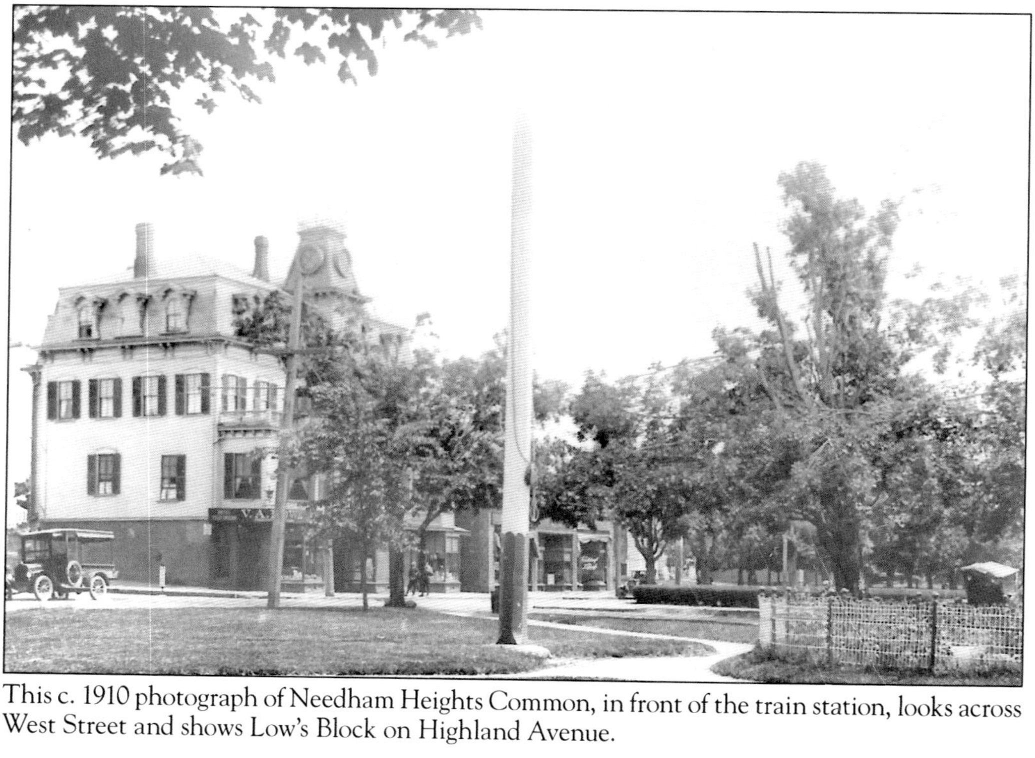

This c. 1910 photograph of Needham Heights Common, in front of the train station, looks across West Street and shows Low's Block on Highland Avenue.

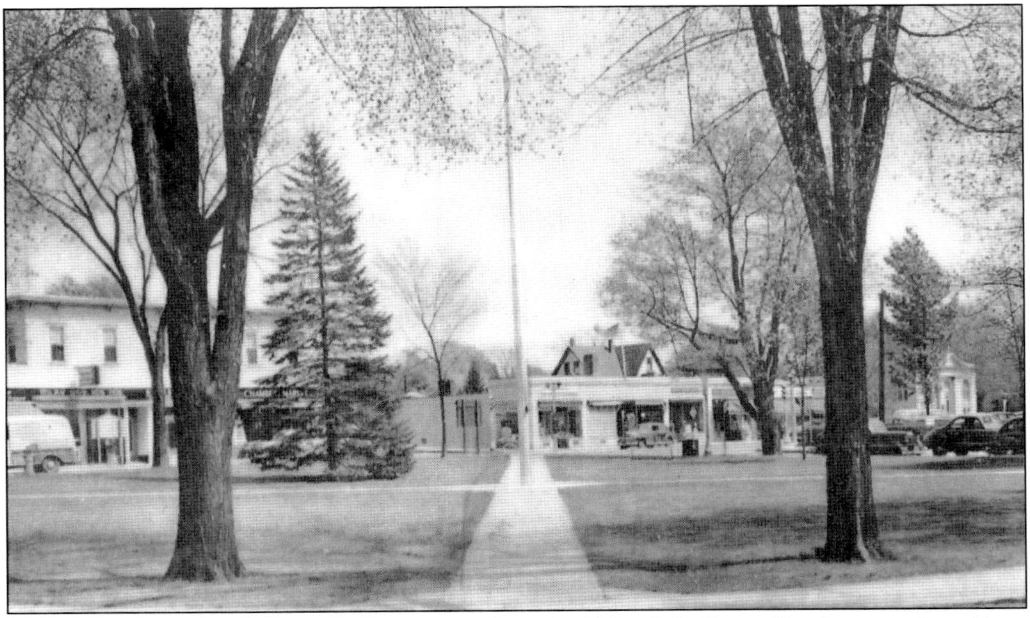

The common at Needham Heights is pictured in the 1940s. The Low's Block was replaced by a single story building. The building that once housed Oliver Crisp's market still stands. The former Carnegie Library, built in 1904, can be seen at far right. In 1915, the building was taken over for office space by the William Carter Company and later served as a bank.

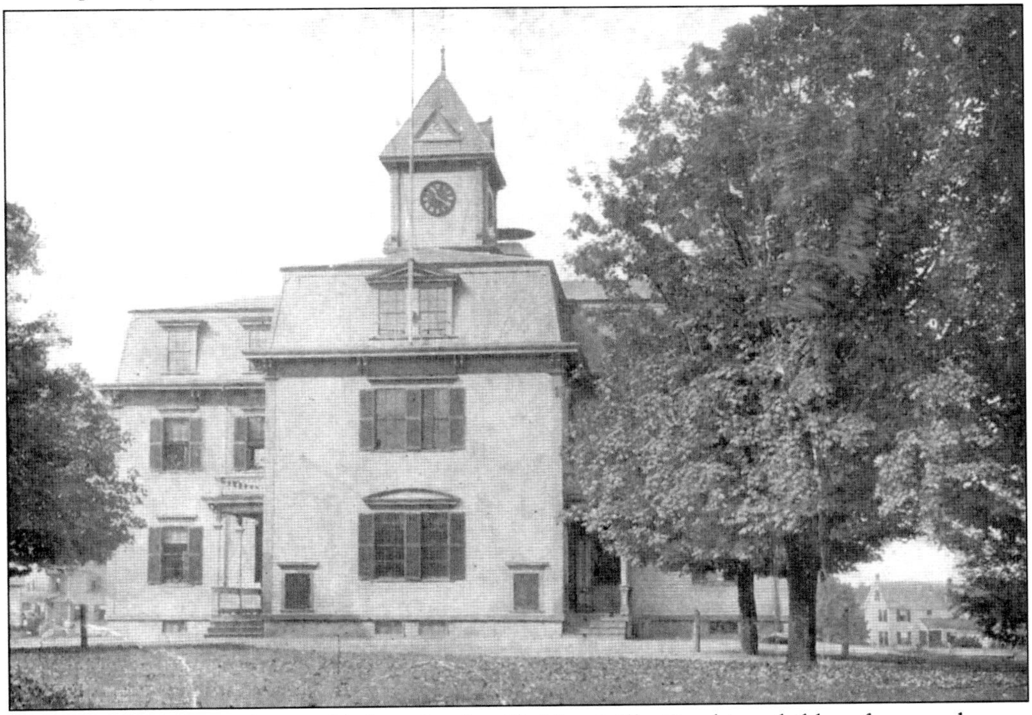

In 1867, the town voted to establish a school at Highlandville. Teaching children from grades one through nine, the school stood at the corner of Highland Avenue and Webster Street. Completed in 1869 at a cost of $7,800, the Avery School, named in honor of Jonathan Avery, offered an education largely for the children of English knitters who had settled in the area.

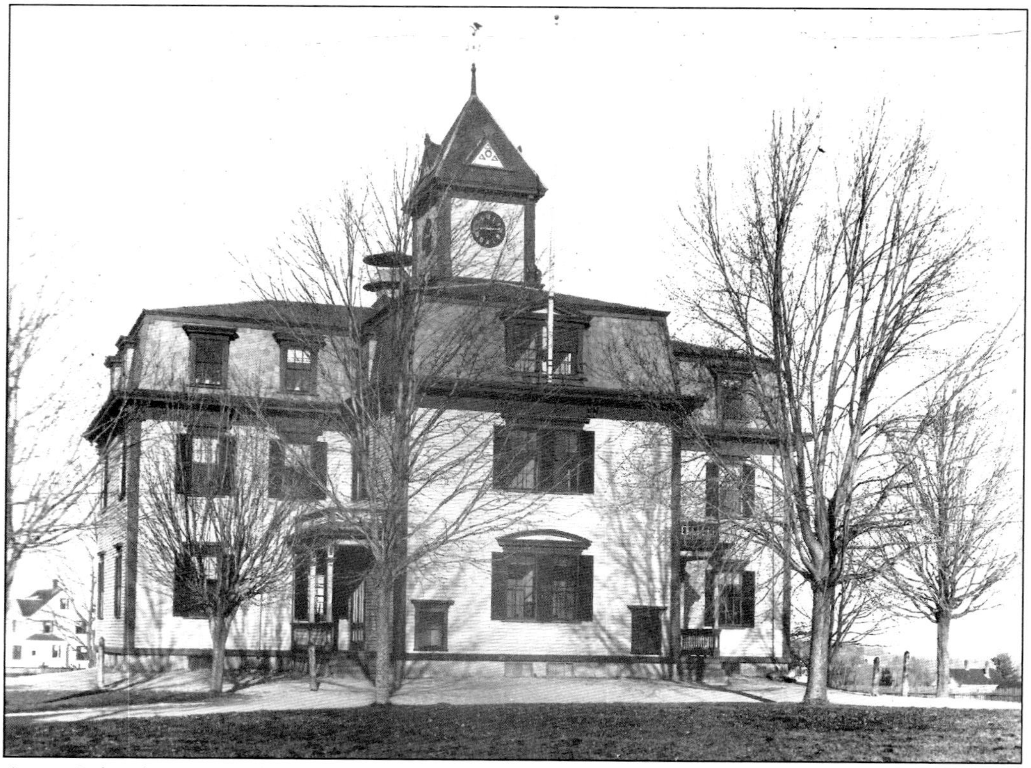

Avery School is pictured around the fall of 1900. At the dedication of the school, Jane G. Avery, daughter of Jonathan and the future wife of William Carter, read a hymn she had written specially for the occasion. (Leonard Dawson Collection of the Needham Free Public Library.)

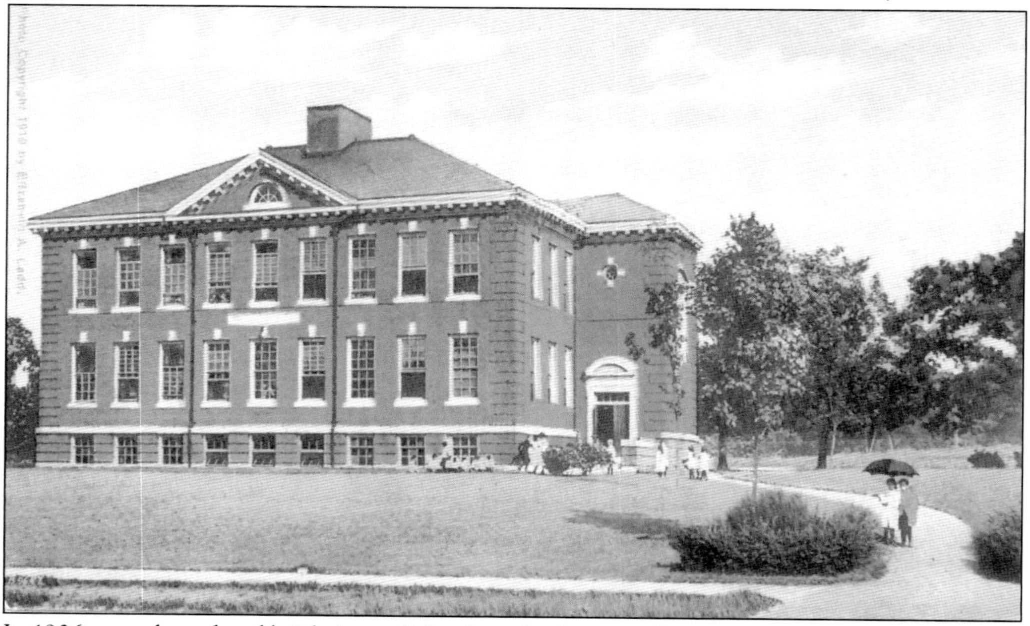

In 1906, an enlarged, red brick Avery School was built across the street from the original wooden structure. Horace Carter donated the land for the new school, and the building cost $23,000. Knitters William Gorse and Joseph B. Thorpe were members of the building committee.

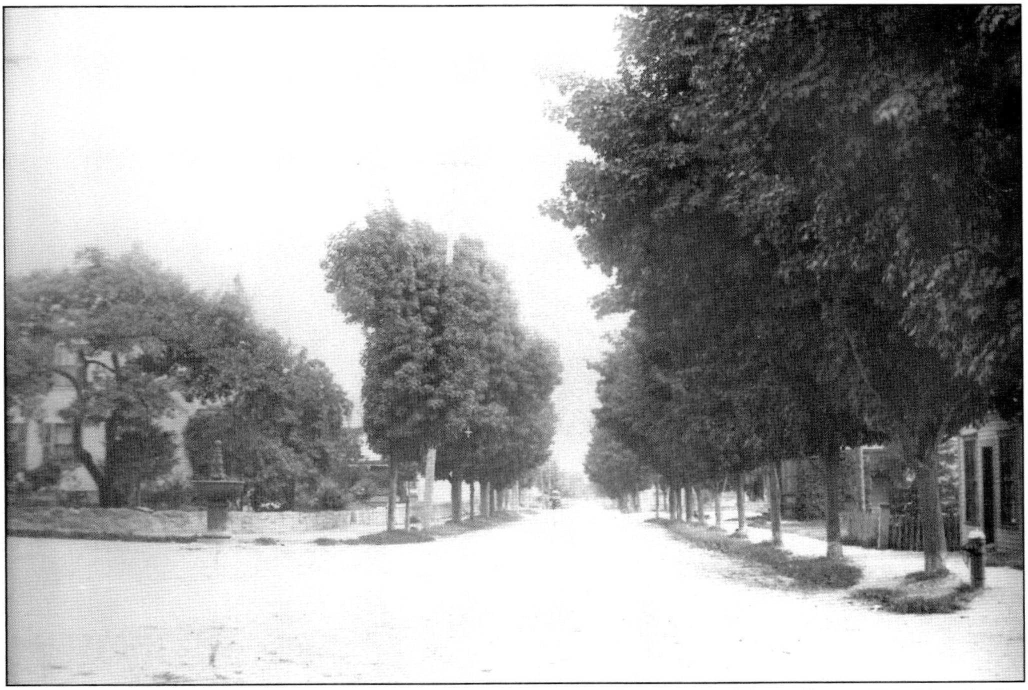

The corner of Hunnewell Street and Highland Avenue was the center of the village of Highlandville, close to the knitting mills and the homes of the knitters, around 1900. (Leonard Dawson Collection of the Needham Free Public Library.)

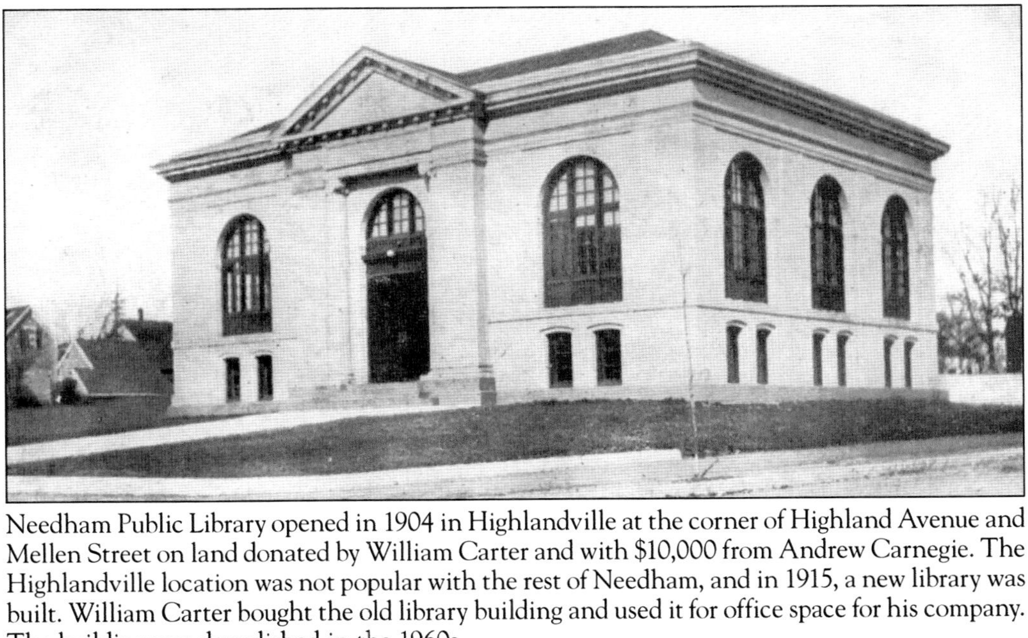

Needham Public Library opened in 1904 in Highlandville at the corner of Highland Avenue and Mellen Street on land donated by William Carter and with $10,000 from Andrew Carnegie. The Highlandville location was not popular with the rest of Needham, and in 1915, a new library was built. William Carter bought the old library building and used it for office space for his company. The building was demolished in the 1960s.

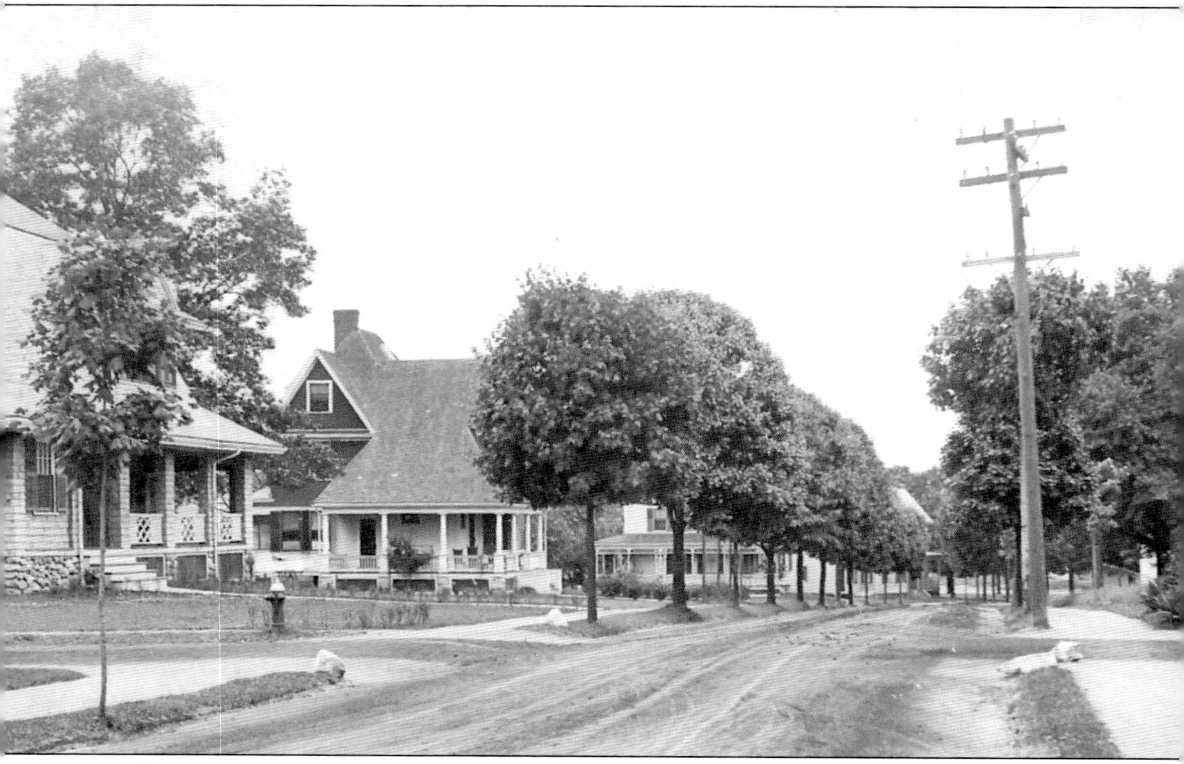

Mark Lee Road, pictured around 1910, shows the elegant houses of some prominent knitters. The short Mark Lee Road intersects with Hunnewell and Webster Streets and Alfreton Road. Born in Matlock, Derbyshire, Mark Lee arrived in Needham in 1853. With his brother John, he made socks and gloves. In 1864, the Lee brothers opened a mill on Highland Avenue, and five years later, they invited William Carter to join them as Lee, Carter, and Company. The Lee brothers' sister became the second wife of William Carter. When Mark Lee retired in 1875, William Carter took over as the sole owner of the mill, now known as the William Carter Company.

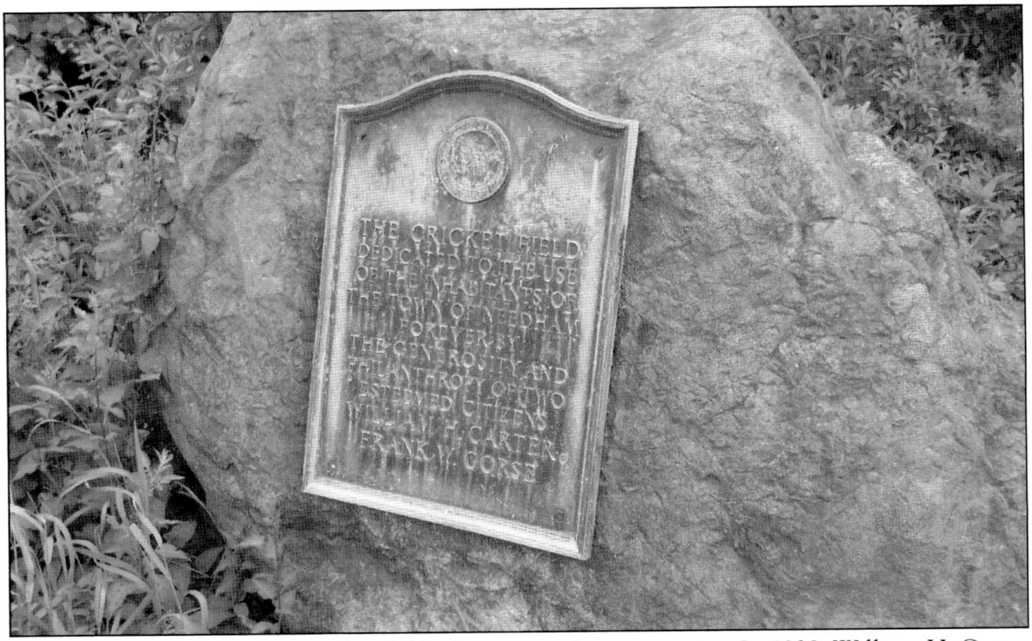

Needham once had several cricket fields, but now only one remains. In 1938, William H. Carter and Frank W. Gorse, sons of prominent English-born knitters, donated the cricket field to the people of Needham. Located on Hillside Avenue near its intersection with Webster Street, the cricket field lies in an area once owned by William Carter. William, Frank, Horace, John, Avery, and Greenough Streets are all named for members of his family.

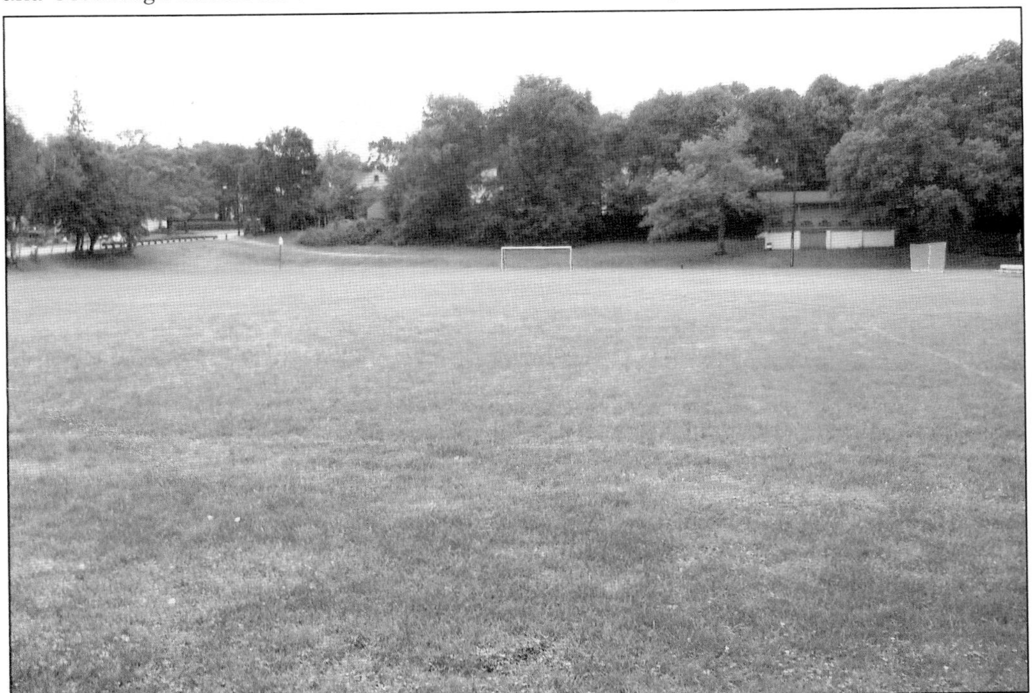

In 1867, the knitters formed the Albion Cricket Club and played on the Kimball estate and later at Avery Park. Late in the 19th century, Needham was known as the cricket capital of New England. This photograph shows the cricket field today, but the game is rarely played in Needham now.

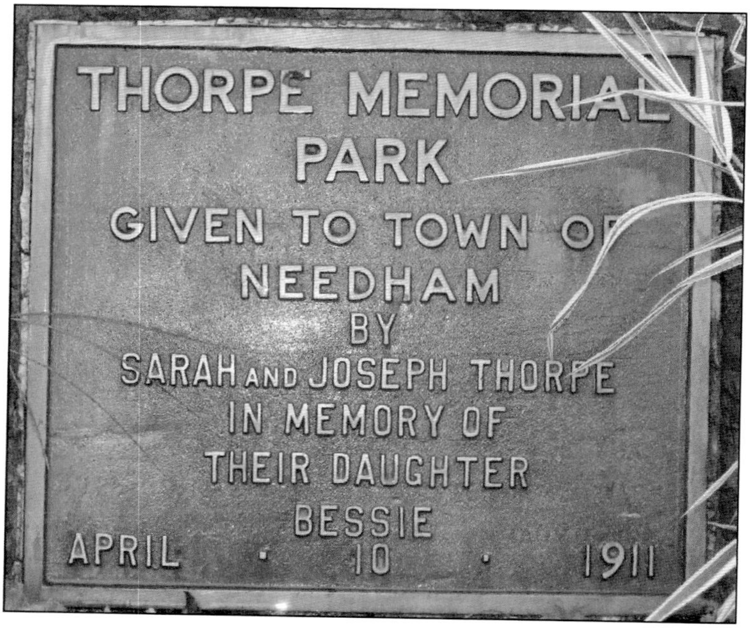

Joseph B. Thorpe was born in Ashfield, Nottinghamshire, and came to Needham at the end of the Civil War. He owned the successful High Street Knitting Company. In 1908, his 17-year-old daughter Sarah Bessie Thorpe died while she was a student in Berlin. In 1911, Joseph and Sarah Thorpe donated the Thorpe Memorial Park in memory of Bessie.

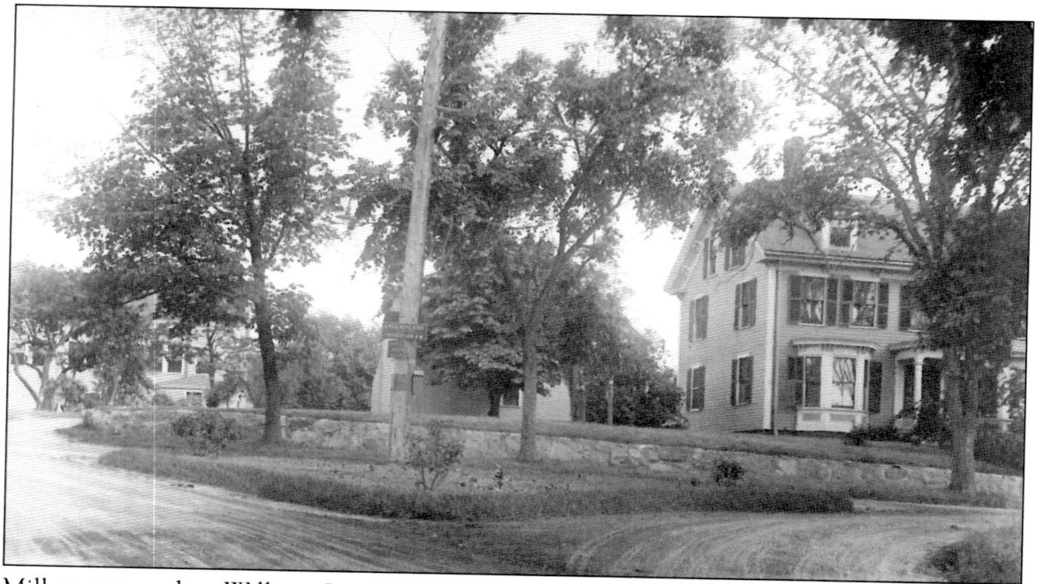

Mill owners, such as William Carter and his sons, lived close to their factories. This photograph shows the large houses on High Street in Needham Heights. Nearby, the Carters built cottages to house the workers in their mills.

Four

Knitters and Their Mills

In 1859, there were 187 knitting mills in the United States using mostly wool, but also cotton and silk. Most mills were small and used machines powered by hand or foot. The Civil War and a fast growing population created a boost for knitwear, prompting the formation of the National Association of Hosiery and Underwear Manufacturers. By the beginning of the 20th century, it claimed over 600 members.

Knitted hosiery and underwear become the leading industry of Needham in the late 19th century, especially in Highlandville. The town had over 40 knitting companies of different sizes. Together the mills employed over 1,000 people, especially immigrants coming from Ireland and Italy. Several hundred more did piece work at home. Most Englishmen arrived poor, but in time prospered and gave back generously to Needham. They were active in establishing the Methodist Episcopal Church and served as town selectmen and members of the school and library committees. John Moseley donated the land on Highland Avenue on which the high school was built. In 1862, his son William joined the 44th Massachusetts Militia and saw battle in North Carolina. Mark Lee Road, Thorpe Park, Thorpe Road, Moseley Avenue, Alfreton Road, and the cricket field commemorate the contributions of the knitters to Needham.

In time, the immigrant knitters joined the Yankee elite families of Needham. In 1884, William Carter, William Moseley, Alexander Lynes, and William Gorse helped form the Needham Cemetery Association. According to its 1884 act of incorporation, the association was formed "for the purpose of acquiring, holding, managing, and perpetuating a place for the burial of the dead in the town of Needham." The Avery School was built in 1906 with Joseph B. Thorpe and William Gorse as members of the committee. Horace A. Carter donated the land on which the Avery school was built.

Most of the knitting mills of Needham remained small. In 1915, the capital of Benjamin Moseley and Company was $62,000; Saxony Mills was $95,000; and Moseley and Company was $50,000. In time, they all failed. By contrast, the William Carter Company had capital funds worth $3,500,000 and grew into an international company.

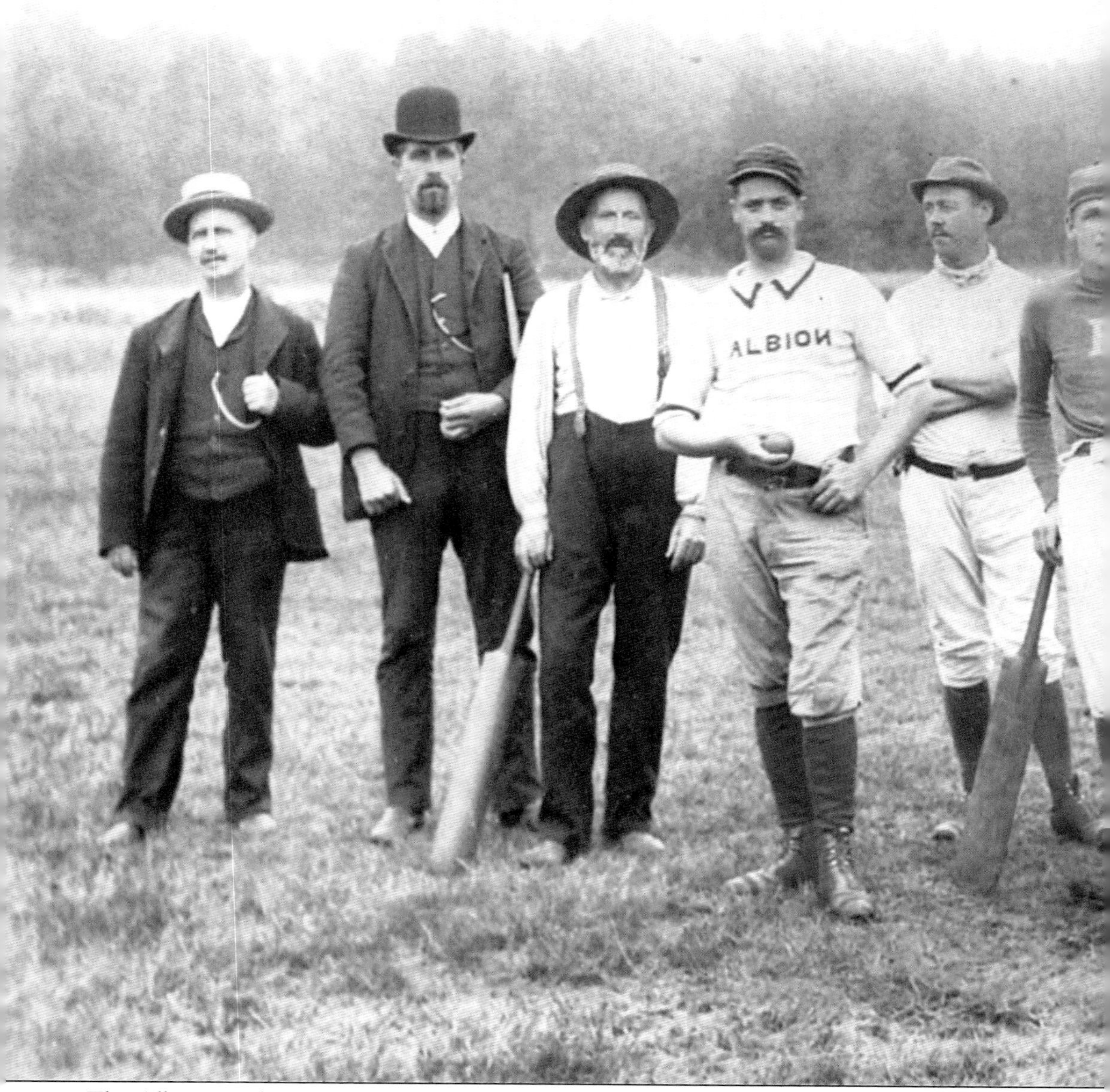

The Albion Cricket Team was founded in Needham in 1867. In the 1880s, Needham was the cricket capital of Massachusetts, and the team was the East Coast champion. Most of the team's members were from the English Midlands. Pictured here are members of the 1885 team posing with bats and wickets. From left to right, they are William Gorse, Levi Searcy, James Dring, George E. Wragg, Fergus Gorse, William Crisp, John Allen, William H. Carter, Abimelech Burroughs, John Beach, Frank Gorse, John Jessup and Henry Patrick. William Gorse and James Dring had

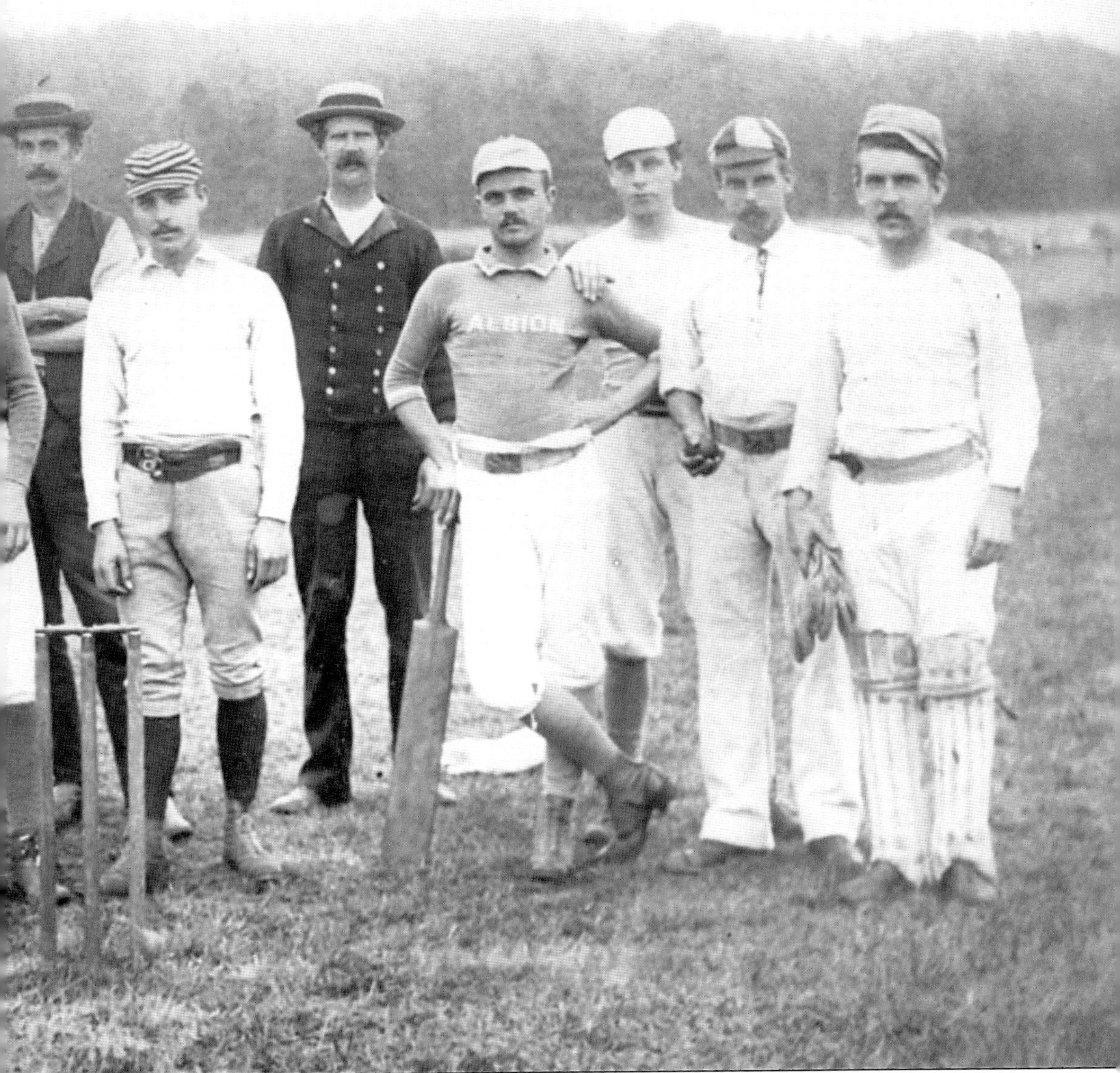

been prominent cricket players in their native England. Young William Carter and Frank Gorse were the sons of prominent knitters, and, in time, would take over the family business. For many years, Carter and Gorse kept their love of the game of cricket. In the 1930s, they donated land in Needham as a cricket field. George Wragg served as Needham's first night policeman and later opened a grocery store in the Moseley building. The Thorpe brothers were also involved with the Albion team.

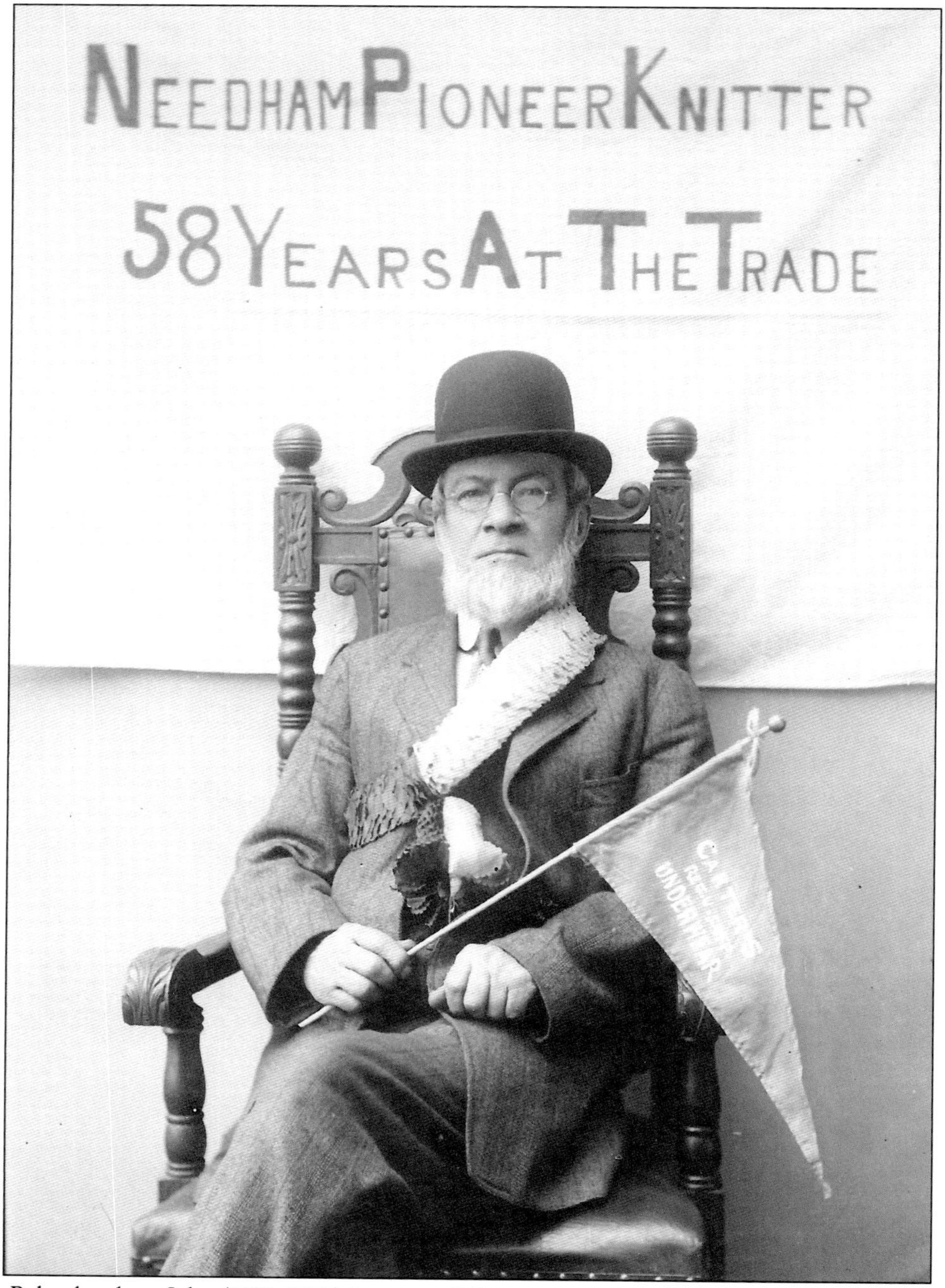

The Beless brothers, John (1826–1903), James, and Thomas, came from Barrow-on-Suir, Leicestershire, England. Thomas, the first to emigrate, sailed on the *Staffordshire* and arrived in Boston in 1852. Together, the brothers established their knitting business at the corner of Greendale Avenue and High Street, Highlandville, making gloves, stockings, and jackets. In 1903, the brothers died within months of each other. H.C Beless owned the Nehoiden Knitting mills and made infants' clothing, and John Beless's daughter Sarah married Joseph Thorpe. Samuel Beless, pictured around 1910 wearing a bowler hat, celebrated 58 years in the knitting trade. He was born in Leicestershire in 1839 and arrived in Needham in 1852. He worked for his father, knitting gloves, stockings, and jackets. Later, he went to work for William Carter.

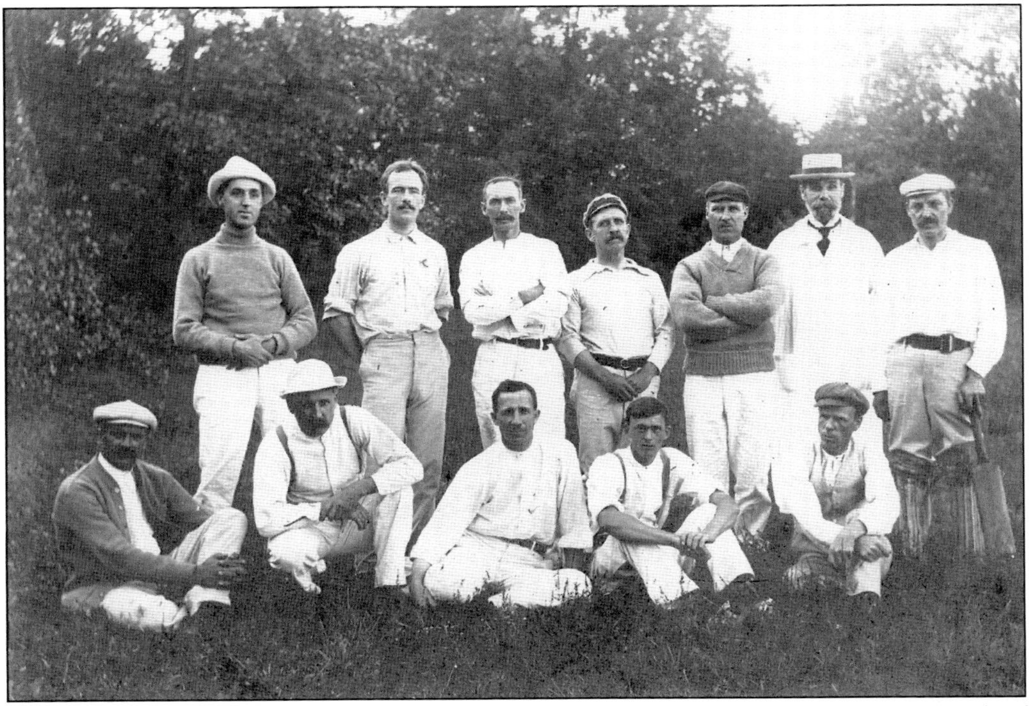

Pictured are members of the Needham Cricket Club during the 1904 season. Comprised mainly of younger men, the team had a few stalwarts, such as Frank Gorse (standing third from the right), who was team captain. To the right of Gorse is Joseph B. Thorpe, umpire, and with cricket bat and pads, William Henry Carter.

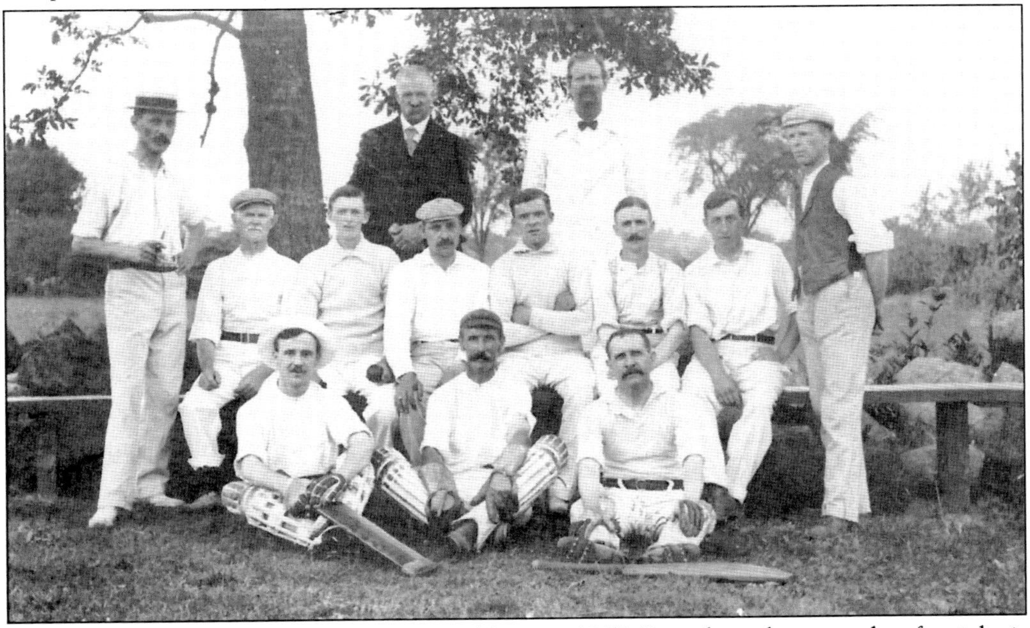

The Highlandville Cricket Club is pictured here in 1907. Seated on the ground at far right is William Henry Carter, still an active member of the cricket team at age 43. William Carter and Joseph Gorse tried valiantly to keep the game of cricket active with their gift of the cricket field to the town of Needham in 1933.

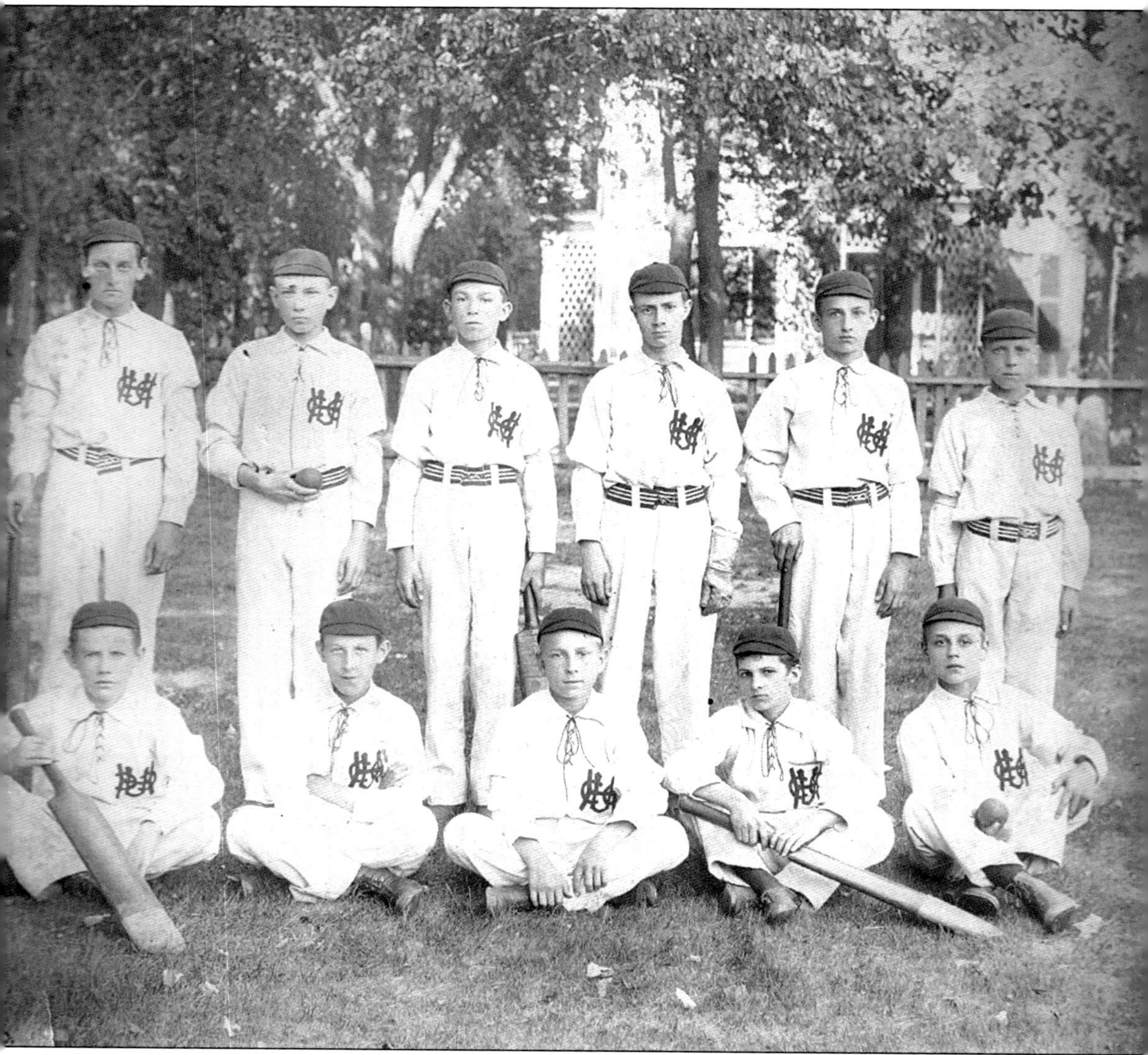

The Needham boys' cricket team is pictured around 1910. The Needham Heights cricket team played on a field near the Avery School. The 1908 season was especially successful, with the team finishing third in its league. The knitters of Needham tried to pass on the game of cricket to the next generation with the formation of a boys' league with little success. Despite the opening of the cricket field, the game in Needham, as elsewhere in the United States, did not catch on. The boys in the picture are smartly outfitted with matching caps, shirts, belts, and long trousers, as well as cricket bats and ball.

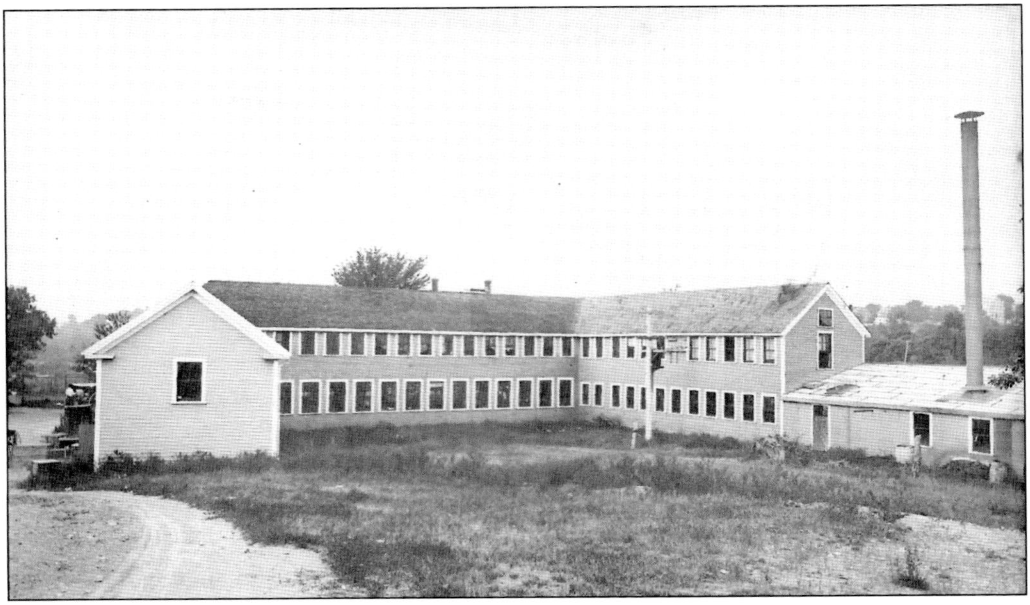

William Roper came from Harwick, Scotland, and settled in Needham in 1881. He opened a small shop on West Street making athletic goods using a hand frame. After his death, his sons Robert and William Jr. expanded the business as Roper Brothers and introduced machinery that made elasticized knitted goods.

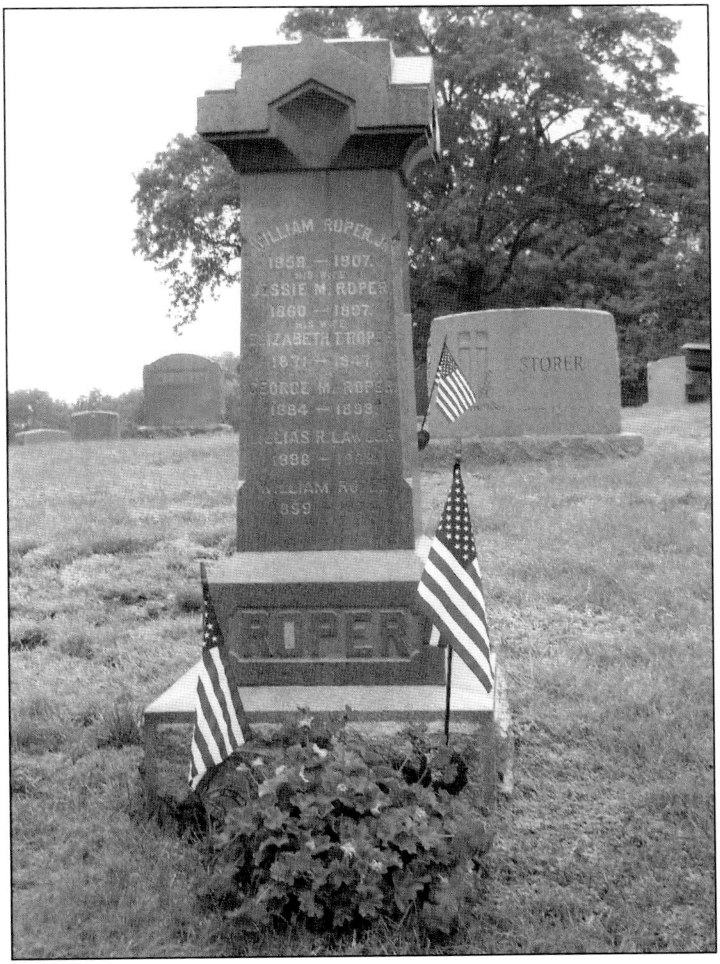

Robert Roper died in 1898 at the age of 42. His brother William Jr. died in 1907, aged 49, and was buried in the Needham cemetery. William's first wife, Jessie, died at the age of 37, and his second wife, Elizabeth, outlived him by 40 years.

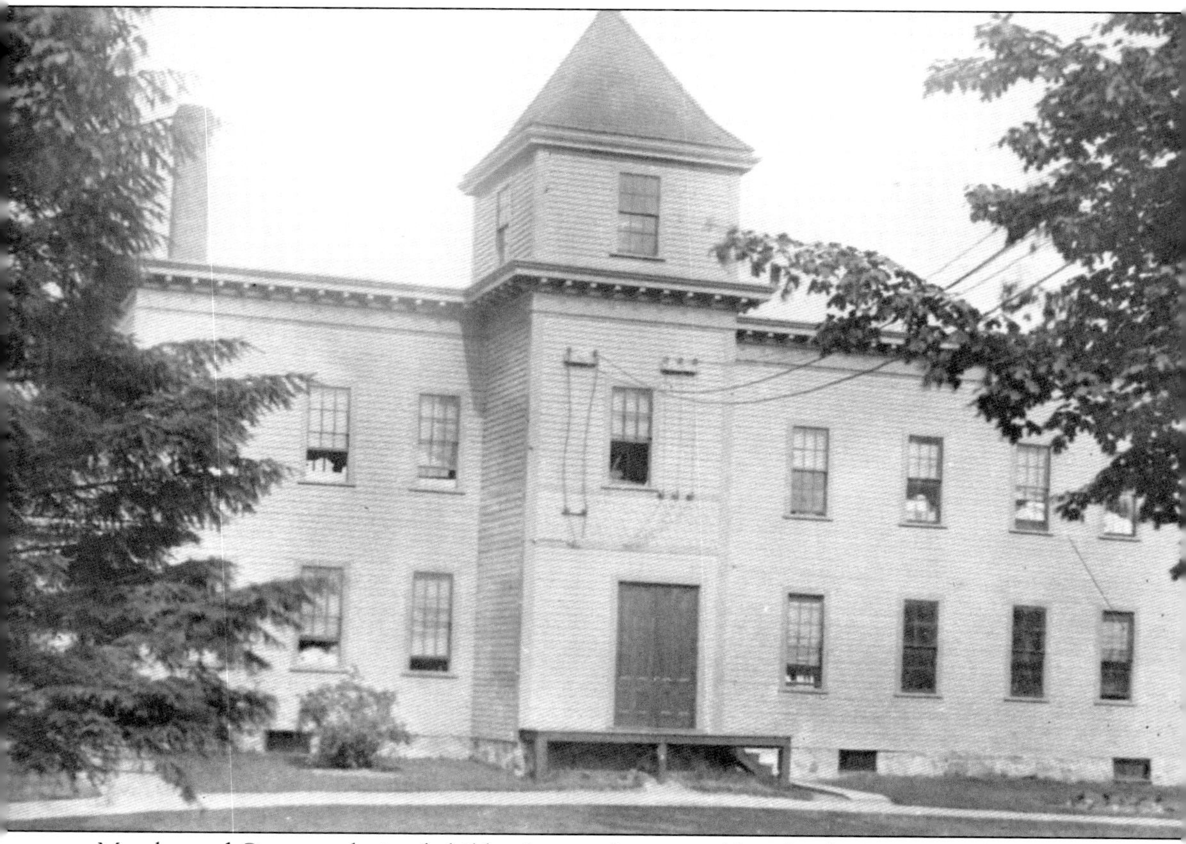

Moseley and Company knitted children's wear that was sold under the Tiny-Wear label. At the time of Needham's bicentennial in 1911, the Moseley mill employed 50 workers. John Moseley was an active member of the First Baptist Church of Needham and served as its treasurer for many years. In 1897, he donated land on Highland Avenue for the high school.

Born in Duffield, Derbyshire, in 1841, William Gorse settled in Needham when he was 20 years old. He was a pioneer in the technique of interweaving rubber with silk, cotton, or wool yarn. William Gorse set up shop at 45 Hunnewell Street making elastic socks and bandages to treat varicose veins and other diseases of the legs. He was active in the Methodist Episcopal Church and a passionate member of the Sons of Temperance.

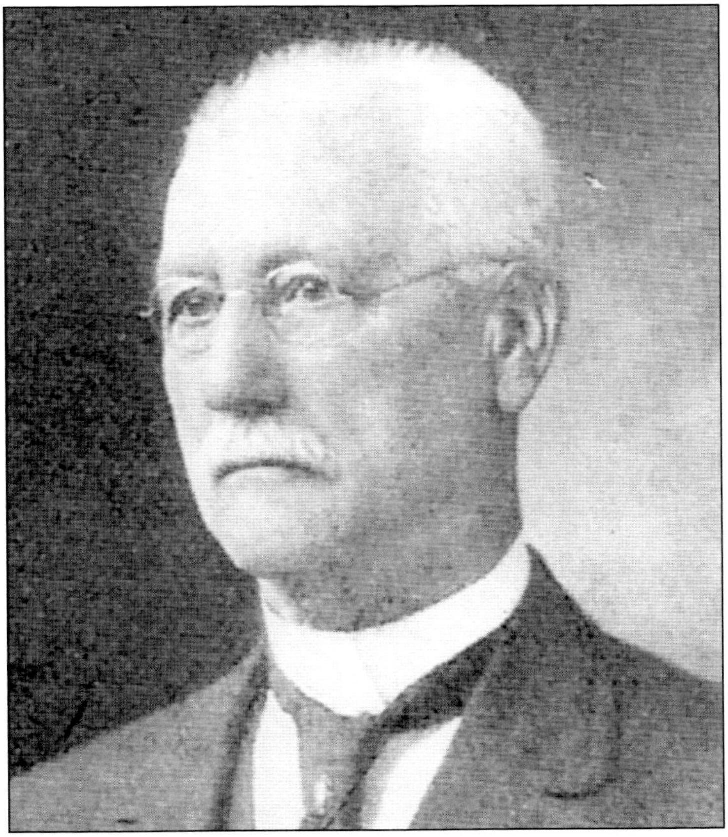

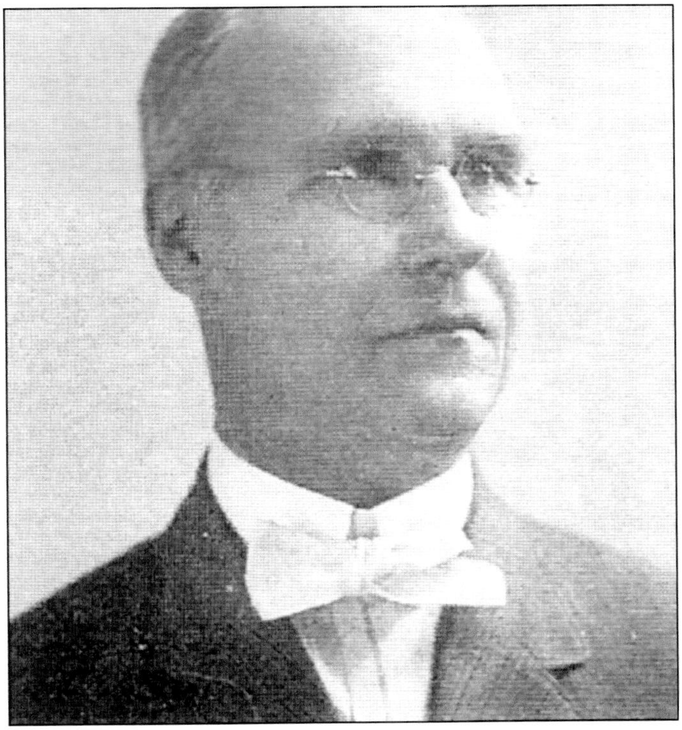

Frank William Gorse started a business similar to that of his father, William Gorse. Frank was a pigeon fancier and won prizes at the 1895 and 1896 Poultry and Pigeon Show at Madison Garden, New York. He was a leading breeder of the Jacobin pigeon and served in 1903 as president of the Jacobin Club.

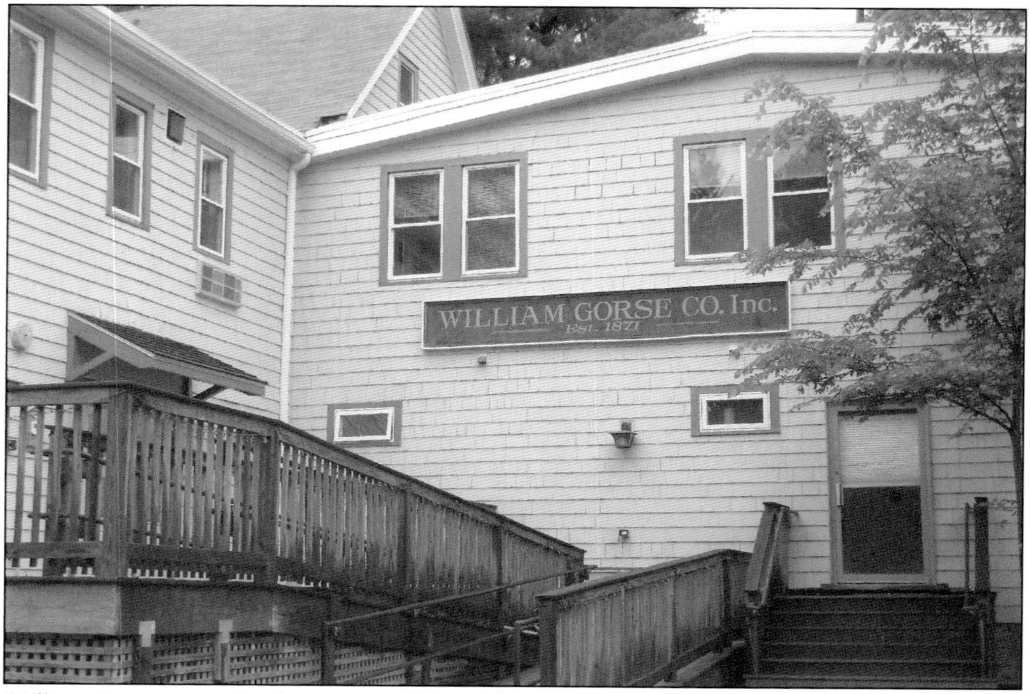

William Gorse started his business in 1871 and his son Frank followed in the knitting trade. Frank bought the Thorpe Mill in 1893, later known as the Thorpe-Gorse mill, on Thorpe Road. The building still stands but is no longer used as a knitting mill.

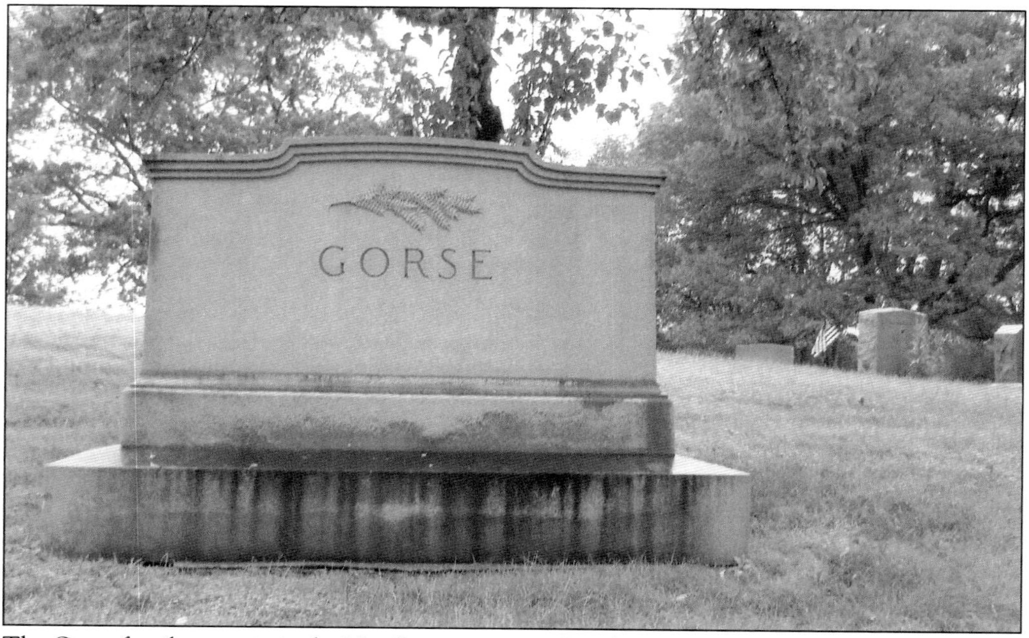

The Gorse family stone is in the Needham cemetery. Frank William Gorse was an active member of the Needham Heights cricket team and excelled as a bowler. Later in his life, he became prominent as a poultry and pigeon breeder. Known as the Doyen of the Jacobin Fancy, Gorse for many years traveled to Great Britain to take part in pigeon shows. Frank William Gorse died in 1938 and was buried near his father.

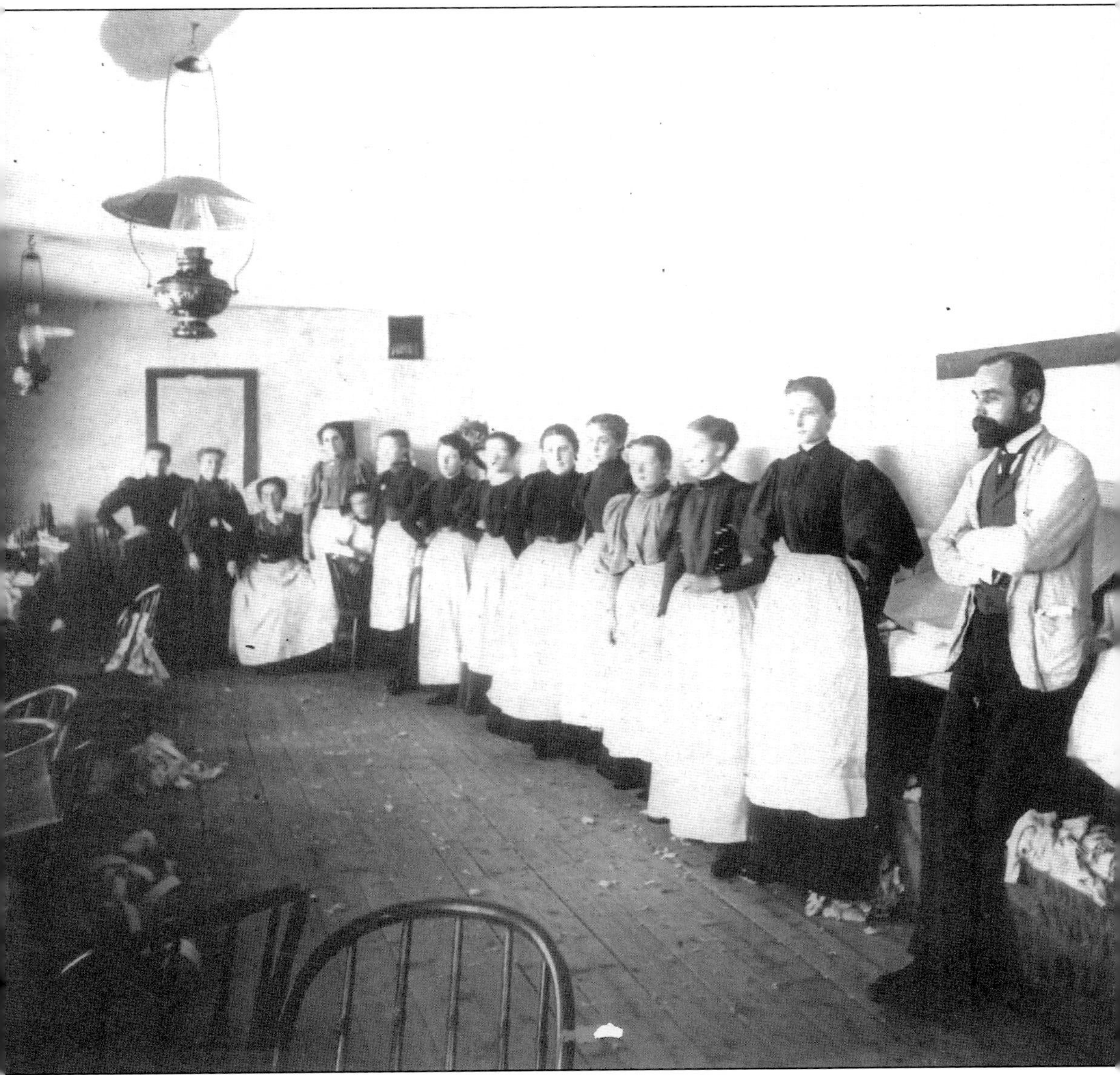

The Thorpe brothers, John, Thomas, Charles, and Joseph, were all knitters and came from Ashfield, Nottinghamshire, England. Joseph Thorpe started the High Street Knitting Company and made children's clothes. He took seriously his civic responsibilities. In addition to his interest in cricket, Joseph Thorpe served as president of the local YMCA, was a town selectman, member of the Needham cemetery board, and raised funds to build the Avery school. Joseph Thorpe is pictured around 1895 inside the mill with his female employees. The workbenches are set close to the large windows, which were the main source of light. In the age before electricity, kerosene lamps suspended from the ceiling were used to light the mill.

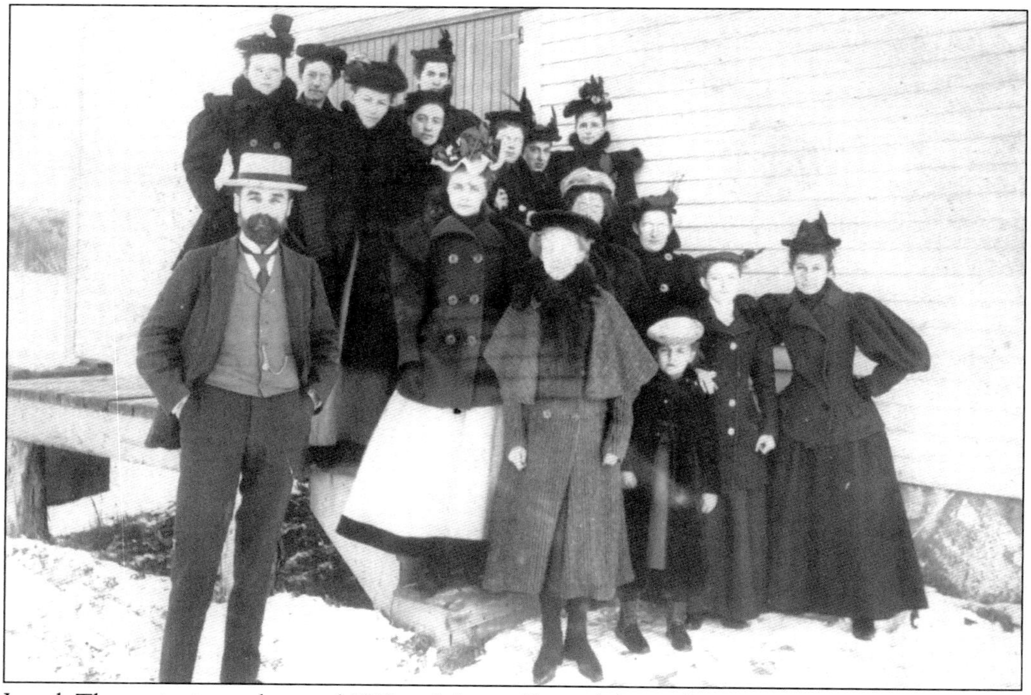

Joseph Thorpe is pictured around 1900 with his staff outside his mill. He was active in the Methodist Church, the Needham YMCA, and the Society of Prevention of Cruelty to Children. Joseph Thorpe sold his business, with some 50 workers, in 1921 to the Nehoiden Knitting Company.

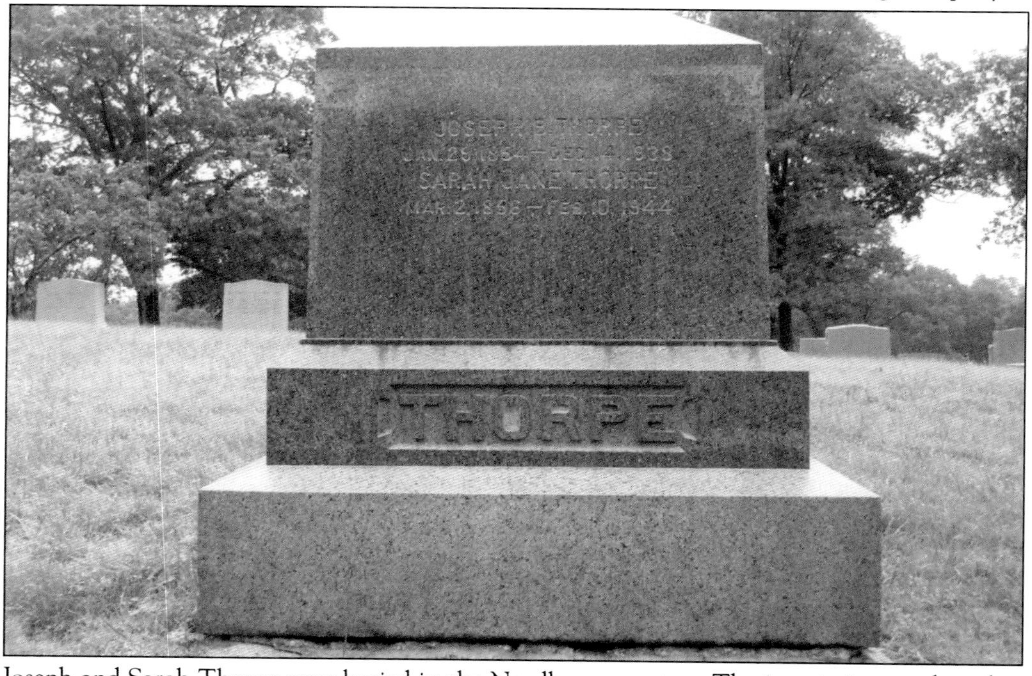

Joseph and Sarah Thorpe were buried in the Needham cemetery. The inscription on the other side of the stone, a poem by Mark Twain, is dedicated to their daughter Sarah Bessie: "Warm summer sun, Shine kindly here / Warm southern wind, Blow softly here / Green sod above, Lie light, lie light / Good night, dear hear, Good night, good night."

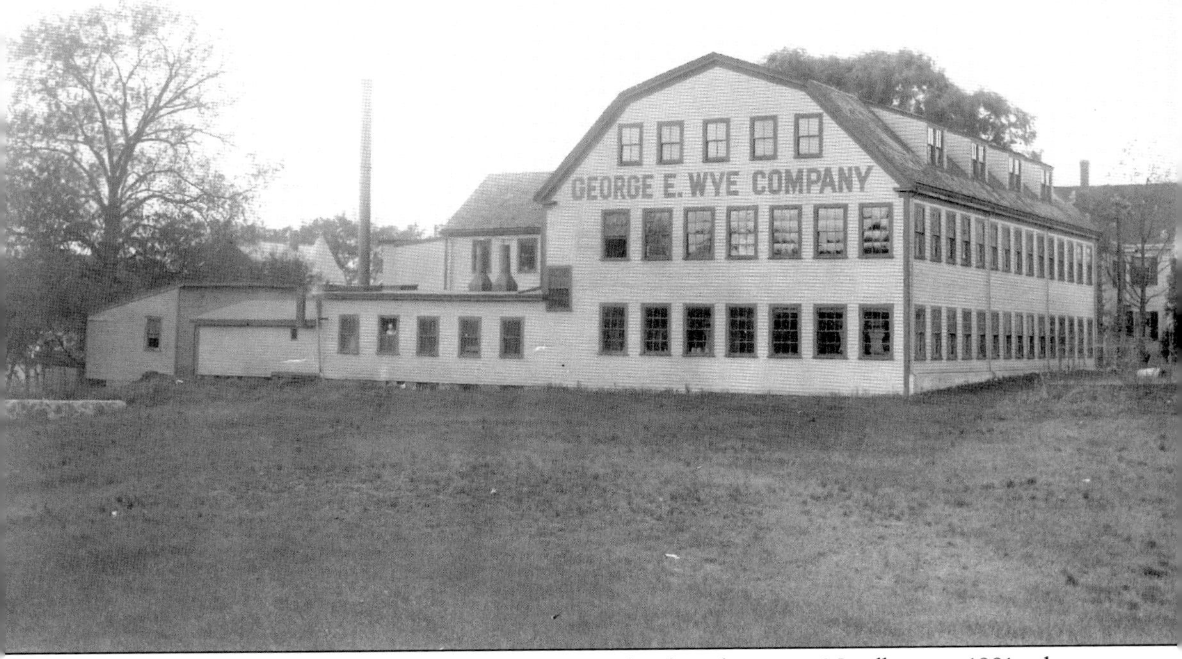

John T. Wye (1839–1929) was born in Leicester, England, and came to Needham in 1881, where he made women's gloves. John was known as a writer of verse and wrote a poem for each Memorial Day for 19 years. His sons, William and George, were born in England and came to Needham several years after their father. The sons continued his business as Wye Brothers and Company at the corner of Pleasant Street and Dedham Avenue. In 1890, the brothers split up, and George set up shop as the George E. Wye Company. William built his mill on Highland Avenue.

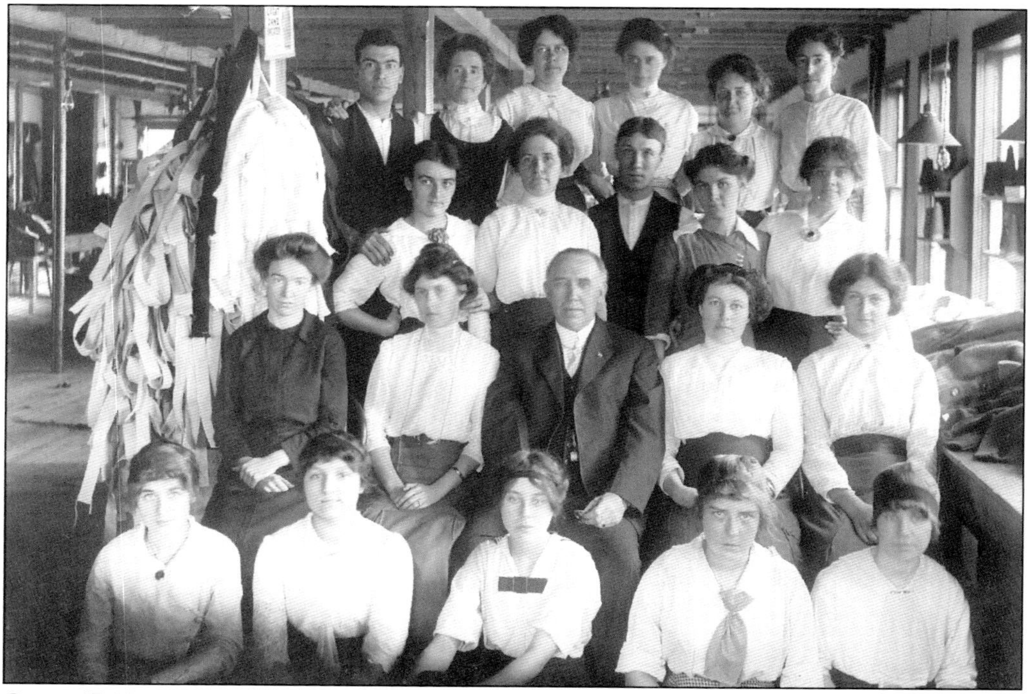

George E. Wye Company incorporated in 1907 with a capital stock of $20,000. The factory was equipped with 65 knitting machines, 30 sewing machines, and a staff of 50. Wye sponsored two floats in the Needham bicentennial parade. In 1911, he had a series of photographs taken to show how his factory worked. This photograph shows Wye and members of his staff. The George E. Wye Company made "Great Dane" sweaters, bathing suits, and jerseys. Wye later expanded to Framingham, Massachusetts.

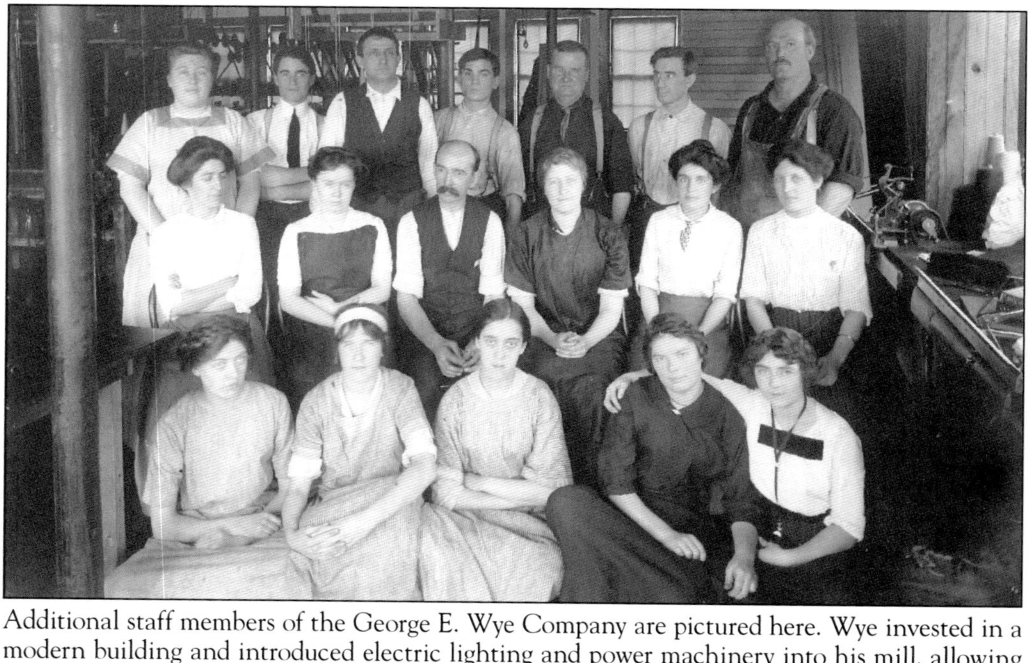

Additional staff members of the George E. Wye Company are pictured here. Wye invested in a modern building and introduced electric lighting and power machinery into his mill, allowing his company to produce more goods using fewer workers.

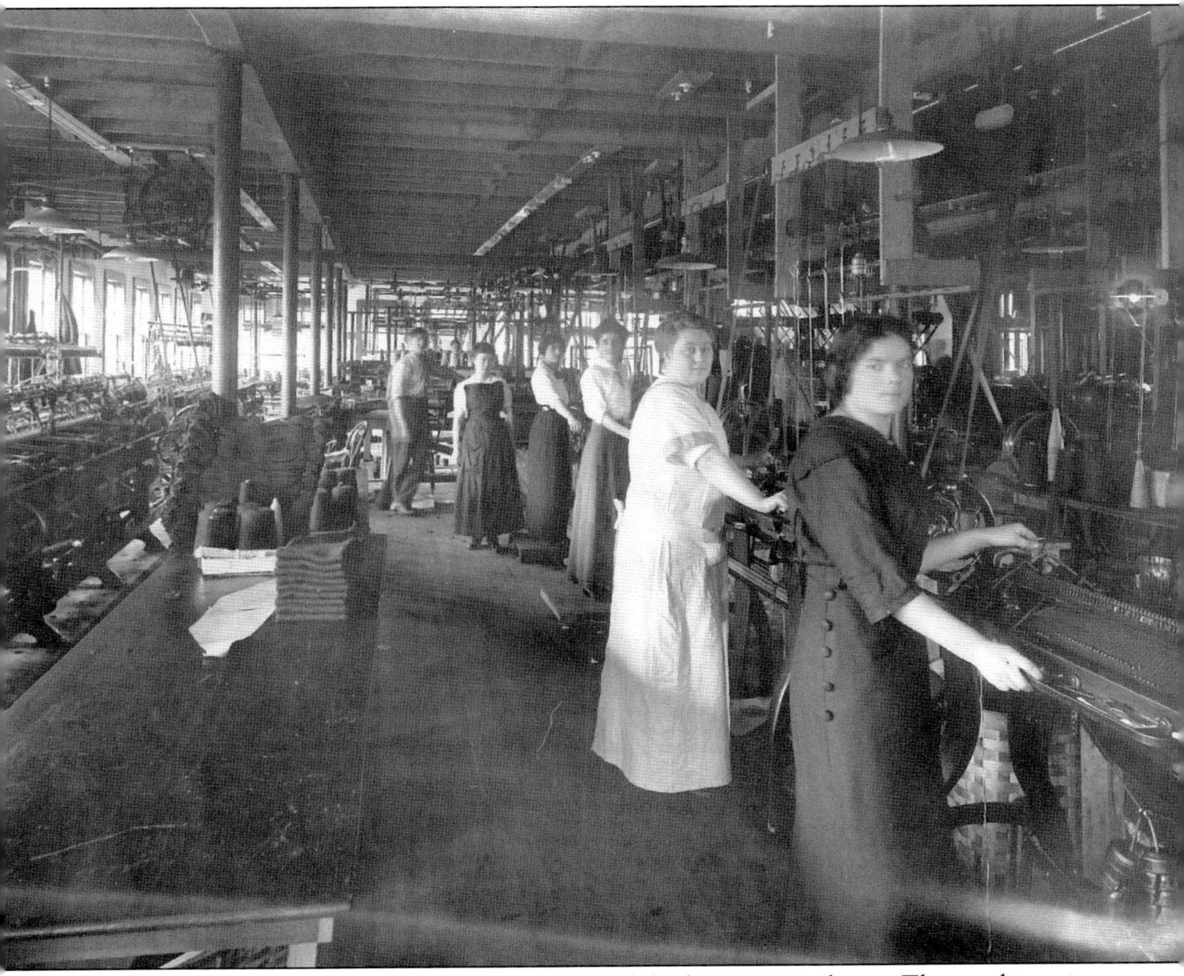

A single worker, standing all day, managed each of the knitting machines. The machines in George Wye's factory were powered by electricity, but still used pulleys attached to the ceiling and belting typical of the age of steam power to turn the machines. Knitters like George Wye faced heavy competition from imports coming from Germany, Great Britain, and Japan. The American Protective Tariff League was formed in 1885 in New York. The declared objective of the league was "to protect American labor by placing a tariff on imports, which would adequately secure American industrial products against the competition of foreign labor." The Payne-Aldrich Tariff Law of 1909 offered some protection to the knitwear manufacturers of Needham.

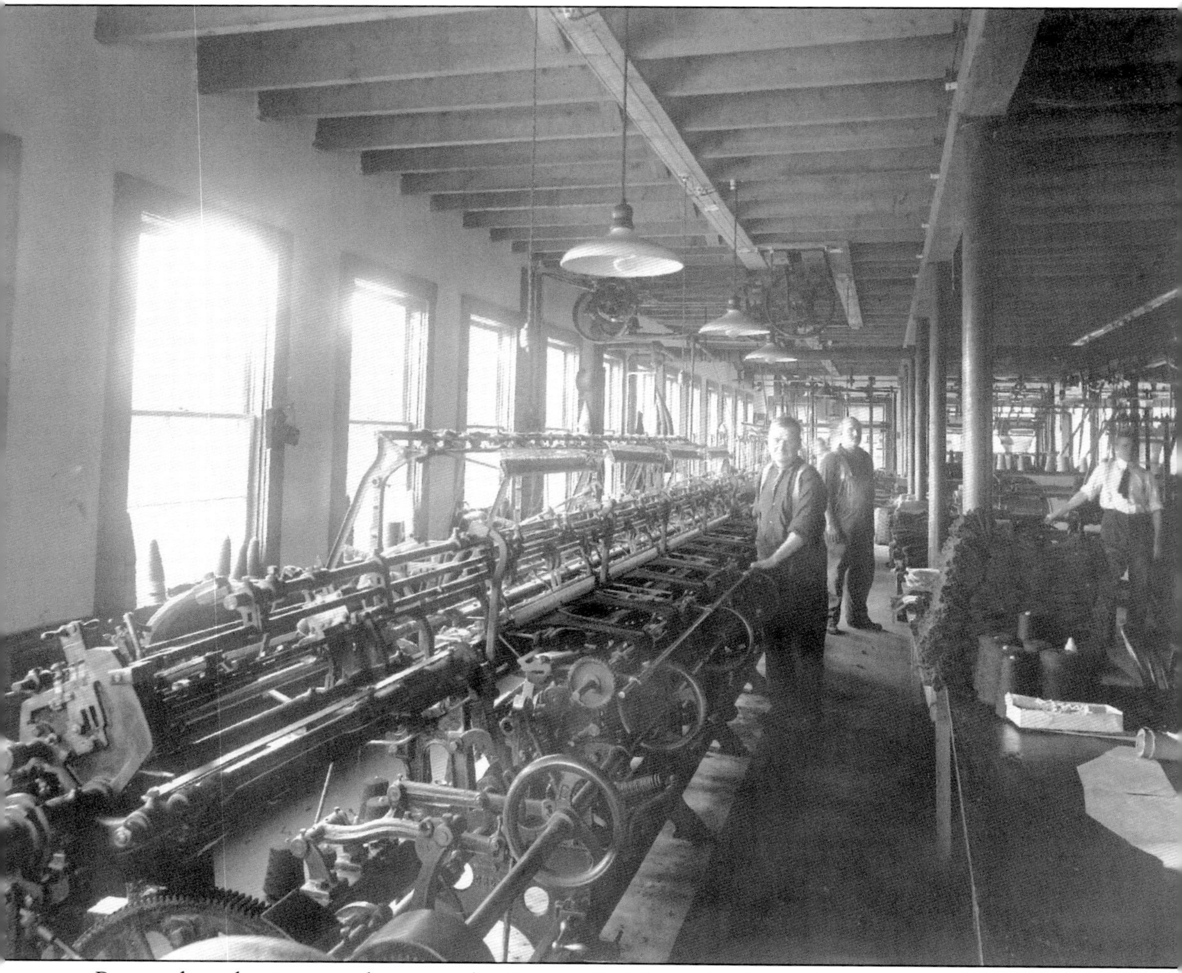

Pictured are hosiery machines at the George E. Wye mill. A number of the male workers are shown operating the machines. These machines required a high degree of maintenance, but were able to knit socks, sweaters, swimwear, and other garments at many times the speed of work done by hand. American companies, such as the Mason Machine Works of Taunton, Massachusetts, manufactured the machinery. The *Textile American*, published monthly in Boston, was the main magazine of the textile trade and provided details of the latest machinery as well as company news.

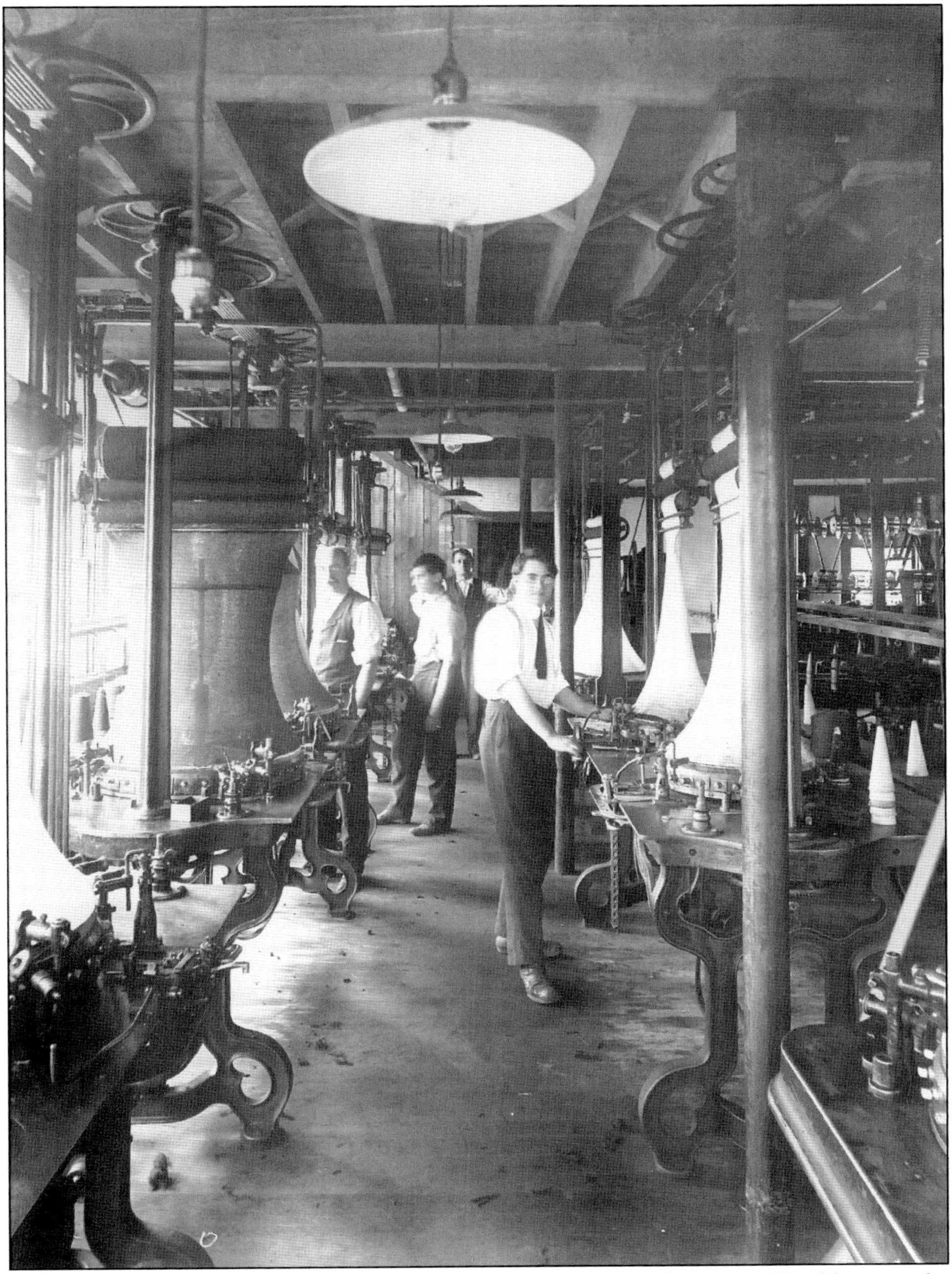

Circular ribbed knitting machines were used to make ribbed underwear, ribbed hosiery, fancy knit cords, sweaters, and swimwear. The elasticity of knitted cloth allows it to fit the shape of the human body. George E. Wye Company was one of many American knitwear companies riding the boom that occurred early in the 20th century. The adaptation of the Wye family to American life was rapid. Two of the sons of William Wye were educated at Harvard College. After Ernest Alfred Wye graduated Harvard in 1902, he traveled to the Philippines, where he worked as a teacher. He later moved to New York and joined his father's company as a salesman serving New York, New England, and Ohio. Percy Edwin graduated Harvard in 1906. Thomas E. Wye was one of some 15 Needham lads who volunteered to fight in the Spanish-American War of 1898.

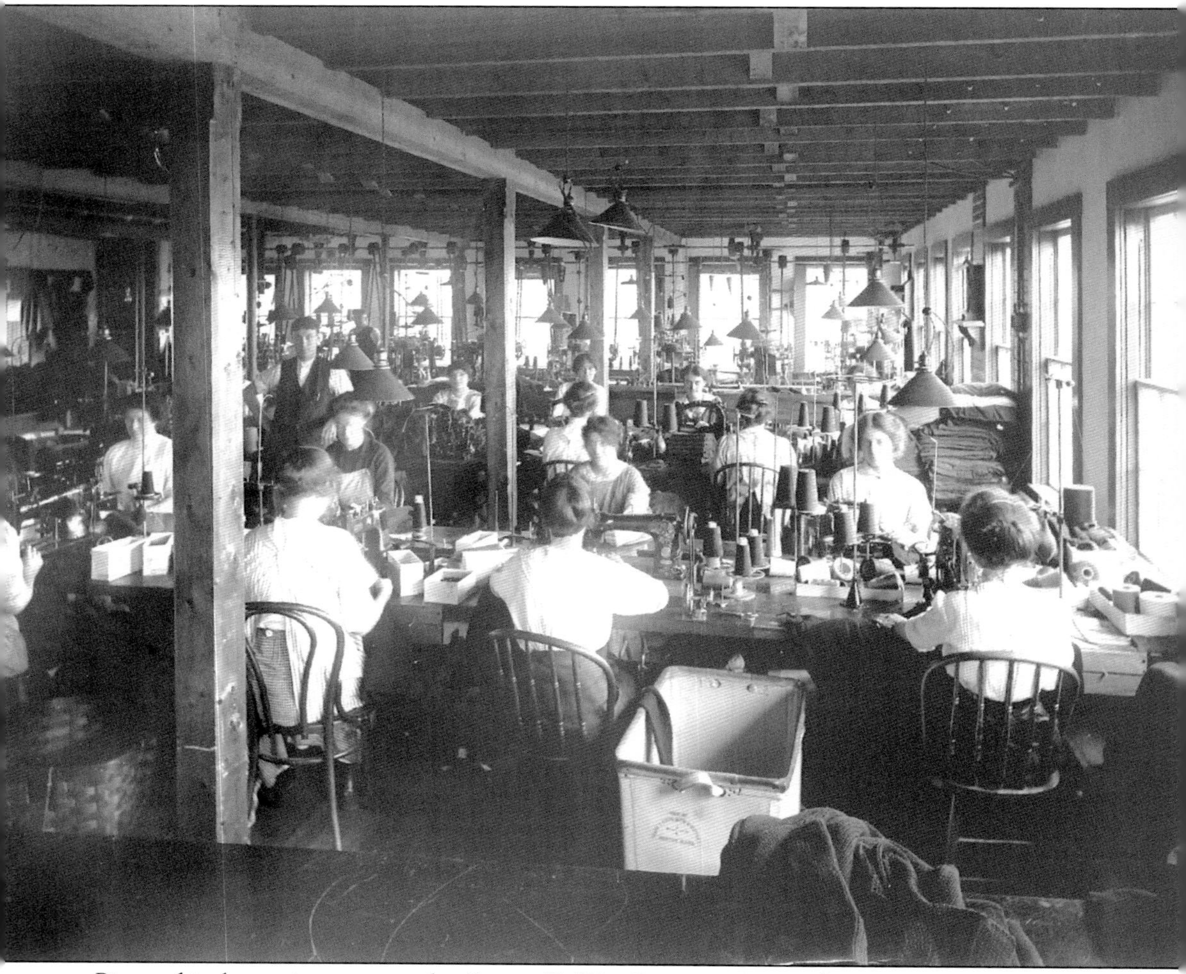

Pictured is the sewing room at the George E. Wye Company. Massachusetts was home to several sewing machine manufacturers, such as Grover & Baker, New Home, and the Boston Sewing Machine Company. By the start of the 20th century, the Singer sewing machine became dominant for home and commercial use. Wye employed 30 female workers in the labor-intensive sewing room of his mill. Using foot-powered sewing machines, the women sewed the sleeves to the trunk of the jerseys and sweaters and added the finishing touches to the bathing suits. The sewing room benefitted from large windows as well as electric lights. A supervisor was constantly on hand to check the work, repair the machines, and help the workers.

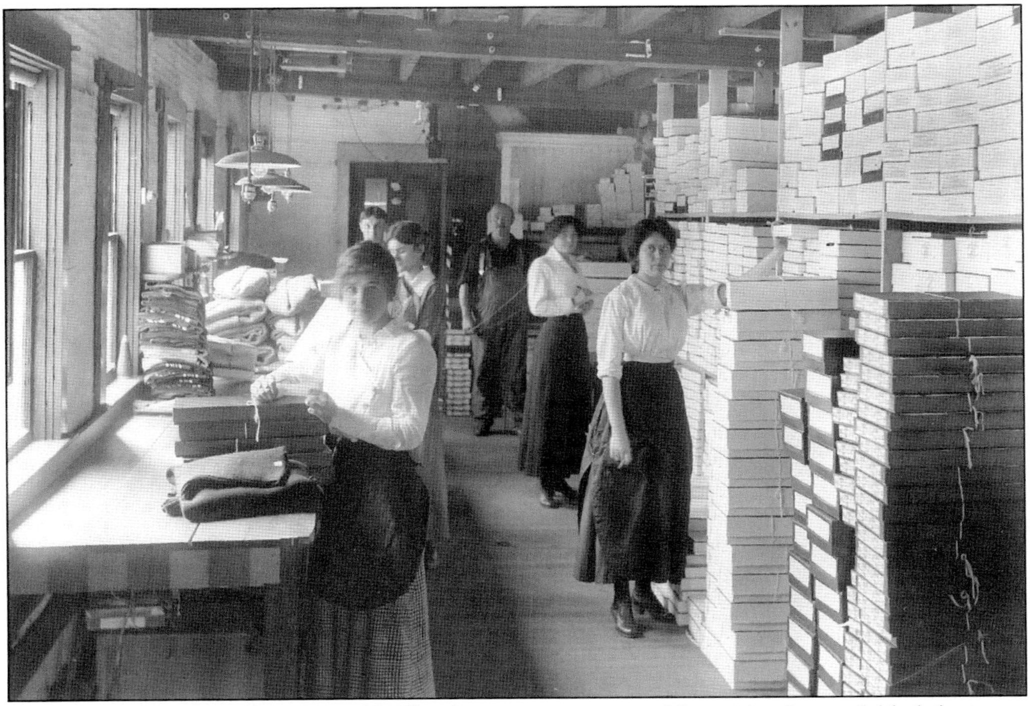

The packing room at the George E. Wye Company is pictured here. Employees folded the items of apparel into boxes that were sent off to department stores for sale or mailed to customers directly from the factory.

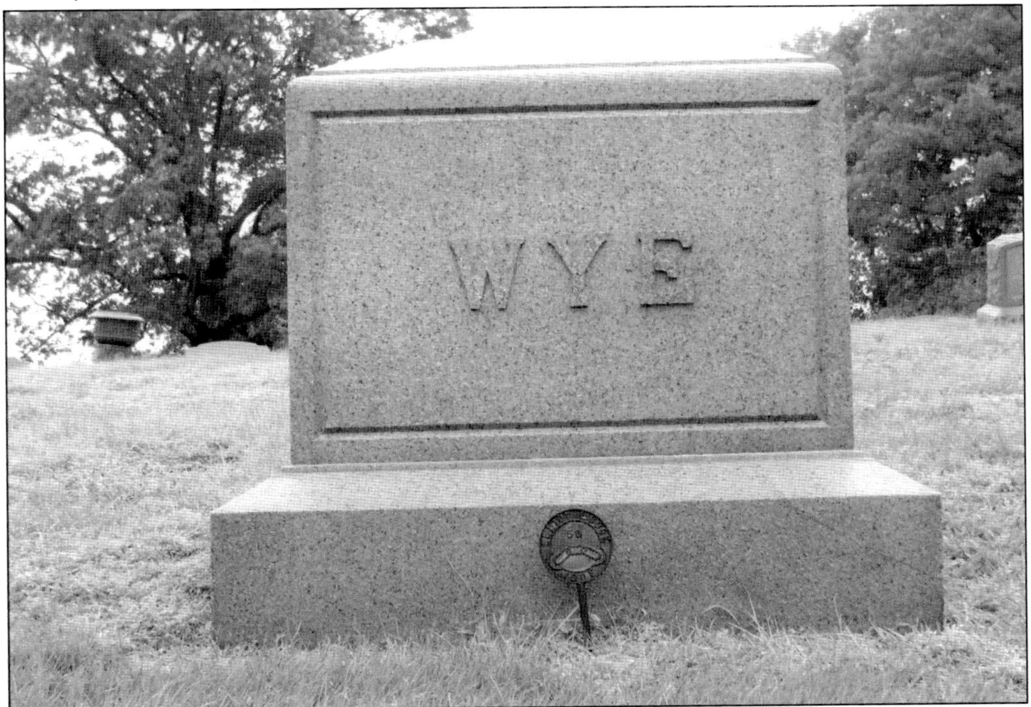

George E. Wye closed his factory in 1925, two years before his death. The Wye family burial plot is in the Needham cemetery.

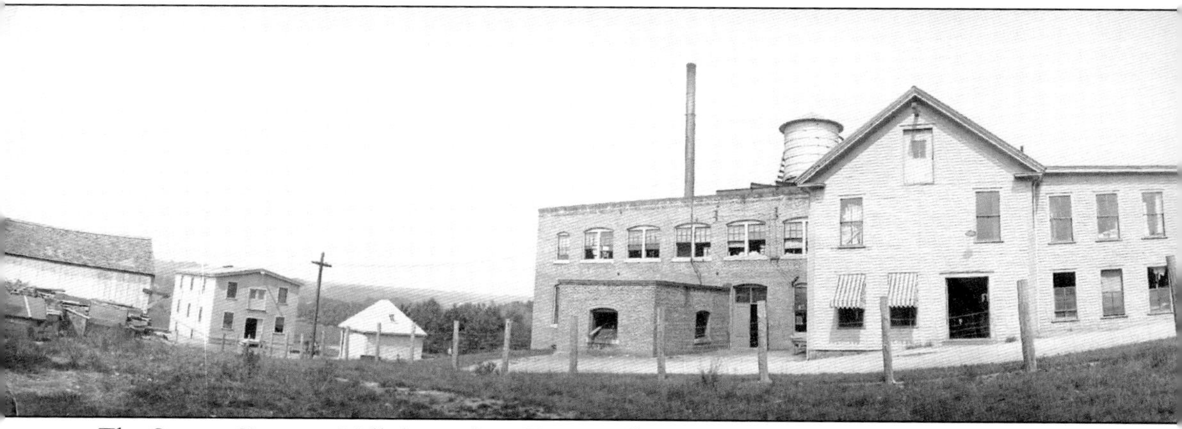

The Saxony Knitting Mill, located on Hunnewell Street in Highlandville, is pictured around 1900. The Saxony Knitting Company was established in 1898. In 1913, it was listed among the 100 prominent hosiery and knitwear companies in Massachusetts. In 1914, the company was granted a patent from the US Patent Office for its new knitting machine. Saxony remained in business until 1931, during the Great Depression. The Saxony knitting mill specialized in infants' and children's underwear, mittens, and sweaters. Saxony was the center of the German knitting industry, suggesting a German connection to this Needham mill.

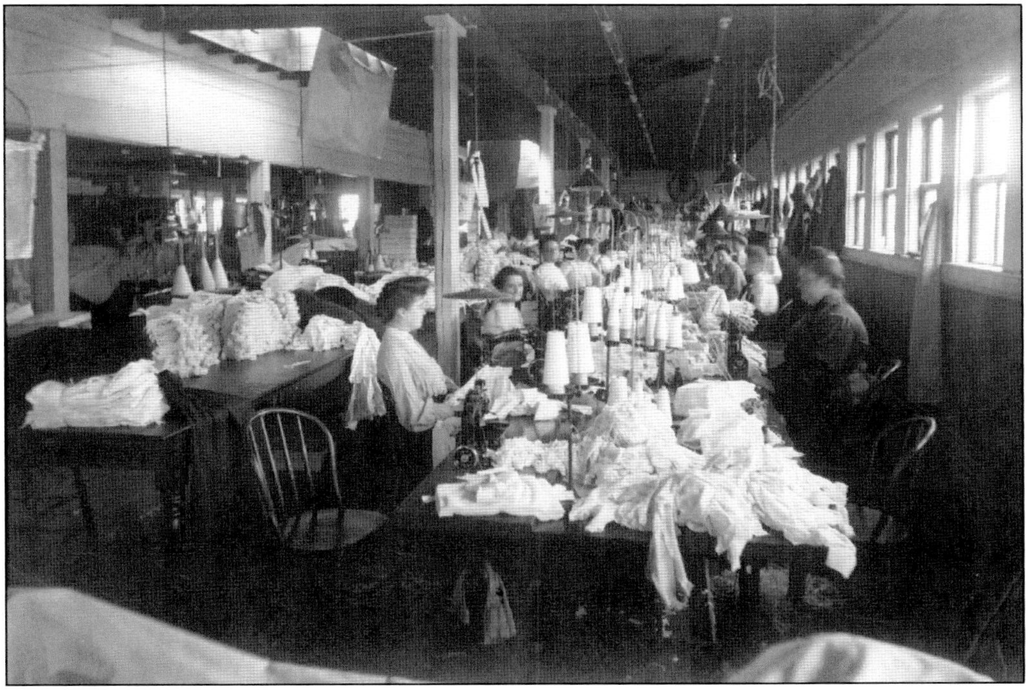

The sewing room at the Saxony Knitting Mill on Hunnewell Street, Highlandville, is pictured around 1910. The large windows to let in light, and the pulleys and belting to run the machines, indicate that the building was erected during the era of gas light and steam power. The electric lights suspended from the ceiling were a recent addition. Here, female workers sewed the machine knitted segments to complete the garments, ready for sale.

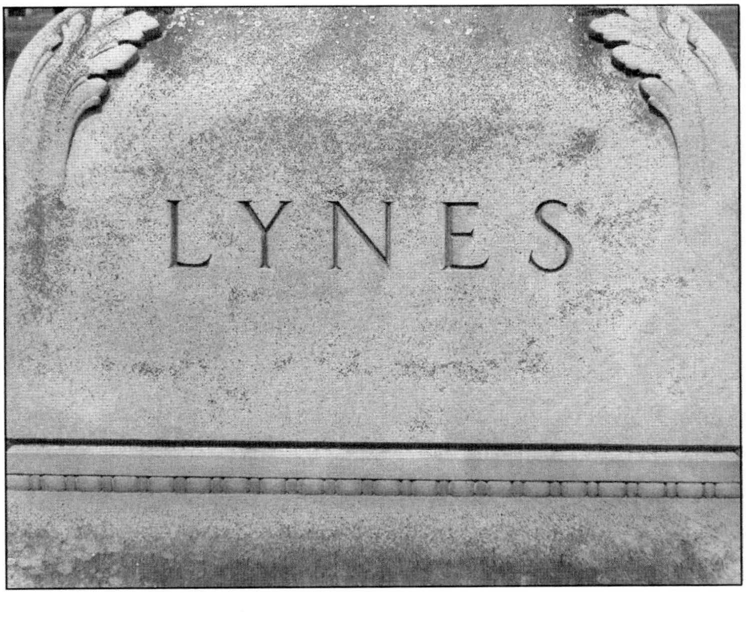

Alexander Lynes was born in Leicester, England, and came to Needham during the time of the Civil War. He owned the Leicester Knitting Company with 70 workers and power machinery. He also employed 100 more who worked out of their homes doing piecework. Lynes specialized in children's underwear, mittens, and sweaters. He died in 1897 and is buried in the Needham Cemetery.

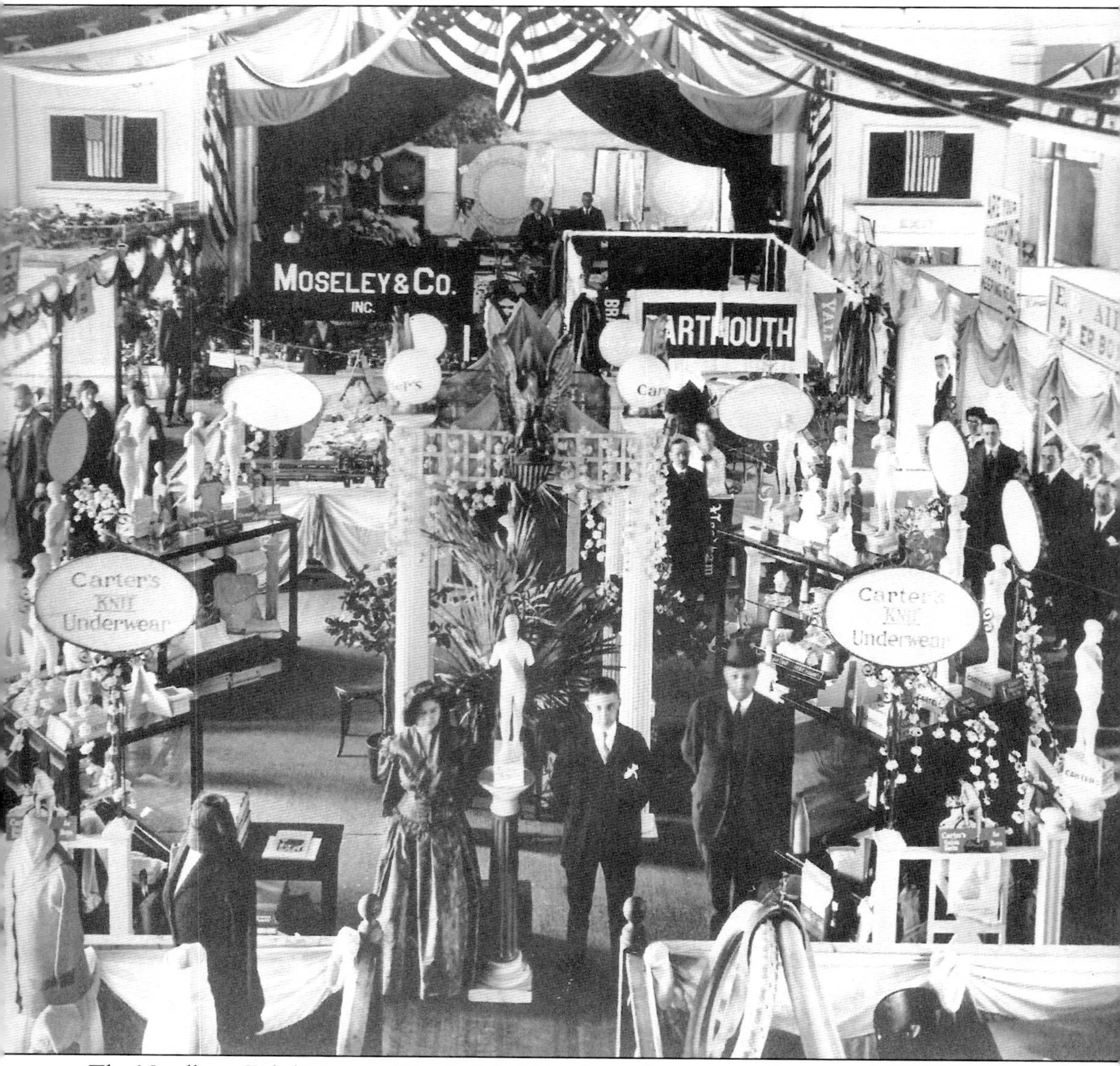

The Needham Exhibition and Festival, held in the auditorium on the second floor of the town hall, was held October 11–12, 1916, and brought attention to the variety of goods manufactured in the town. In front is the large exhibit of Carter's knit underwear, while Moseley and Company occupies one of the stalls in the rear. In addition to knitwear, Needham was home to William Bourne and Son Piano Factory, several small shoe shops, paper mills, and a glue factory. Several greenhouses along Highland and Central Avenues provided flowers for the Boston market. (Leonard Dawson Collection of the Needham Free Public Library.)

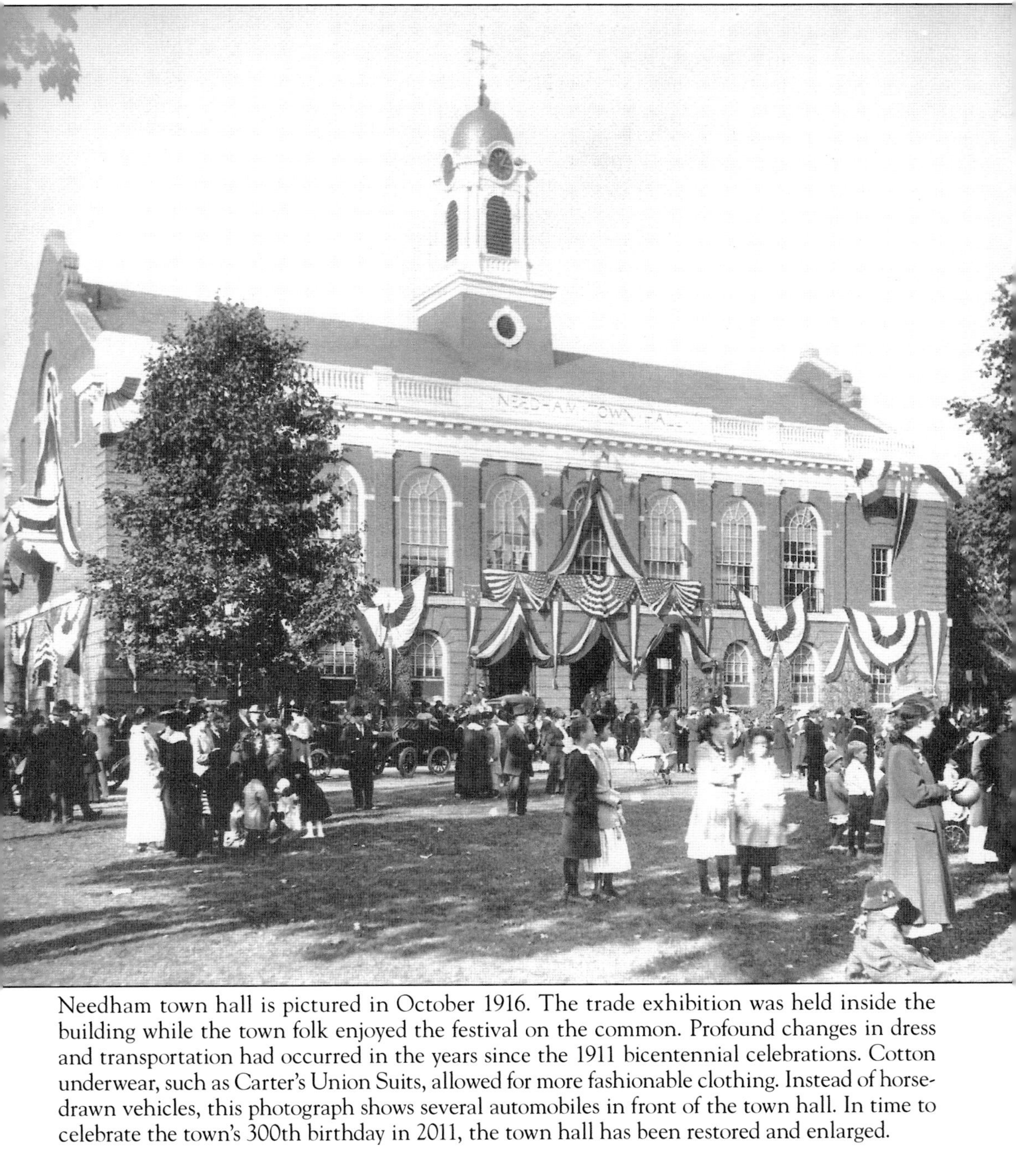

Needham town hall is pictured in October 1916. The trade exhibition was held inside the building while the town folk enjoyed the festival on the common. Profound changes in dress and transportation had occurred in the years since the 1911 bicentennial celebrations. Cotton underwear, such as Carter's Union Suits, allowed for more fashionable clothing. Instead of horse-drawn vehicles, this photograph shows several automobiles in front of the town hall. In time to celebrate the town's 300th birthday in 2011, the town hall has been restored and enlarged.

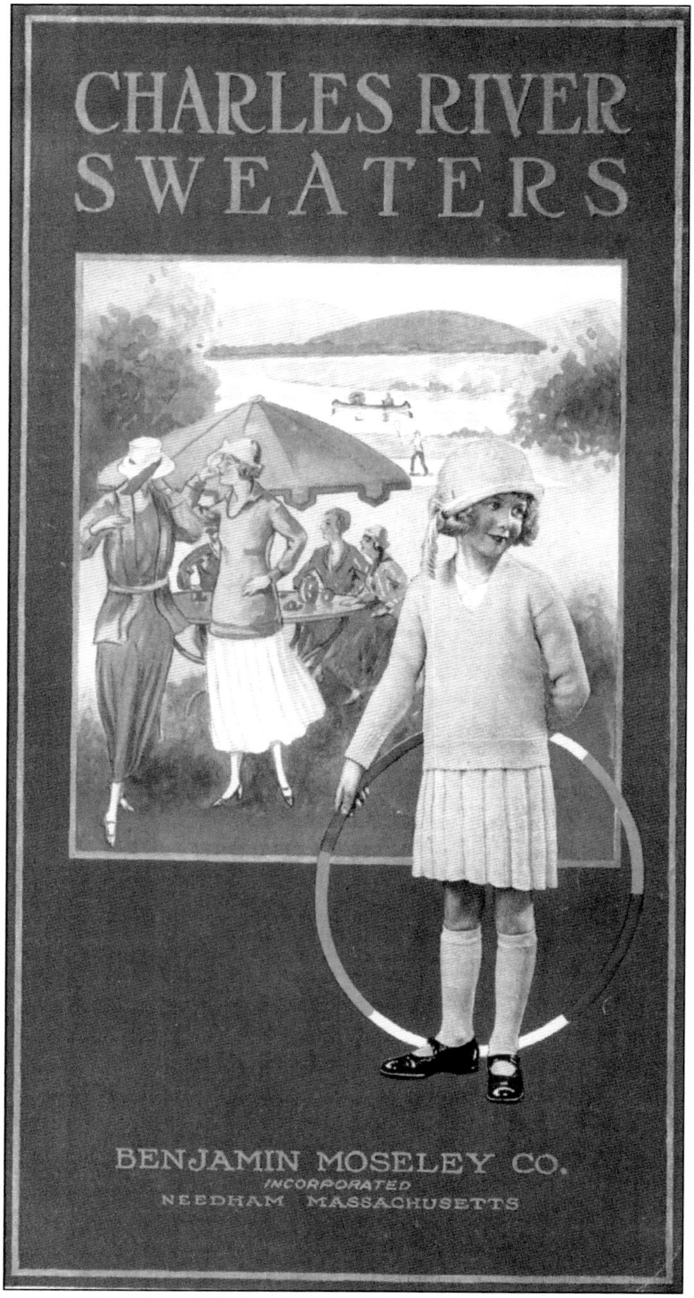

Several of the descendants of English knitters who came to Needham during the second half of the 19th century followed in the trade. Charles Bartlett Moseley of Highlandville graduated in 1900 from Brown University and then joined his father's company. Benjamin Moseley started his knitting business around 1918. Benjamin Moseley and Company, at 849 Highland Avenue, Needham Heights, made fancy Charles River knitted sweaters and sportswear for the whole family. In 1921, Benjamin sold his stake in the business to Frederick Bailey, who kept the name as Benjamin Moseley & Company. Bailey installed English made machinery in the mill. With the number Needham 0368, the company had one of the earliest telephone lines in the town. Benjamin Moseley and Company remained in business until the 1950s.

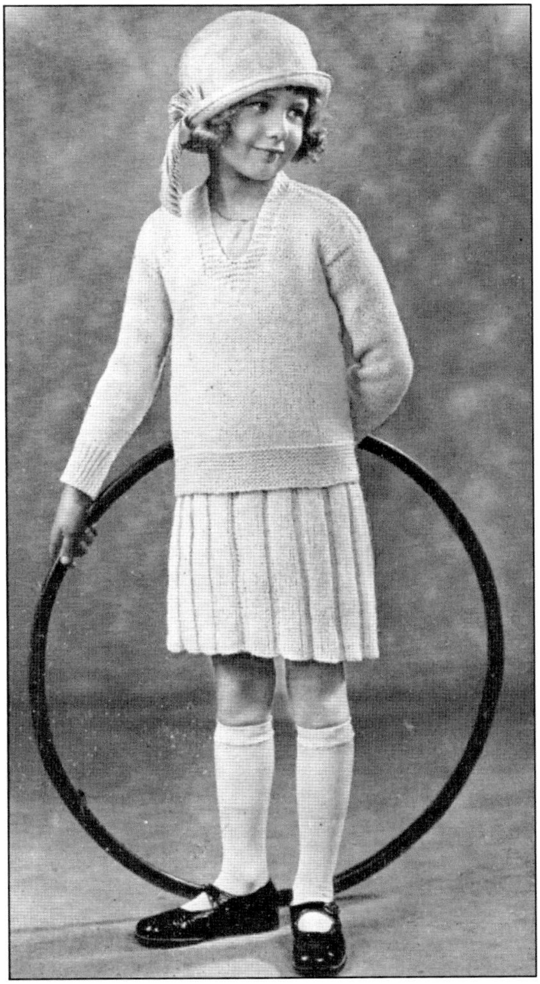

Shown here is knitted woolen clothing for girls from a 1920s Benjamin Moseley catalog. The garments were offered in various colors including black, white, lavender, scarlet, and green. Two-piece suits (jersey and skirt) for a girl one to two years old cost $3.50. Two-piece suits for a girl aged seven or eight cost $6.75, and for a girl aged 11 or 12, the retail cost was $7.75. Two-piece suits for boys (jersey and trousers) were less expensive by $1 or $2. Children's five-piece suits cost $7.50 for a child one to two years old, and up to $9.50 for a child nine to 10 years old.

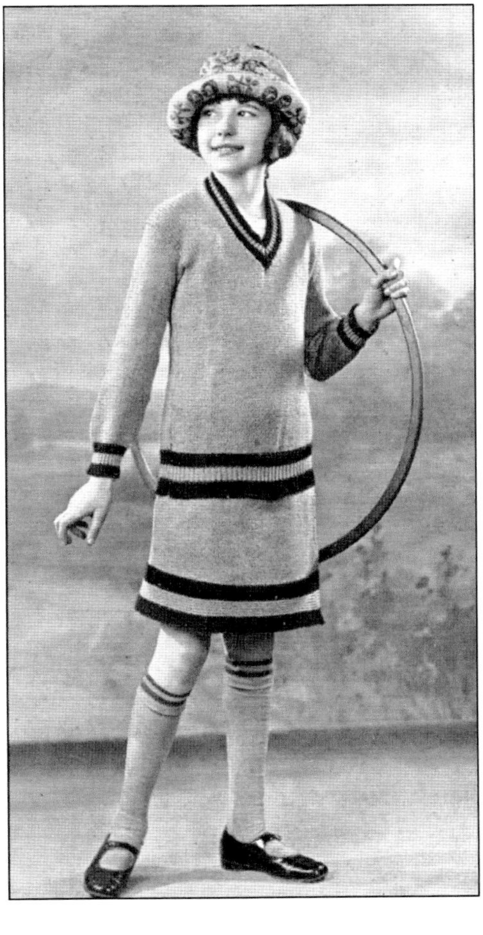

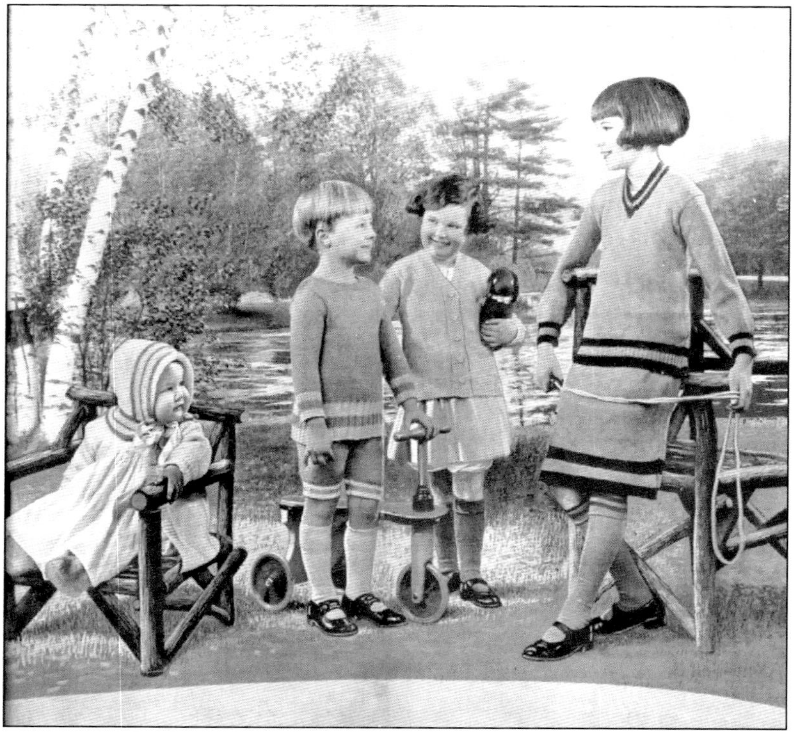

This is Benjamin Moseley's knitwear for toddlers to children aged 10 years for boys and girls. A five-piece suit for a toddler cost $7.50 and $9 for a child aged 10 years. Scarves and mittens were extra at 75¢ each.

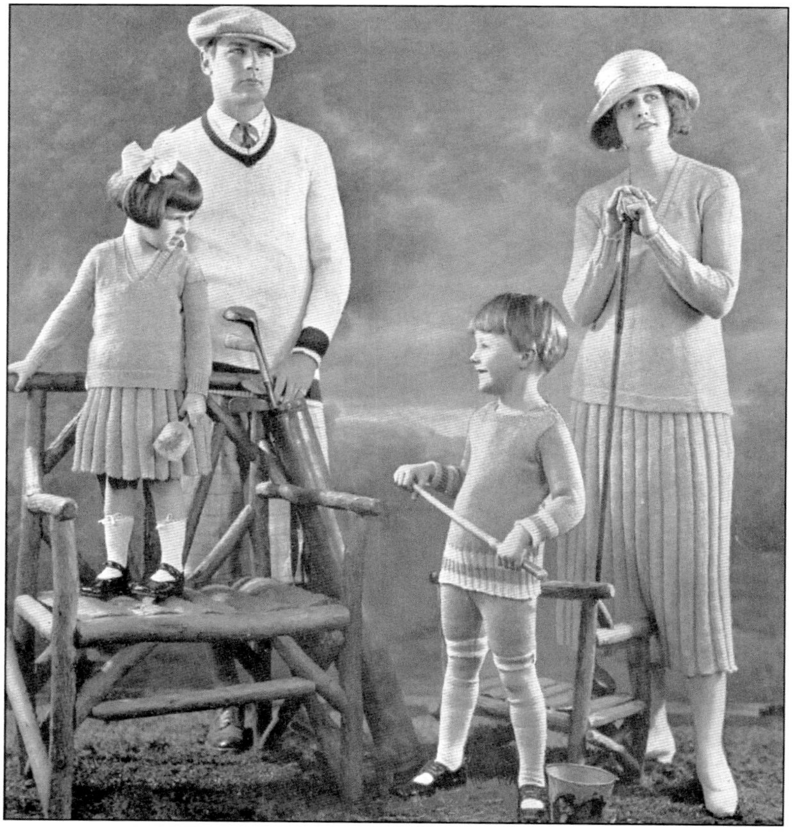

Golf anyone? Benjamin Moseley made worsted knitwear for the whole family. The garments were "hand-finished and full-fashioned." In the 1920s, a lady's golf sweater cost $4.50 and a skirt was $10. A man's golf sweater cost $6. Camel hair sweaters cost $8.

Five

The William Carter Company

William Carter, as the most successful of the Needham knitters, deserves a separate chapter. He was born on February 25, 1830, in the ancient market town of Alfreton, Derbyshire, in the heart of the English Midlands. Like many others, Carter learned to make hosiery only to find that the power machines of the industrial revolution made obsolete the hand and foot operated knitting machine. At age 26, leaving behind his wife, Hannah, and son, Frank, he emigrated to the United States. With the help of Alexander Lynes and William Moseley, he came to Highlandville in 1860 and bought a small house, where he set up his knitting frame in the kitchen and made cardigan jackets and woolen underwear. Hannah enjoyed only a few years in America before she died in 1862 at the age of 33.

William Carter married Martha Lee, whose brothers Mark and John became his business partners in a knitting mill on Highland Avenue, close to the railroad station. Martha bore him William Jr., Mary, Horace, and John before she died at the age of 31 in 1873. When the Lee brothers left the business, Carter continued as the William Carter Company. With the introduction of power equipment, the company grew rapidly. In 1874, Carter married Jane Greenough Avery, the youngest child of Jonathan Avery and a descendant of the Avery family, who had arrived on the Mayflower. Their children were Lucie and Roscoe.

William Carter bought the mill at Rosemary Lake and converted it into Carter's Knitting Mill No. 2. In addition to expanding his business into underwear, Carter developed land in Needham, contributed to his church, and gave funds to build the town library.

Believing that he could reduce costs through expansion, in 1909, Carter bought a third mill in Springfield, Massachusetts. By 1910, the William Carter Company employed 1,400 workers and was one of the largest knitting companies in the United States. During World War 1, Carter's contracted with the US government to provide two million shirts and drawers, and its mills began producing 55,000 garments a week. William Carter died on July 16, 1918, aged 88 years. In the 1950s, Carter's demolished its Needham mill on Highland Avenue, and in its place built administrative and executive headquarters. After a presence of nearly 130 years, the William Carter Company finally left Needham in 1989.

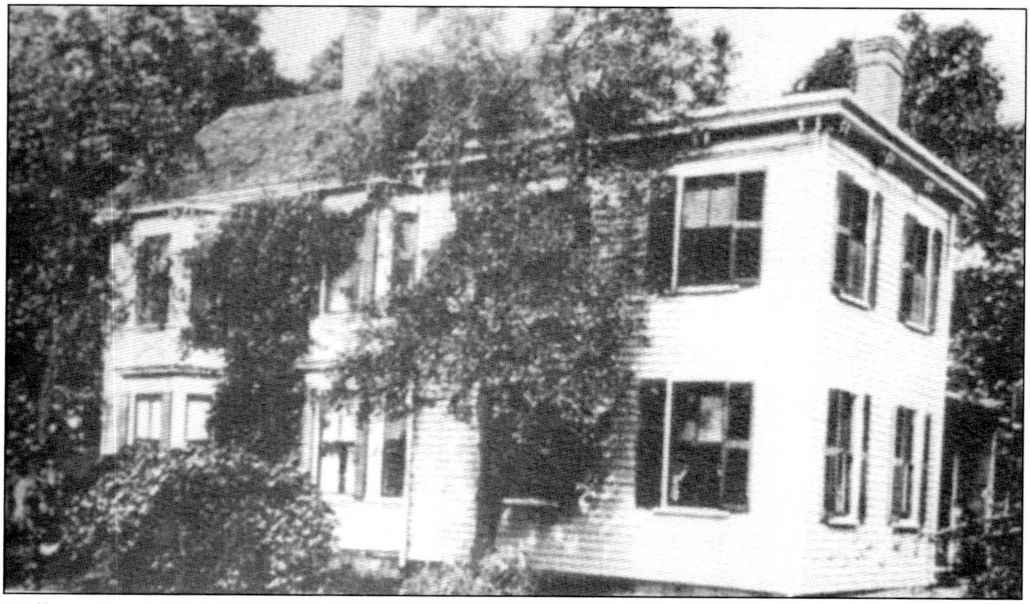

William Carter came to Needham in 1860 and set up as a framework knitter. His house was situated on the present site of the Needham Heights Post Office at the corner of Highland Avenue and Hunnewell Street. It was William Carter's home from 1865 to 1898.

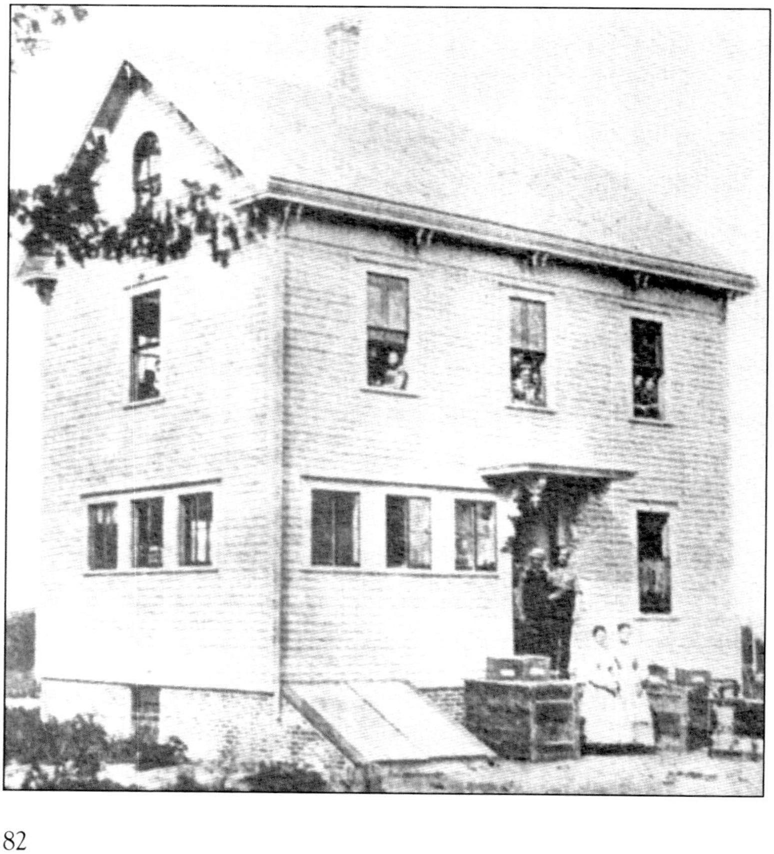

The small house, which was later enlarged, cost him $175. The kitchen served as the first workplace for the knitting frames to make Carter knitwear. Five years later, the enterprising Carter built his first workshop. This photograph shows his workers leaning out of the upstairs windows and at the front door.

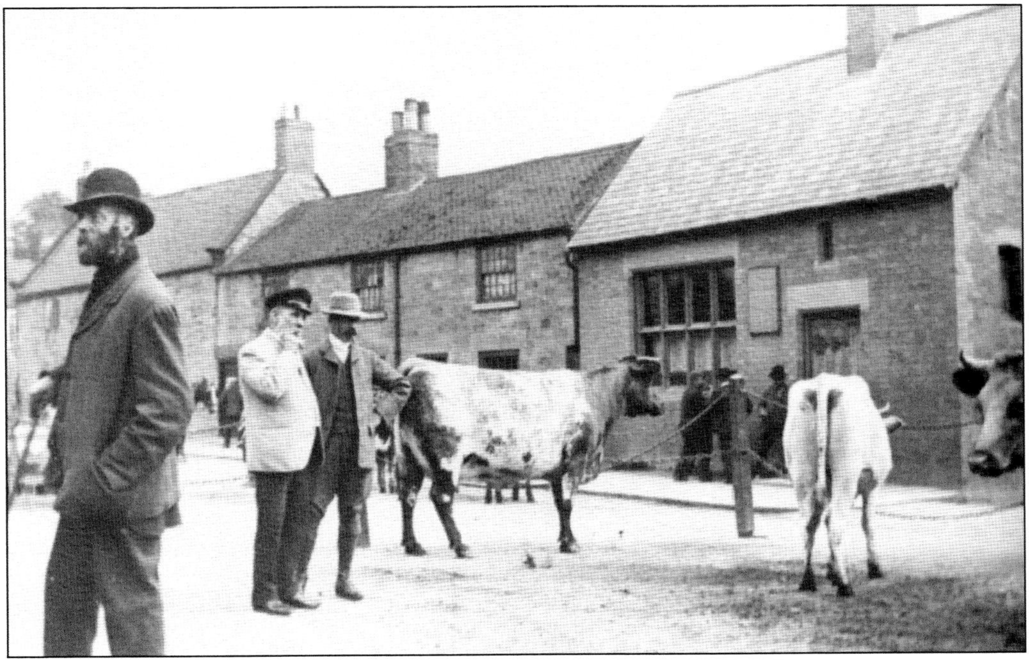

William Carter was born in Alfreton, Derbyshire, in 1830. The town in the English Midlands was at the center of the English hosiery and knitwear home craft industry. After achieving success in America, Carter often visited the town of his birth during the summer months. He built a grand home in Needham on a short road he named Alfreton Road. William Carter is pictured second from the left around 1890 on one of his visits to Alfreton.

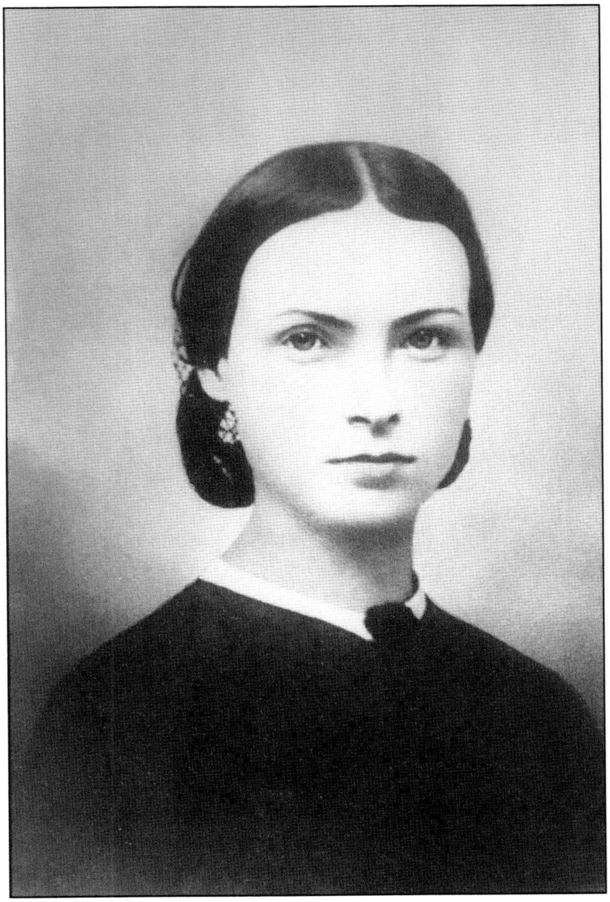

Martha Lee was 22 years old when she became William Carter's second wife. She was a sister to his business partners, Mark and John Lee. Martha had four children, William (born 1864), Mary, Horace (1869), and John. She died in 1873 at the young age of 31. In 1874, Carter married for the third time.

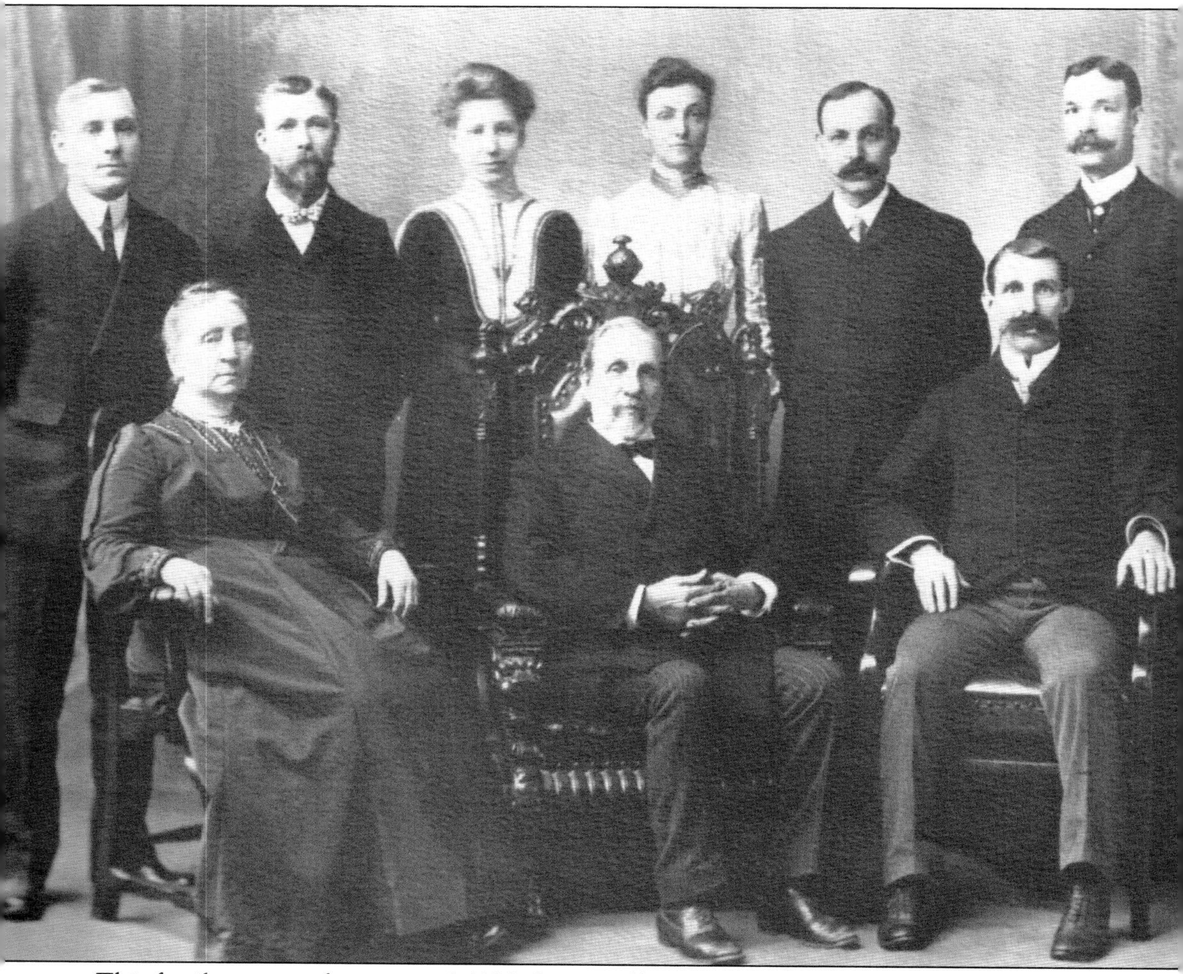

This family portrait from around 1900 shows William Carter seated with his third wife, Jane Greenough Avery Carter. Seated on his left is Frank, his oldest son. Frank's mother was Hannah Truman, who died in 1862, soon after coming to Needham from England. Standing from left to right are Roscoe, John, Lucie, Mary Elizabeth, William, and Horace. John, Mary, William, and Horace were the children of Martha Lee, Carter's second wife. Roscoe and Lucie were the children of Jane G. Avery Carter, his third wife.

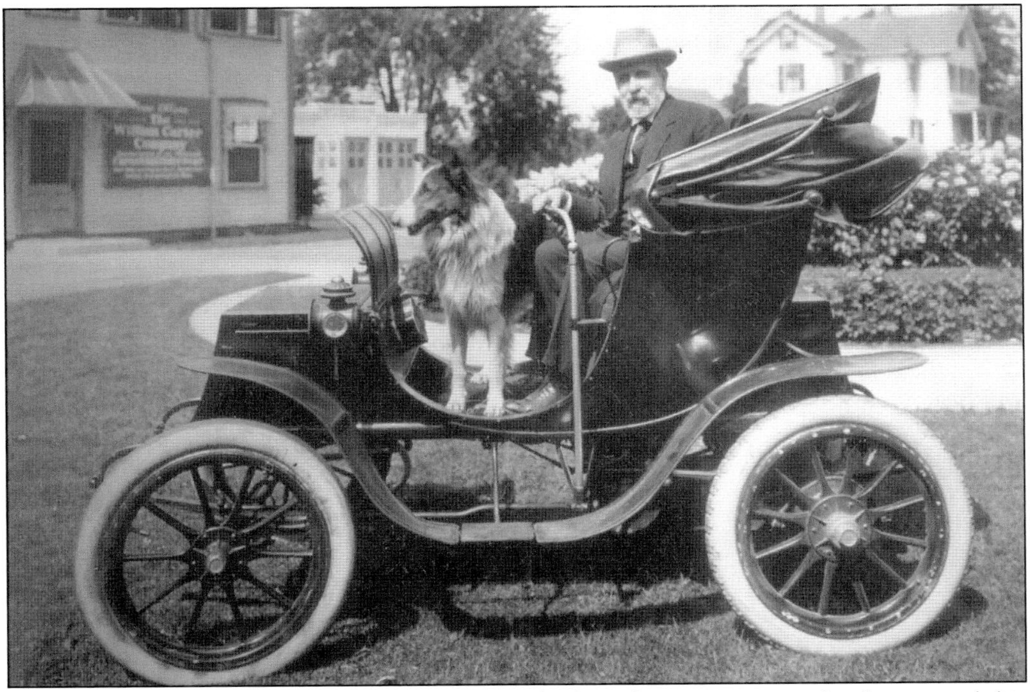

William Carter is pictured around 1910 sitting in his horseless carriage near his factory with his favorite dog. The car was kept by the family until 1942, when it was donated as scrap metal to support the war effort.

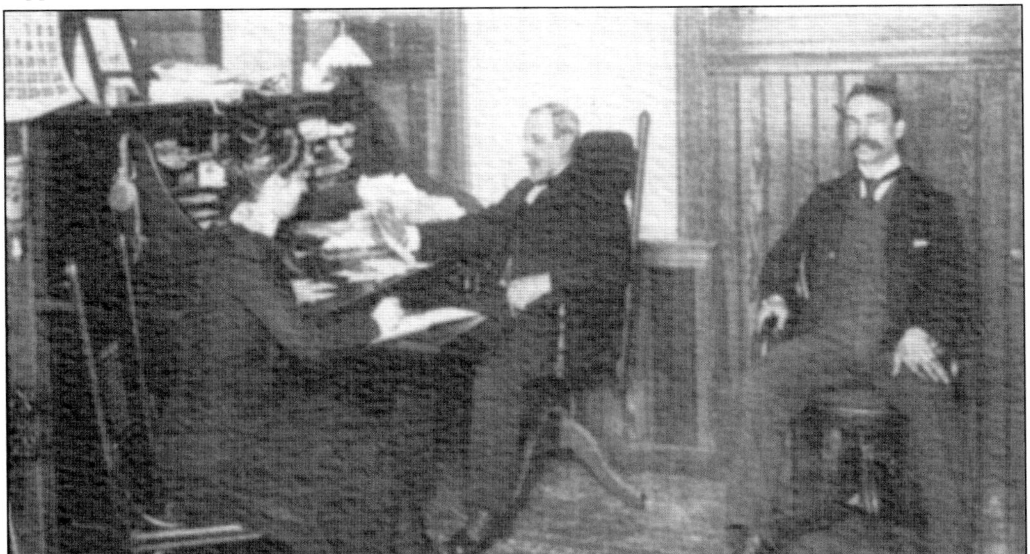

William Carter is pictured in his office dictating a letter to his secretary around 1900. Seated at right is the dapper Horace Albert Carter, born in Highlandville in 1869. At age 16, his father informed him that he was to "come to the mill to work tomorrow morning." After his father died in 1918, Horace was appointed vice president and treasurer of the William Carter Company. Horace served Needham on the school committee, as trustee of the Methodist Church, and as president of the Needham National Bank. Upon the death of his older brother William, he served as president of Carter and Company from 1955 until his death on May 2, 1959, at the age of 90.

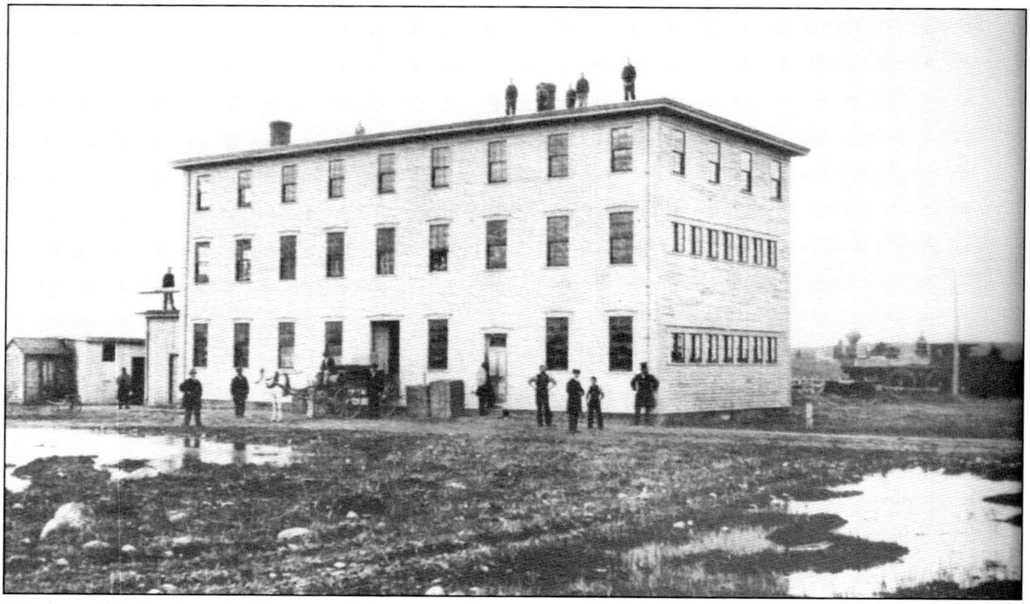

Mark and John Lee built a small knitting factory on Highland Avenue. In 1869, they invited William Carter, their brother-in-law, to join them in a partnership as Lee, Carter, and Company. By 1875, the Lee brothers moved on, leaving William Carter as the owner. A locomotive is seen leaving Highlandville station at the rear of building.

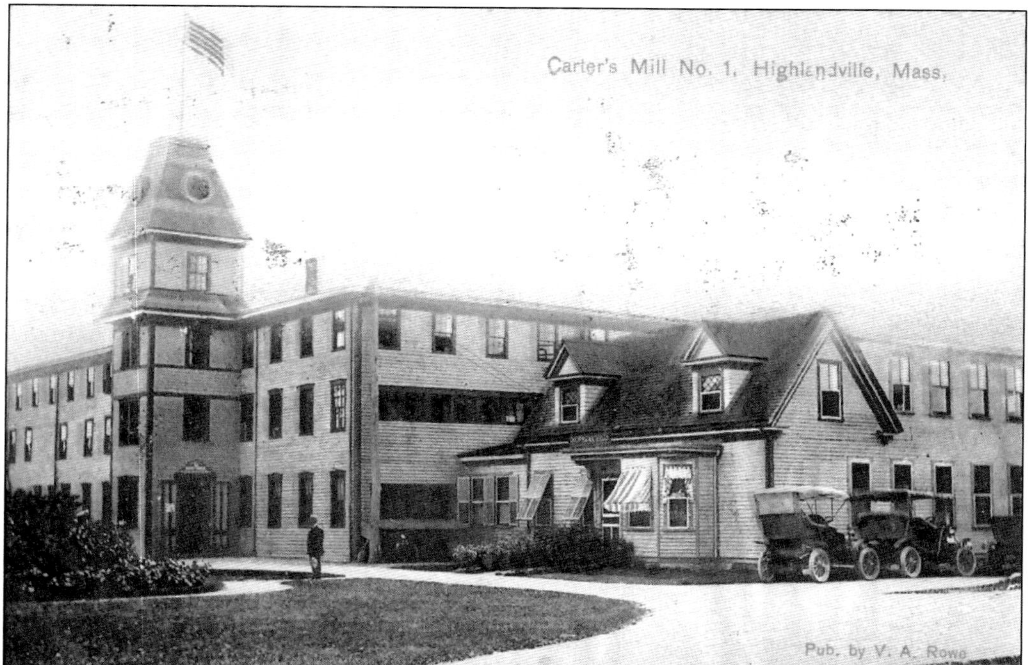

This photograph shows Carter's Mill around 1910. William Carter enlarged the building originally constructed for Mark and John Lee. Carter's was now one of the largest manufacturers of underwear in America.

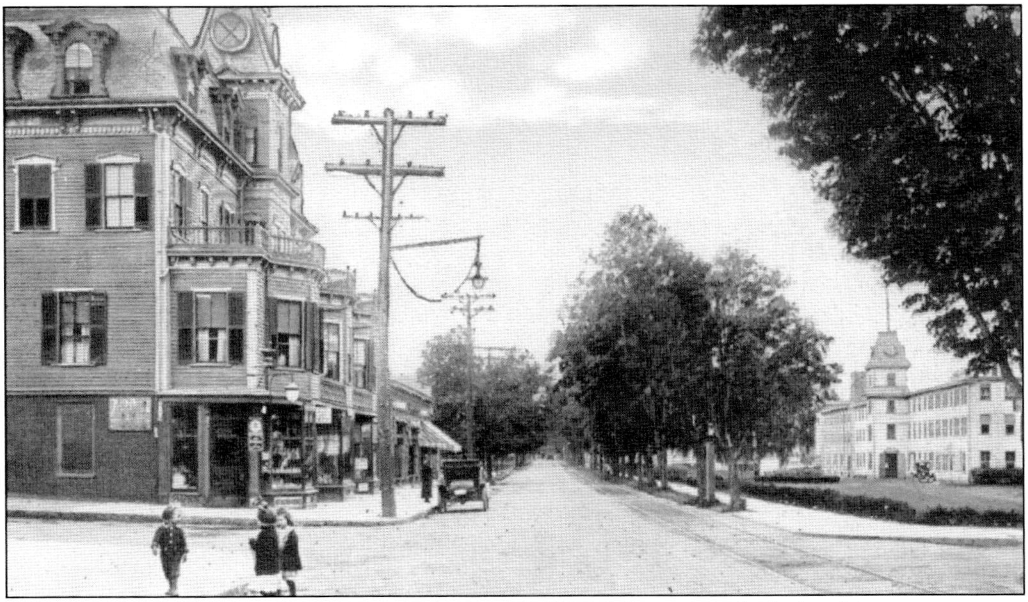

At right is the Carter Mill No. 1 around 1910. Highland Avenue linked the old town center at Great Plain Avenue to the industries of Needham Heights. Note the trolley track that linked Needham to Newton, with connections into Boston. The knitting mills with hundreds of workers and their proximity to the railroad station encouraged the opening of stores. The large building with the clock tower was the Low Block with a pharmacy and meeting halls. Nearby were J.J. Whetton's general store, Oliver Crisp's market, the post office, and Highland Hall, where the fraternal organizations of the knitters held their meetings.

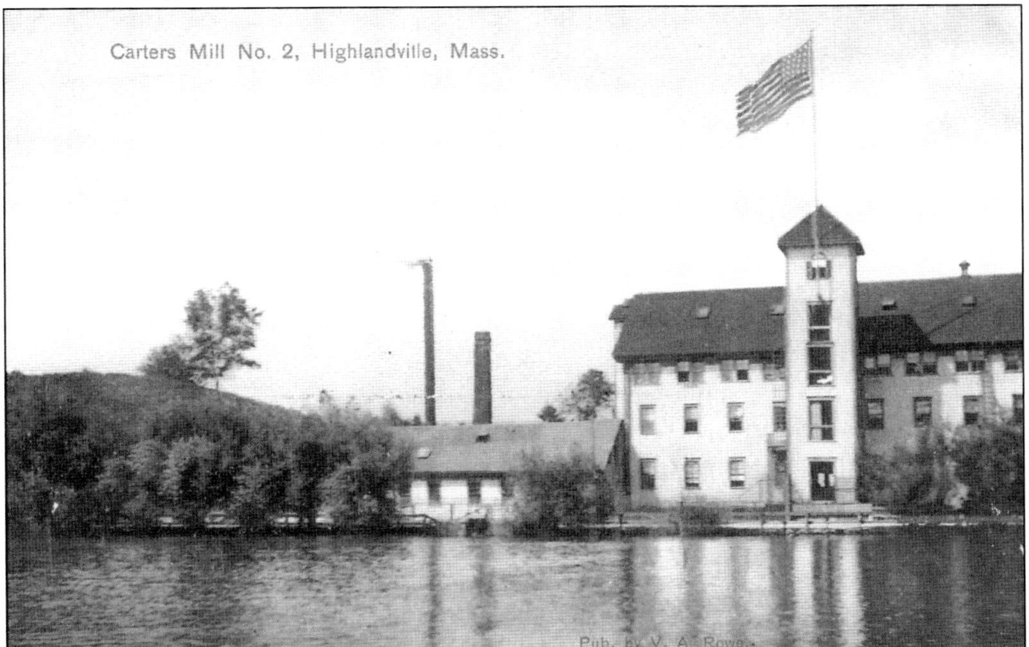

Carter Mill No. 2 is pictured around 1915. The original mill on Rosemary Pond depended on waterpower. Late in the 19th century, a steam plant was built and the mill was enlarged. From 1902, the mill was used by Carter's to make Union Suit underwear.

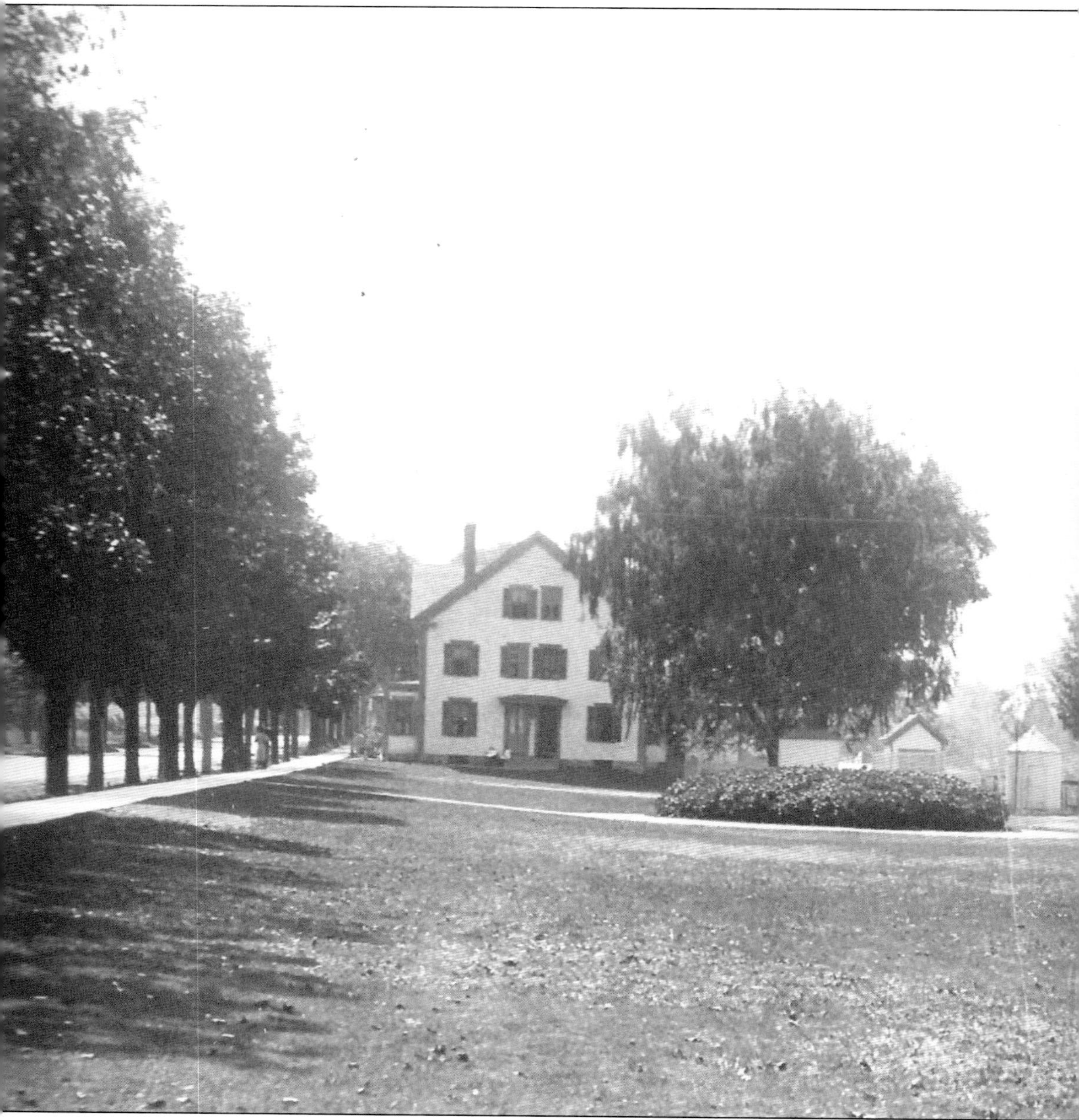

The January 1908 issue of *American Textile Magazine* reported on the success of the William Carter Company. His goods sold widely in the United States and abroad. The magazine article states that Carter was "frequently called upon to fabricate hosiery for no less distinguished a person than the then Duke of Wales, now King Edward." This 1911 photograph shows Carter's

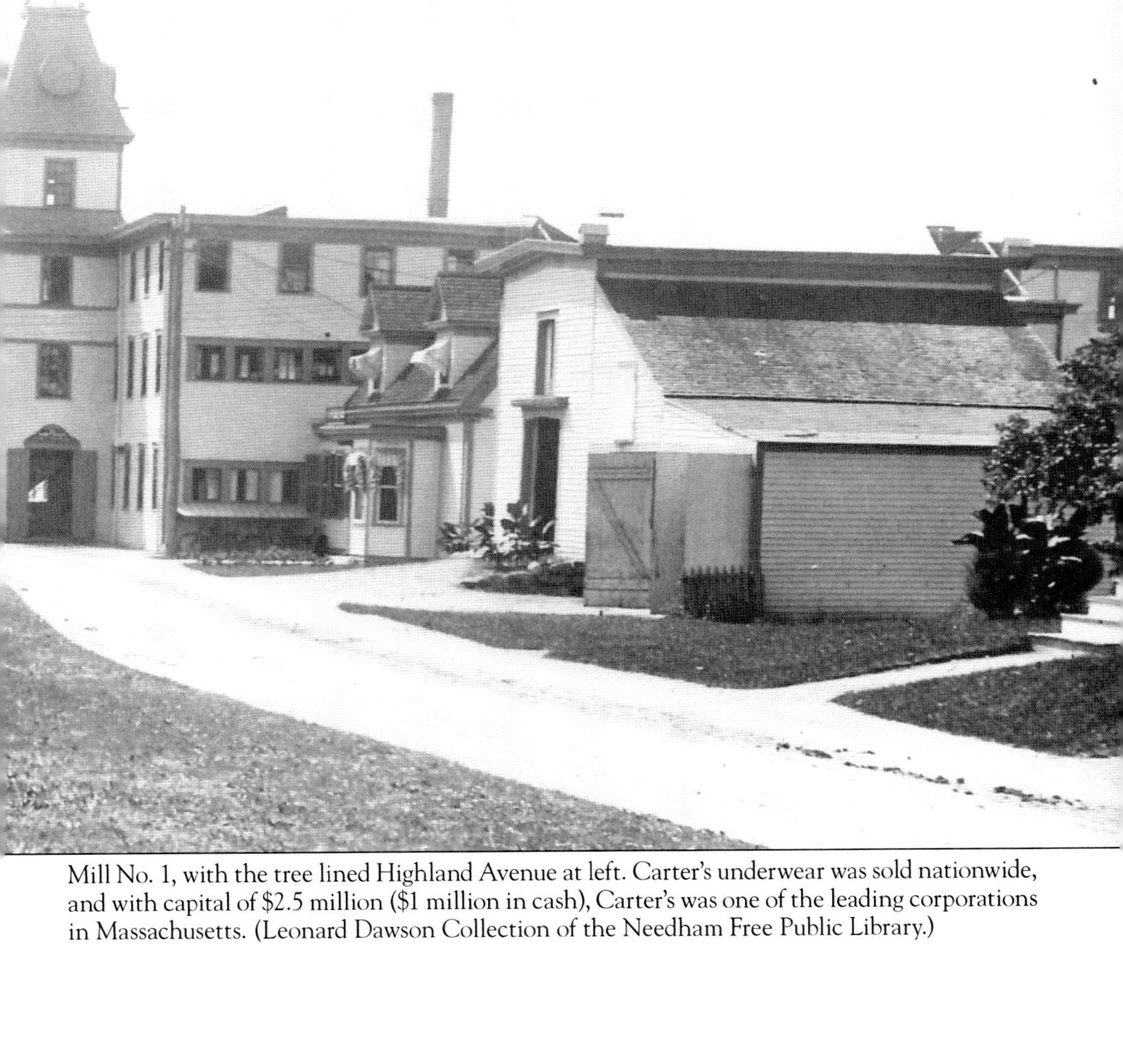

Mill No. 1, with the tree lined Highland Avenue at left. Carter's underwear was sold nationwide, and with capital of $2.5 million ($1 million in cash), Carter's was one of the leading corporations in Massachusetts. (Leonard Dawson Collection of the Needham Free Public Library.)

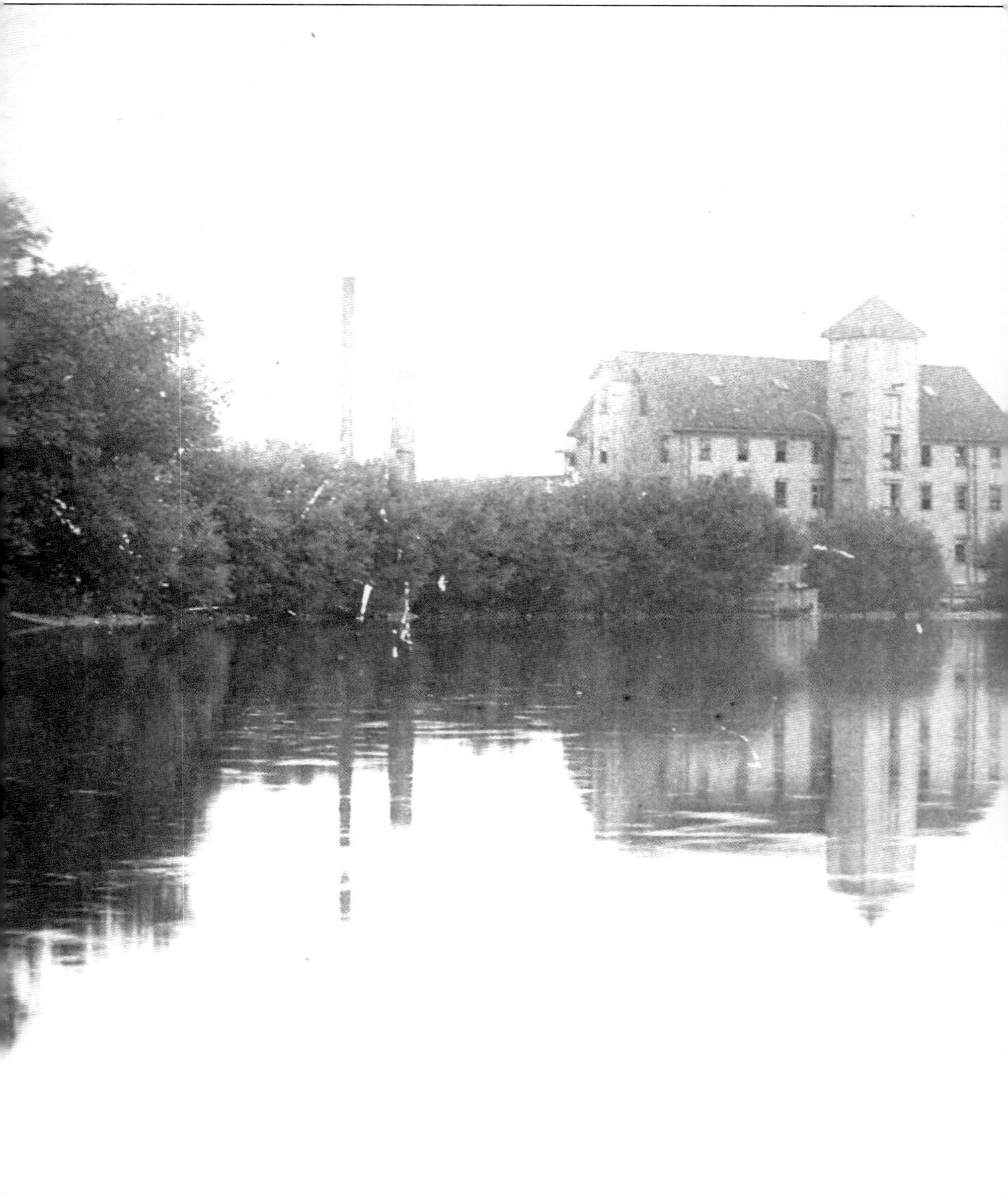

Lemuel Lee dammed the stream to create Rosemary Pond. A water-powered mill at Rosemary Pond was built before the Civil War as a beaver hat manufactory. Galen Orr bought the building in 1851 as a cotton-batting mill. Later, it served as a gristmill. In 1866, the Ashwell Manufacturing Company bought the mill and used it to make socks. Later, it was used also to make underwear. In 1888, William Carter bought the mill at a bargain price, leasing it to the Union Cycle Company

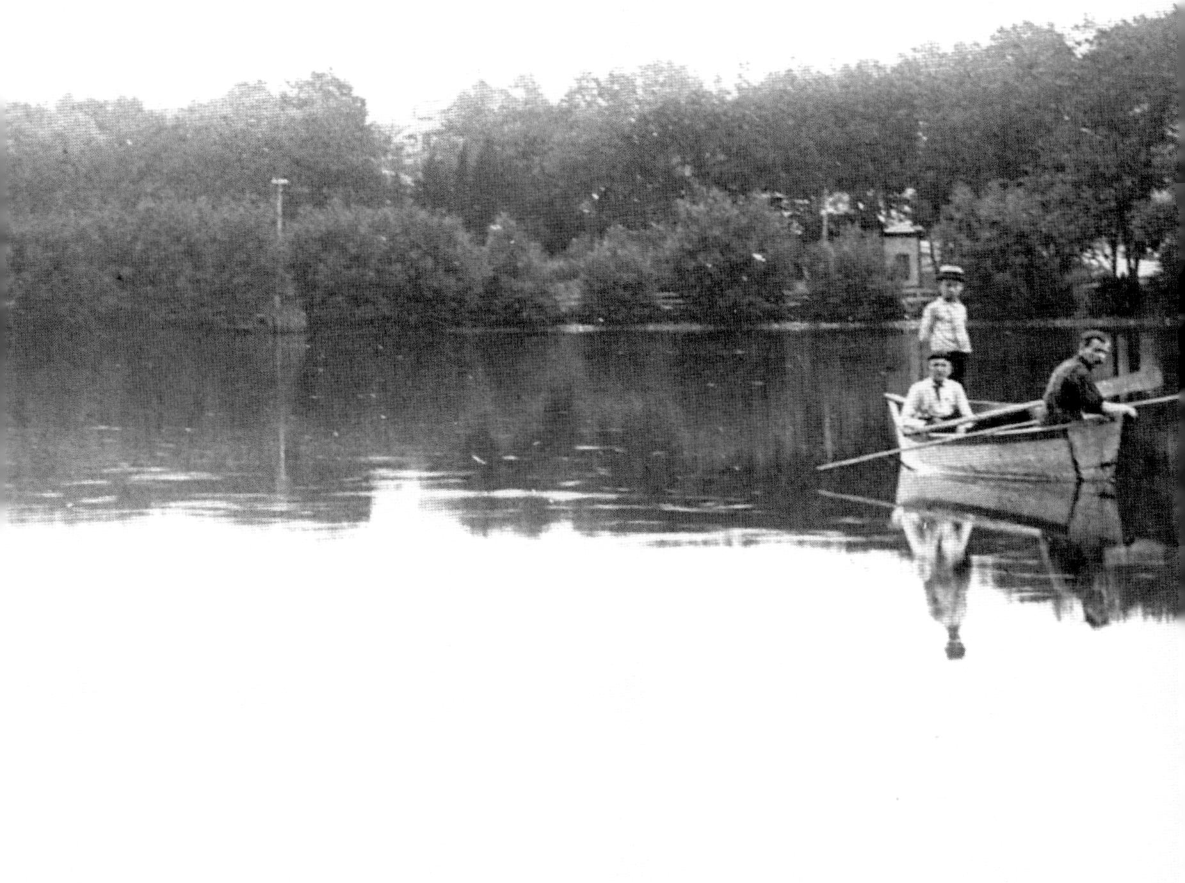

to make bicycles. In 1902, Carter refurbished the building into an underwear mill called Carter's Mill No. 2. To beautify his property, in 1909, Carter installed four swans on the pond and built a swan house. He also placed his motorboat on the pond for his pleasure. After Carter's left the property, it was used by the Tillotson Corporation to make rubber goods. (Leonard Dawson Collection of the Needham Free Public Library.)

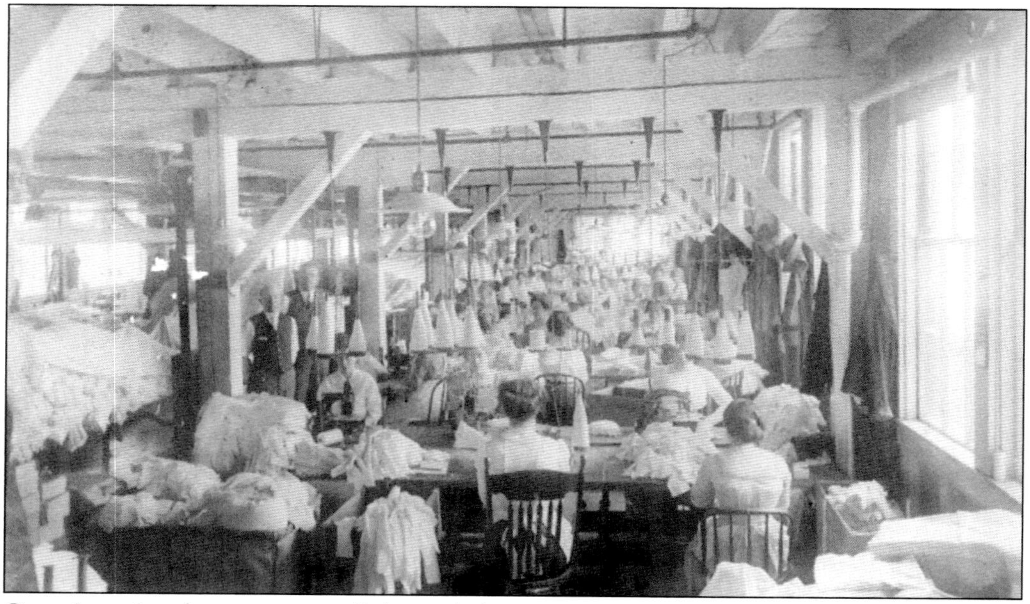

Carter's sewing department, staffed mainly by women, was where the knitted components of socks, mittens, gloves, and underwear were sewn together into garments. Overhead electric lights supplemented the light coming in through the large windows in the mill. Average annual wages in knitwear mills in 1899 were $268, and in 1904, it was increased to $303, which was still less than $1 a day.

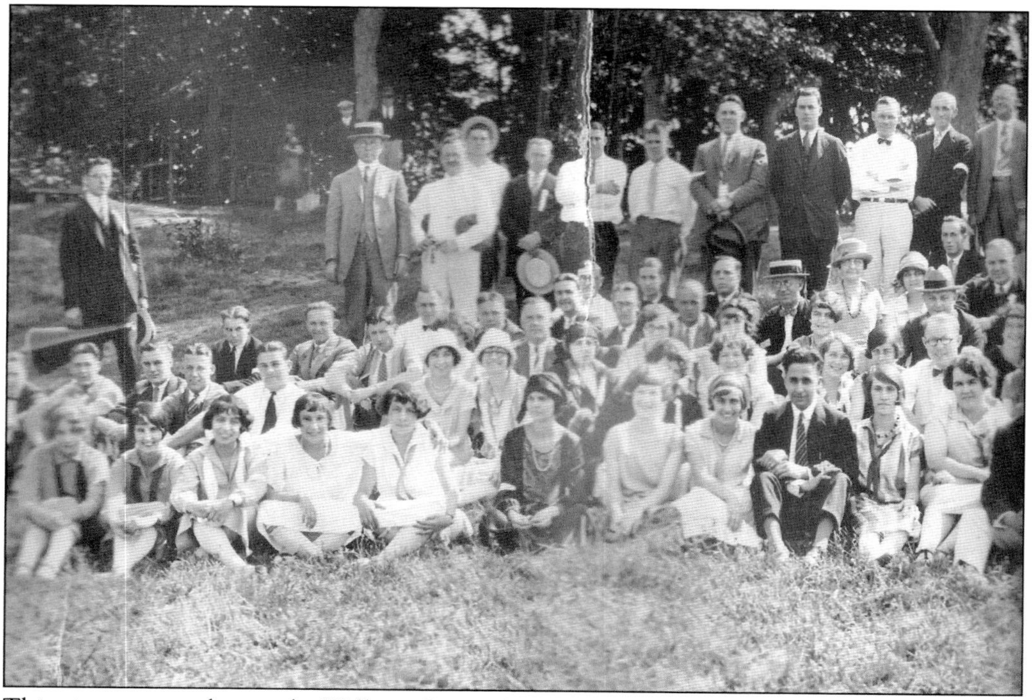

This picture was taken at the William Carter Company's outing at Nantasket in the summer of 1925. It was a dismal year for the Boston Red Sox, who won only 47 games and lost 105 to finish last in the American League. The Boston Braves had a better year, winning 70 games and losing 83 to finish fifth in the National League.

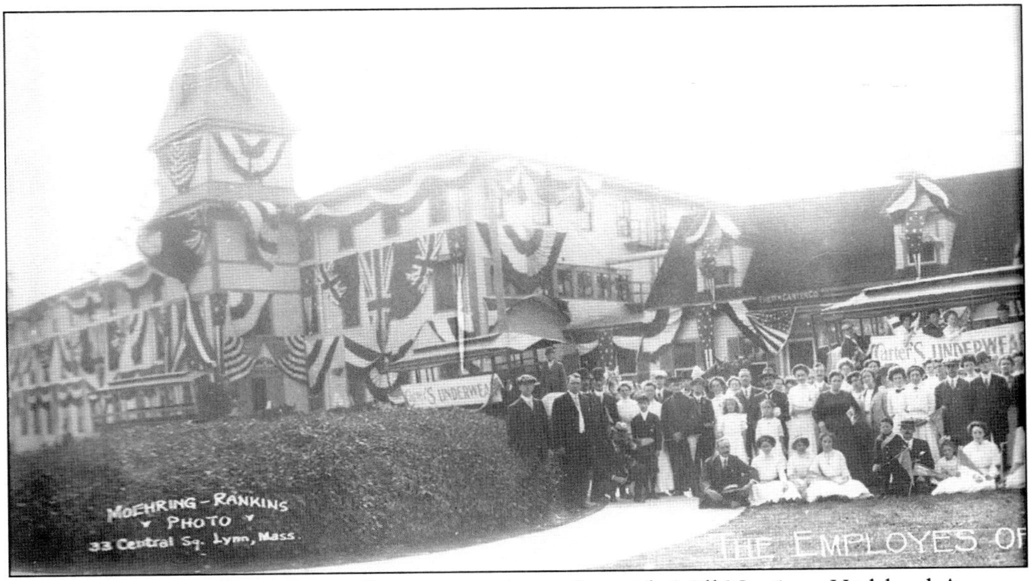

The staff of the William Carter Company is pictured outside Mill No. 1 on Highland Avenue, Needham Heights, in 1910. The managerial staff, who are wearing waistcoats and ties, are grouped on the left and right and flank the mill workers, who are mostly women. In 1910, with two mills in Needham and one at 33 Morris Street in Springfield, Massachusetts, Carter's employed 1,400 workers and was one of the leading knitting companies in America.

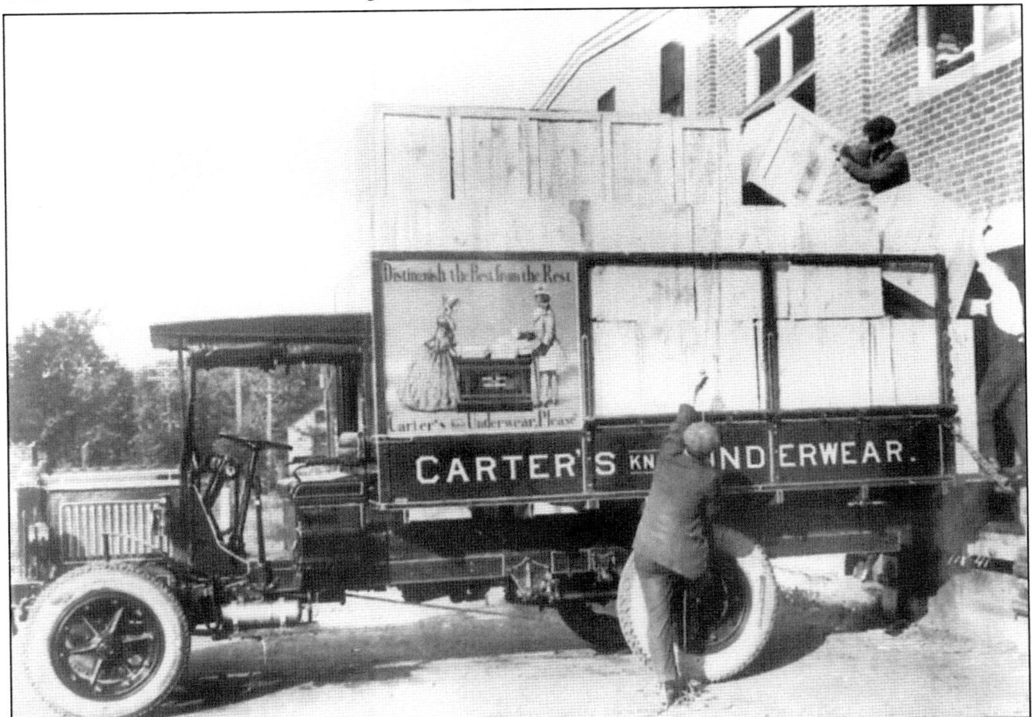

By 1900, Carter's moved from knitted gloves, socks, and jackets to underwear. This c. 1920 photograph shows one of the company delivery vans loaded high with wooden crates of underwear that are going to supply department stores across the nation and abroad. Carter's made Union Suits, or one-piece woolen underwear, for flexibility and warmth during the winter months.

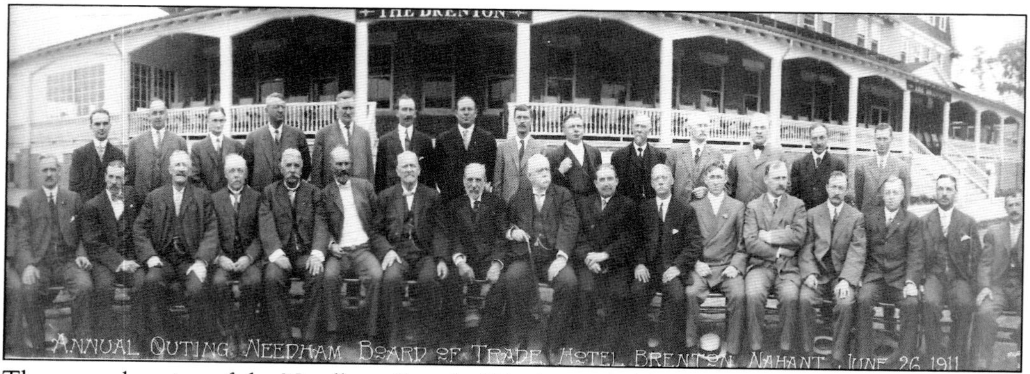

The annual outing of the Needham Board of Trade was held at the Hotel Brenton, Nahant, on June 26, 1911. As the town's leading industrialist, William Carter is seated front and center in the place of honor. Seated to his left are Judge Emery Grover and another knitter, William G. Moseley. Town selectman and officials make up the other members of the group. (Leonard Dawson Collection of the Needham Free Public Library.)

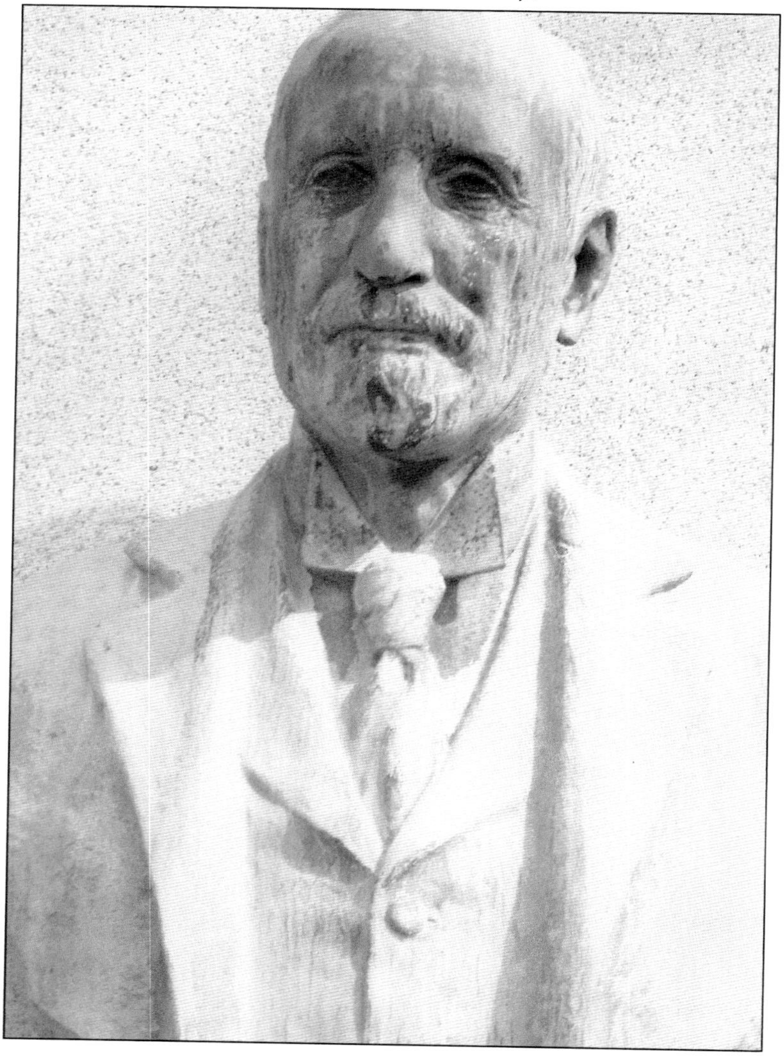

William Carter, the "grand old man" of Needham and one of the captains of American industry, died at his home at Alfreton Road on July 16, 1918, aged 88. The tolling bells of the nearby First Methodist Episcopal Church announced his death. He was buried in the Needham Cemetery.

Founded in 1842, the Methodist Episcopal Society became the spiritual home of many of the English knitters who settled in Highlandville. In 1874, William Carter helped raise $1,000 to buy land from Jonathan Avery. Alexander Lynes, president, with Mark Lee, secretary, and William Carter, treasurer, raised $10,000 to build and furnish this church, which was completed in the late 1870s.

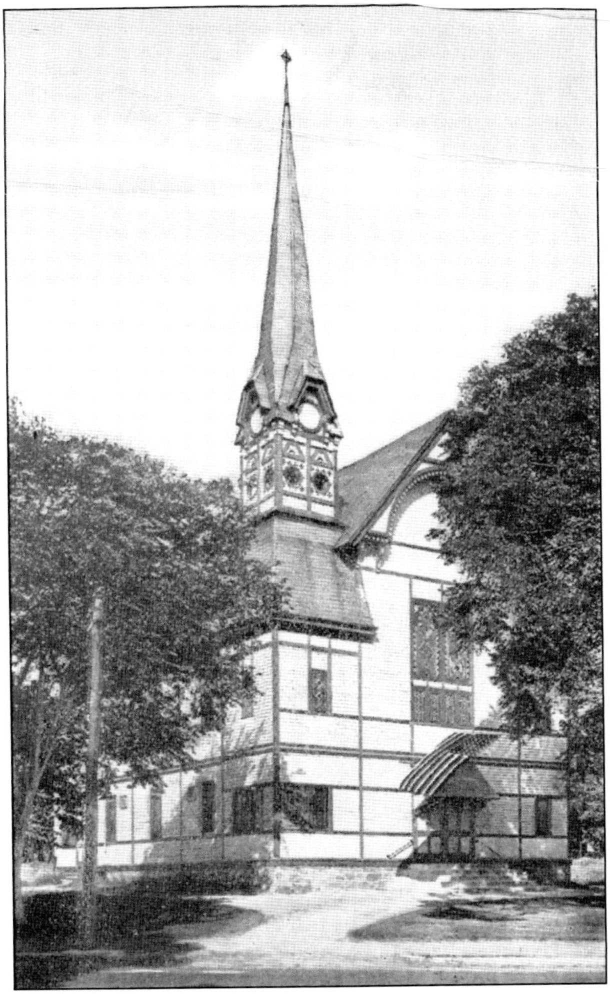

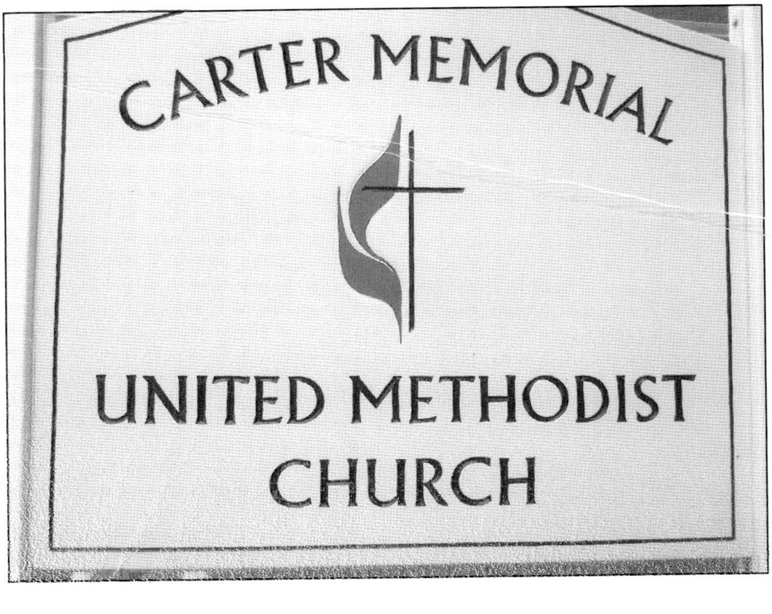

The Carter Memorial United Methodist Church, in the heart of Needham Heights, stands at the corner of Highland Avenue and Hunnewell Street. The church was rebuilt in the 1950s with funds donated by the Carter family, who were pioneers in children's clothing.

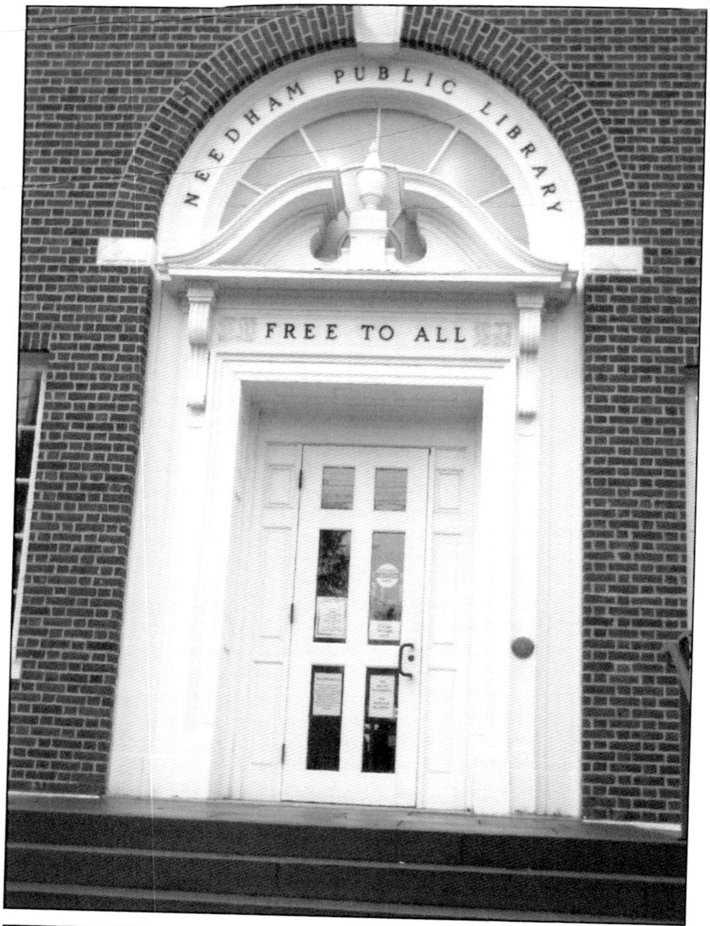

William Carter donated a parcel of land at the corner of Rosemary Street and Highland Avenue. As chairman of the building committee, he raised $40,000 to build a new library, completed in 1915, stacked with 40,000 books. A commemorative plaque and his portrait still grace the library to this day.

The William Carter School on Highland Avenue is pictured in 1979. Built in 1921 and named in honor of the founder of the William Carter Company, it remained a public elementary school until 1981. The building was torn down and replaced by an apartment complex. (Leonard Dawson Collection of the Needham Free Public Library.)

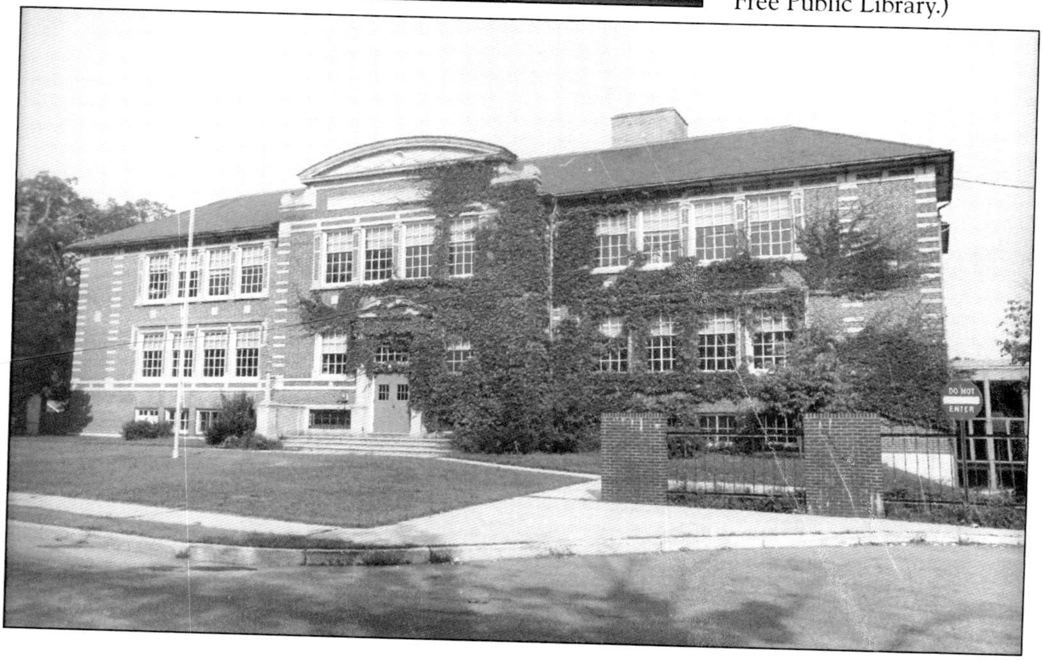

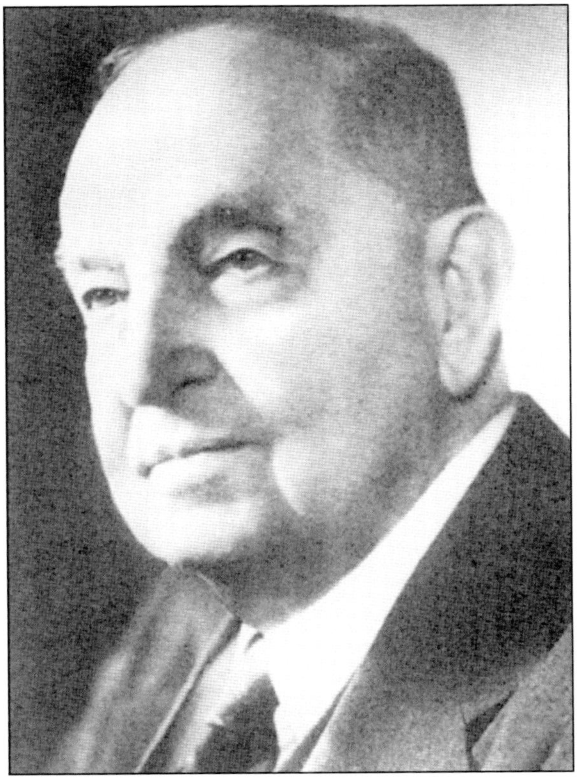

All five of William Carter's sons worked in his company. William Henry, born in 1864 in Highlandville, was the most successful of the Carter sons. He was elected as a Republican to serve in the 64th and 65th US Congress (1915–1919). He did not seek reelection, but chose to run the William Carter Company after his father died. During his 37-year tenure as president, The William Carter Company bought three mills in the American South. His brother Horace Albert (born in 1869 in Highlandville) was president of the company from 1955 to 1959 and continued the move to the South.

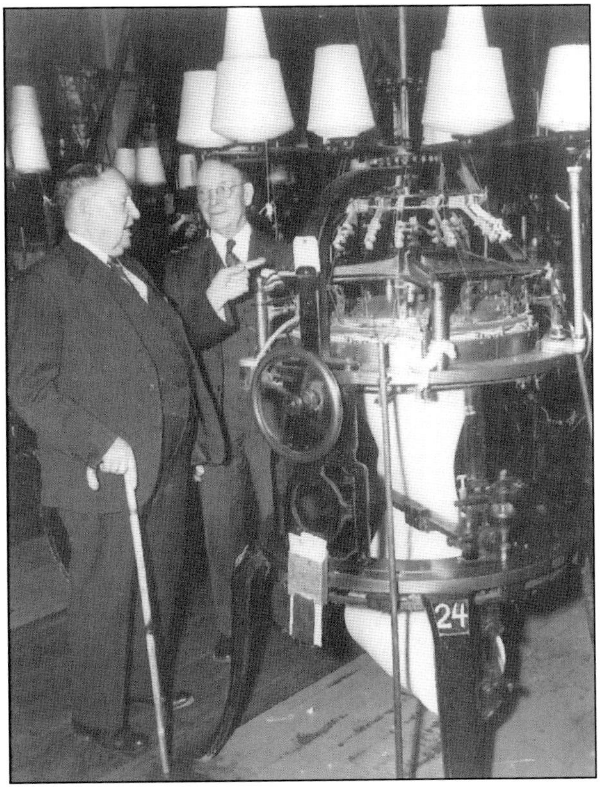

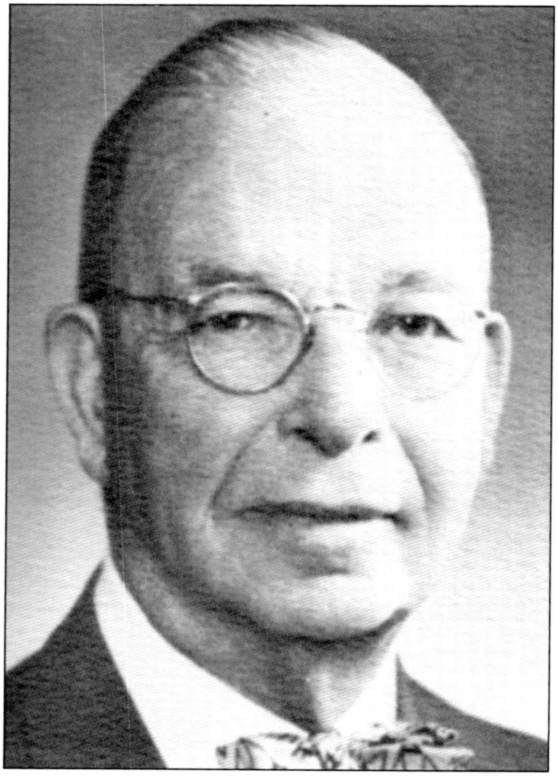

Horace Albert Carter had an artistic side and published a book of poems. Already in their seventies in the 1940s, he and his brother William still kept a firm grip on the company established by their father. During World War II, the company's production increased. Production in Needham was about to end as the William Carter Company moved garment making to the South and shifted from underwear to children's clothing.

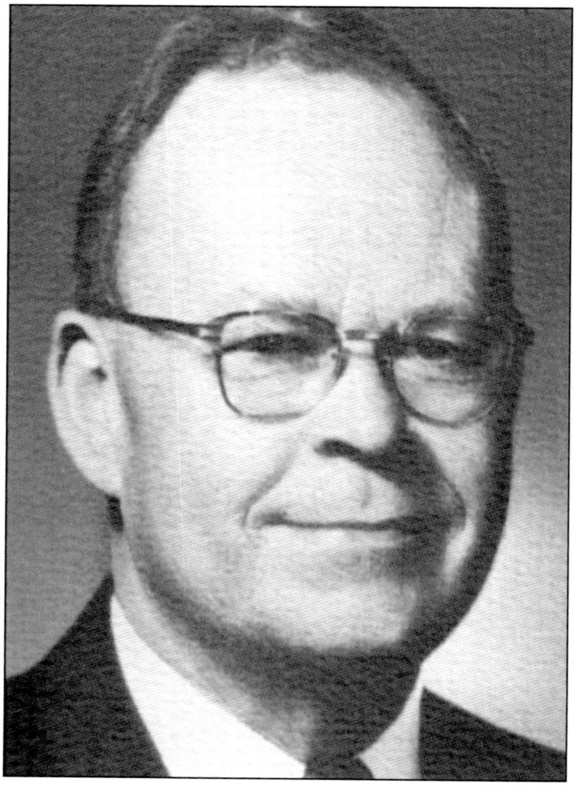

Lyndall Frederick Carter, son of Horace A. Carter, succeeded his father as president of the William Carter Company in 1959. After graduating from Phillips Exeter Academy, Lyndall attended Williams College and Harvard Graduate School of Business Administration. Lyndall started his career at Carter's in the administrative office, working up to assistant treasurer in 1928, first vice-president in 1944, and executive vice president in 1956. Lyndall served as president of the Needham Rotary Club and director of the Needham National Bank. Under Lyndall, the company expanded by buying mills in Mississippi and Pennsylvania. Lyndall Carter died in 1973, and his son Dana was a member of the fourth generation of Carters to take a senior position in the company.

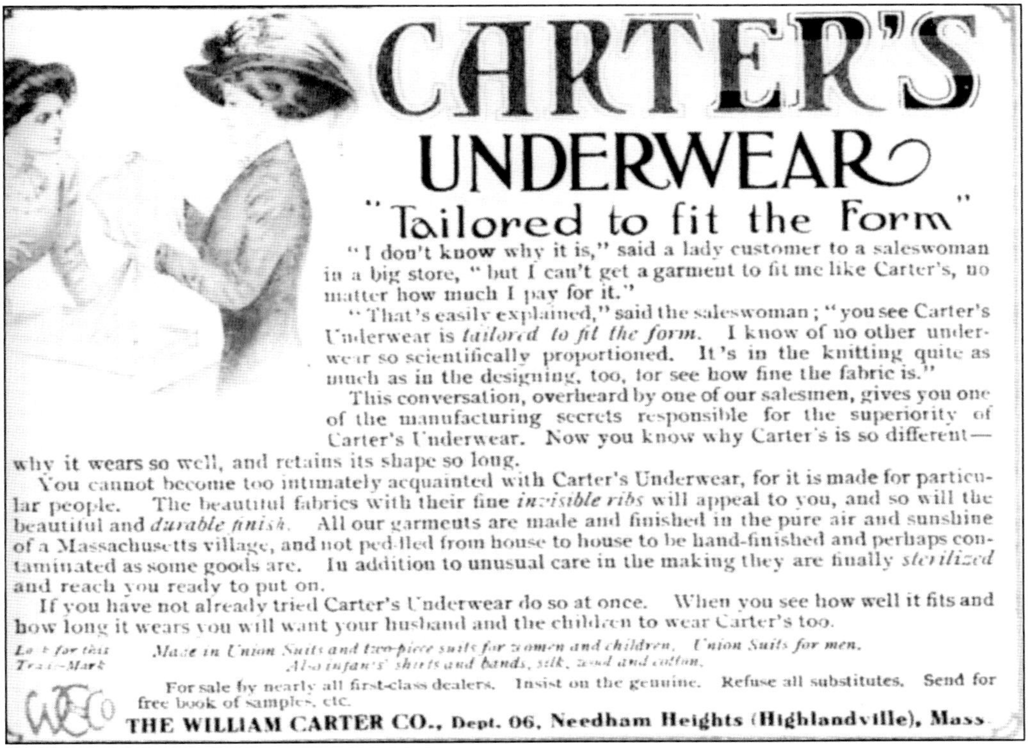

"Tailored to fit the Form," reads a 1909 Carter's advertisement. The bicycle craze of the late 19th century and a desire for comfort shifted women's clothing away from corsets and petticoats. Starting early in the 20th century, Carter's form fitting underwear was, according to the advertisement, "made and finished in the pure air and sunshine of a Massachusetts village."

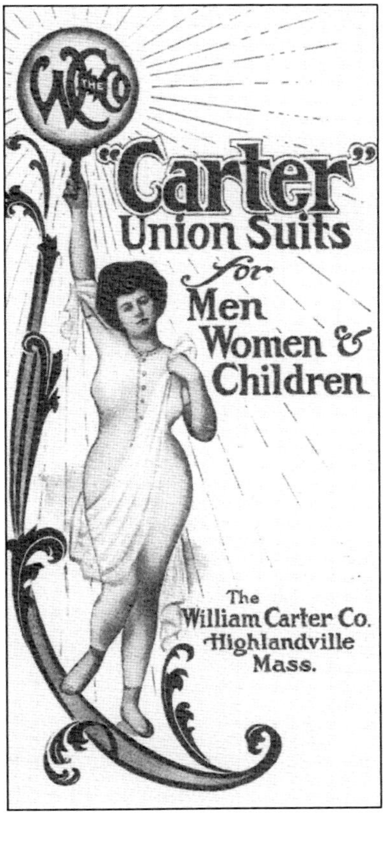

Carter's Union Suits were for men, women, and children. Introduced late in the 19th century as emancipation from multilayered and restrictive women's clothing, the Union Suit gained popularity among men and boys as well.

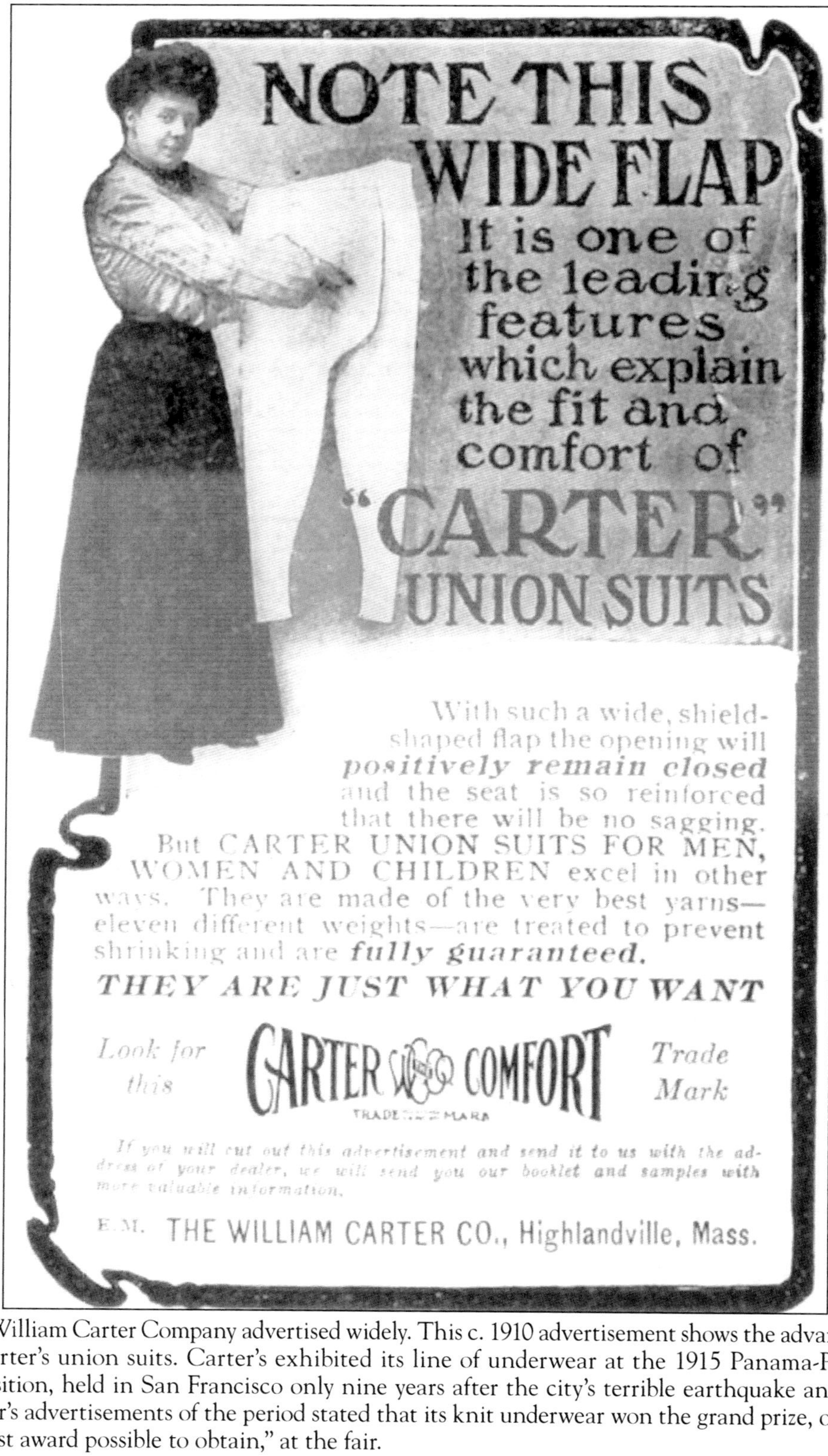

The William Carter Company advertised widely. This c. 1910 advertisement shows the advantages of Carter's union suits. Carter's exhibited its line of underwear at the 1915 Panama-Pacific Exposition, held in San Francisco only nine years after the city's terrible earthquake and fire. Carter's advertisements of the period stated that its knit underwear won the grand prize, or "the highest award possible to obtain," at the fair.

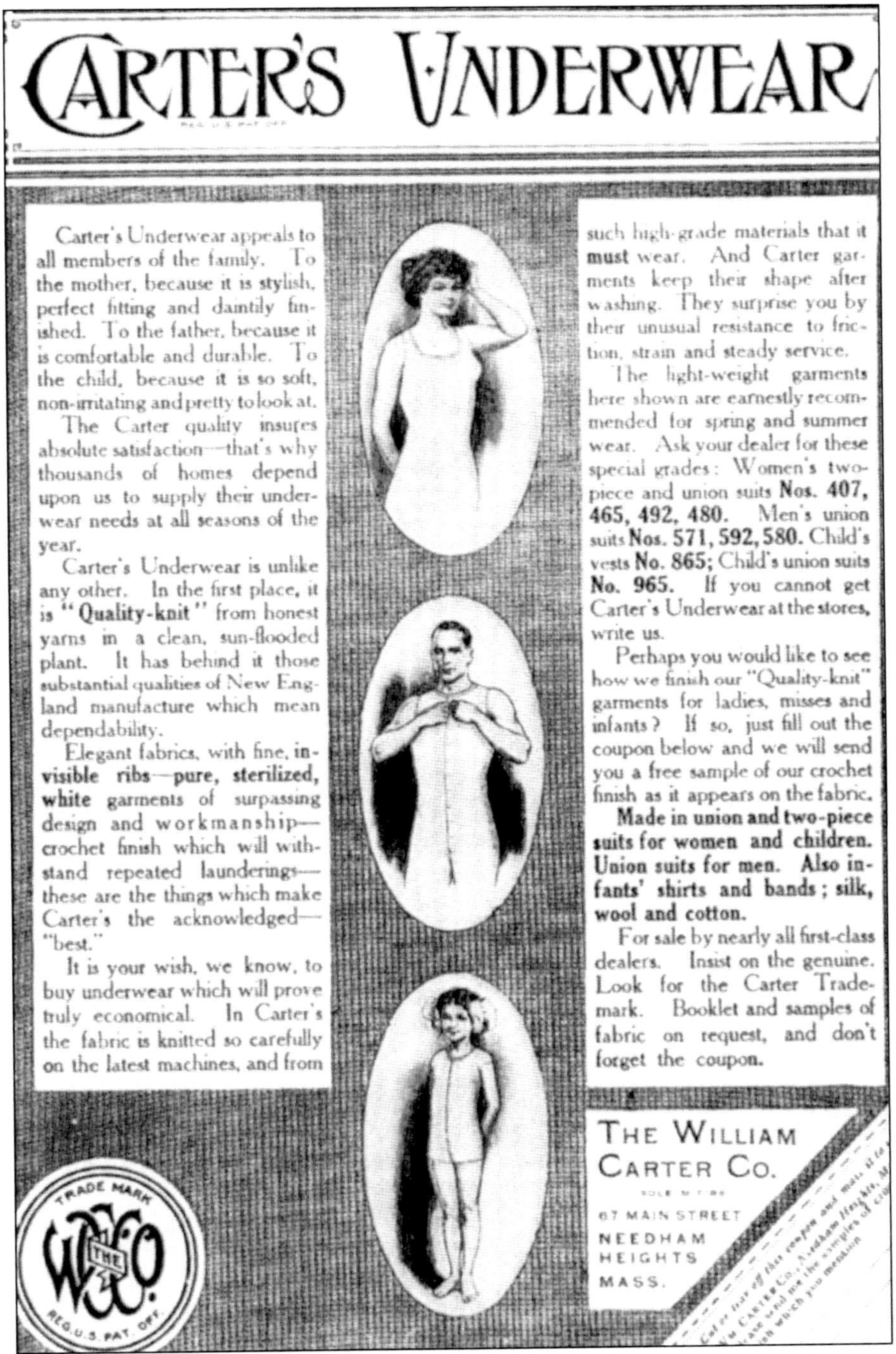

In the 1920s, Carter's was still selling the one-piece Union Suit but was also advertising two-piece underwear. These "Quality-knit" garments were sold in department stores across the United States, as well as in markets abroad. Carter's used the latest machines and first class materials, yet sold its garments at a fair price. For the mother, Carter's underwear was stylish, a perfect fit, and dainty. For the father, it was comfortable and durable, and for the child, it was soft and nonirritating. Carter's of Needham Heights advertised that it offered one-piece Union Suits or two-piece suits. According to advertisements, Carter's garments "kept their shape after washing."

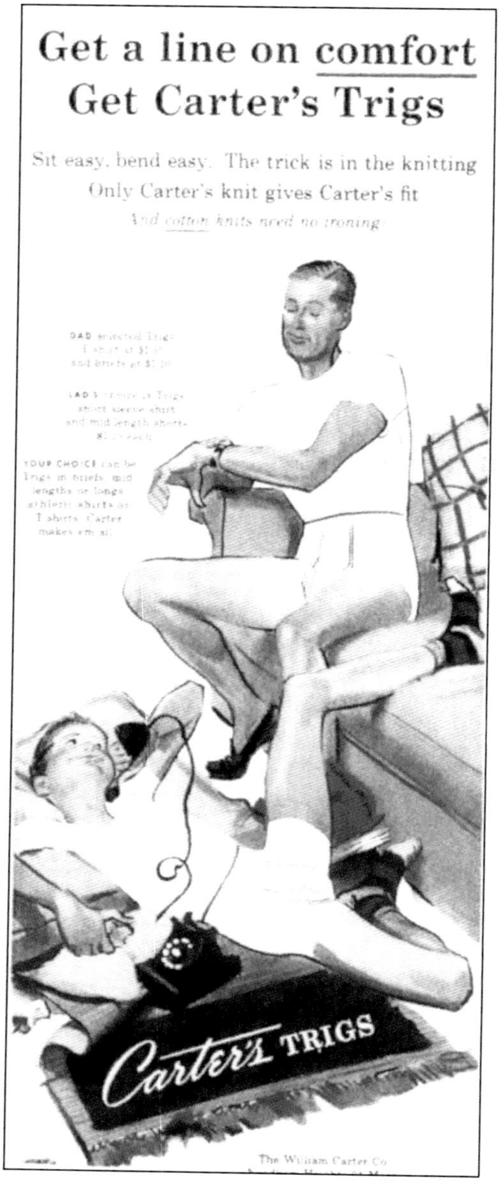

In the 1940s, Carter's moved from the one-piece Union Suit to the comfort of cotton knitted Trigs, or separate undershirts and briefs. Taken from the word to signify smart and neat in appearance, Trigs were easy to wash and needed no ironing.

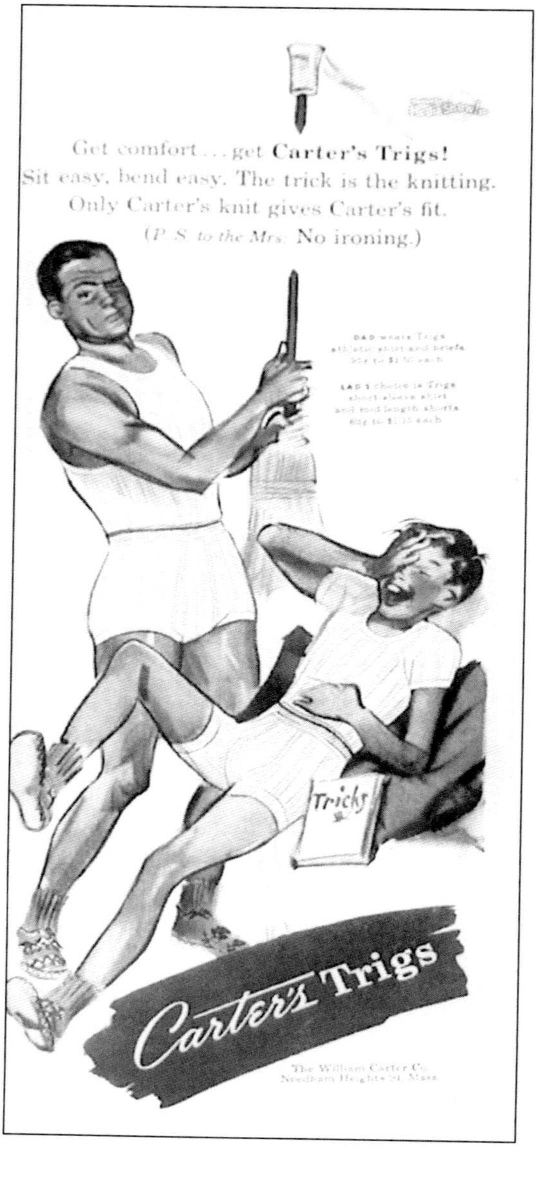

Carter's Trigs were for the active boys and men interested in comfort and flexibility. Formality and hard work were less emphasized, replaced instead by love of sports and having fun. Made of cotton, Trigs did not itch.

Starting in the 1950s, Carter's switched from underwear to infants' and children's clothing. Carter's made clothing for girls up to size 14 and boys up to size 18. Carter's apparel included light clothing for hot weather and sweaters and coats for the winter months.

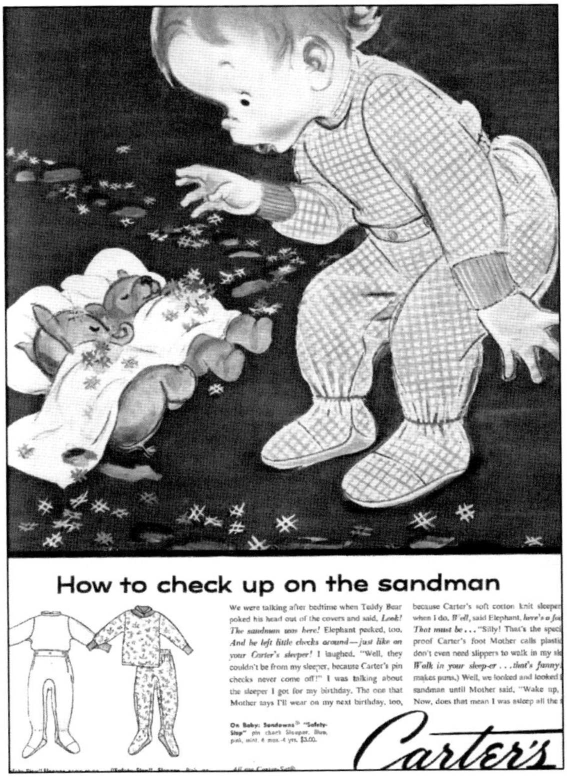

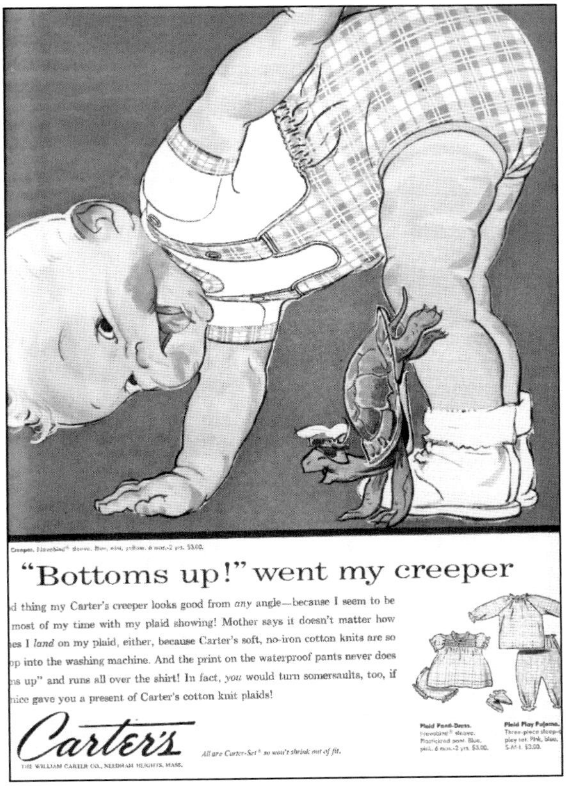

Carter's expanded its line of infant and children's clothing beyond department stores by opening its own factory outlets. Here, goods were offered at discount prices as well as two-thirds-off bargains at twice-yearly sales.

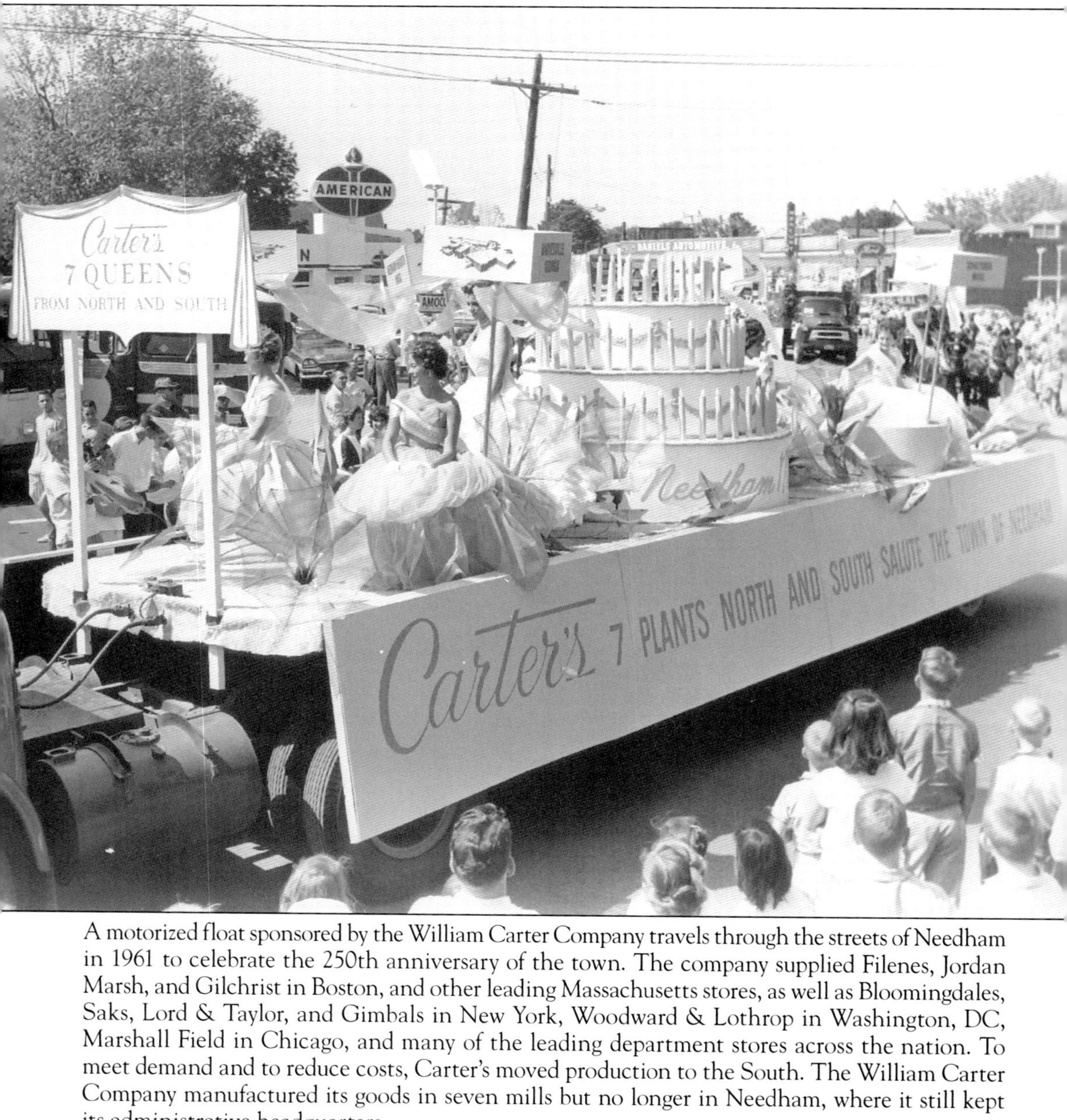

A motorized float sponsored by the William Carter Company travels through the streets of Needham in 1961 to celebrate the 250th anniversary of the town. The company supplied Filenes, Jordan Marsh, and Gilchrist in Boston, and other leading Massachusetts stores, as well as Bloomingdales, Saks, Lord & Taylor, and Gimbals in New York, Woodward & Lothrop in Washington, DC, Marshall Field in Chicago, and many of the leading department stores across the nation. To meet demand and to reduce costs, Carter's moved production to the South. The William Carter Company manufactured its goods in seven mills but no longer in Needham, where it still kept its administrative headquarters.

Six

1911

William G. Moseley, manufacturer of silk, elastic stockings, and underwear, served as the town moderator from 1899 until 1911. Early in 1911, Moseley appointed 21 prominent citizens to plan Needham's bicentennial celebration, scheduled for September of that year. The men selected mostly came from the old families, but three of the knitters—William Carter, Joseph B. Thorpe, and William Gorse—were also included. William Carter's wife, Jane Greenough Avery Carter, wrote the bicentennial poem.

On September 17, the town hall had been beautifully decorated and was ready for the bicentennial banquet. The climax of the bicentennial celebrations was the parade held on September 19, 1911. Dozens of floats, marching bands, and civic groups participated. The most impressive among them were the floats sponsored by the "Principal Industries of the Town," especially the knitters. The William Carter Company presented 16 horse-drawn barges carrying employees showing the latest knitting machinery. The Carter exhibit took five minutes to pass a given point and was the largest feature of the whole parade. Next came the Moseley and Company float pulled by two horses with a display of the knitting process from yarn to clothing. On the float were six small children dressed smartly in knit caps, leggings, and sweaters and accompanied by two adults. The signs on the side of the float displayed the company's Tiny-Wear trademark and "Moseley & Company, established 1880." George E. Wye Company, a knit goods company at the corner of Pleasant Street and Dedham Avenue, had two floats. One depicted a Shaker village and "Ye Knitting of 1711," and the second float, "Knitting of 1911," showed a modern sweater making machine, a power sewing machine, and modern office equipment, such as the telephone and typewriter. A number of the knitting mills were gaily decorated for the celebration.

Change was in the air as displayed by the New England Telephone and Telegraph exhibit and the Edison Company float. The era of manufacturing in small towns with local management would soon be over, to be replaced by national and even international companies.

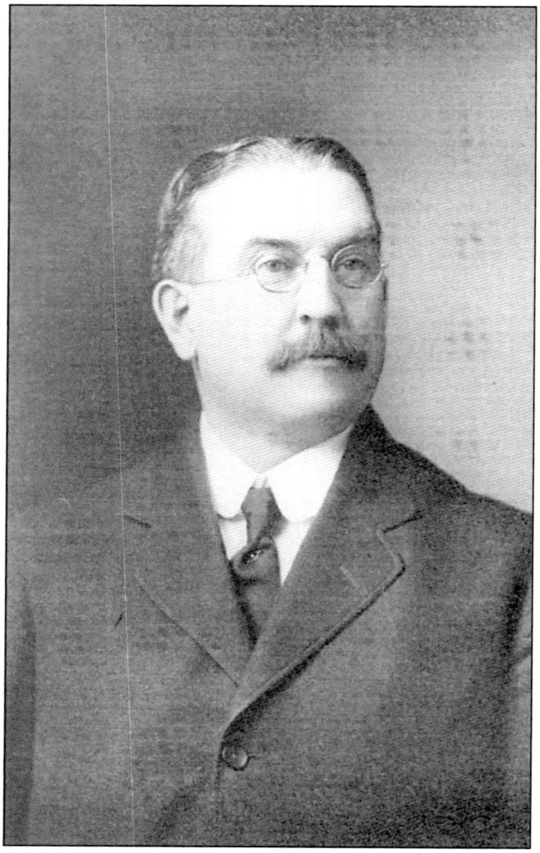

William G. Moseley served as town moderator from 1899 until 1911, when he organized the bicentennial celebration. With his brother John, in 1888, he established Moseley and Company, makers of knitted hosiery and children's underwear. In 1893, William Moseley with William Carter and others petitioned to establish the Needham street trolley system, with one line running from Wellesley to Dedham along Great Plain Avenue and another line running along Highland Avenue into Newton. William Moseley helped establish the Needham Cooperative Bank.

To celebrate the 1911 bicentennial, the Moseley Building, at the southeast corner of Great Plain Avenue and Chestnut Street, and other prominent buildings were festooned with bunting. Built in the 1870s, the Moseley Building was the town's main commercial block, and in the 1890s, held the town offices. Thomas Crossman, who ran a shop in the Moseley Building, won the prize for the best decorated store to celebrate the bicentennial.

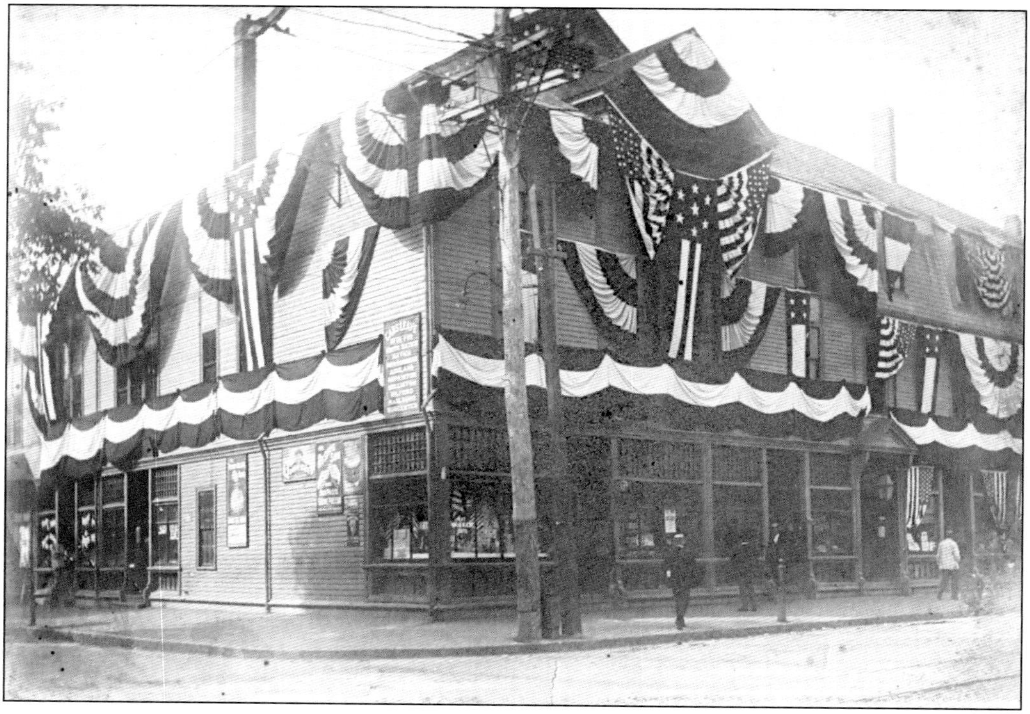

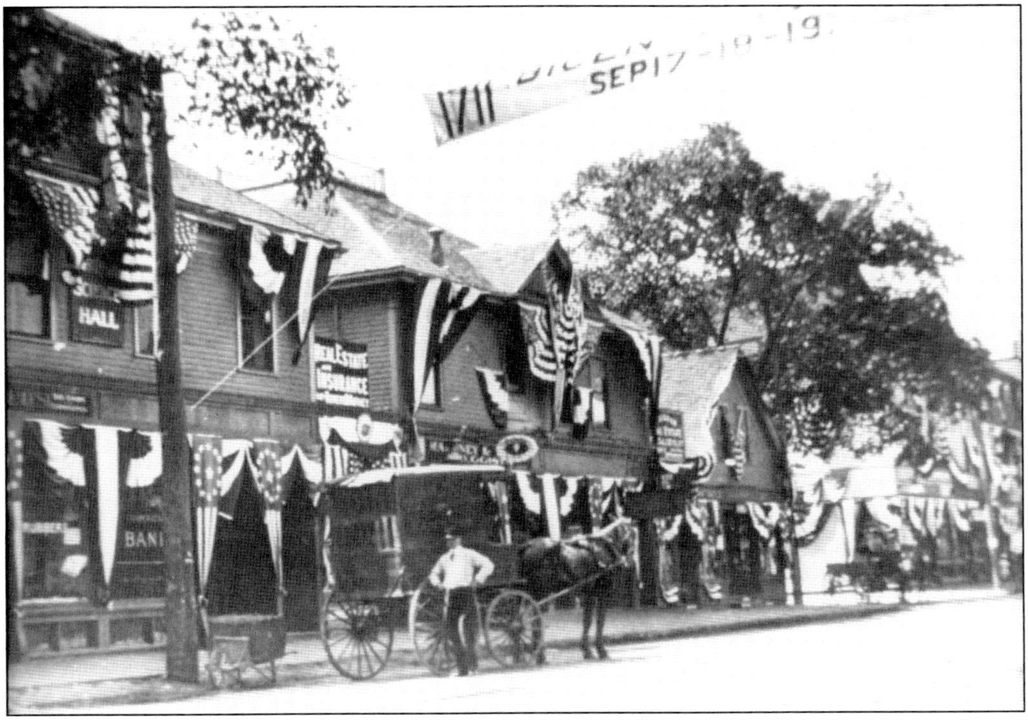

The stores near the corner of Highland Avenue and Great Plain Avenue were decorated in honor of the bicentennial. The wagon on Great Plain Avenue in front of the insurance and real estate office is from the Dedham Custom Laundry. (Leonard Dawson Collection of the Needham Free Public Library.)

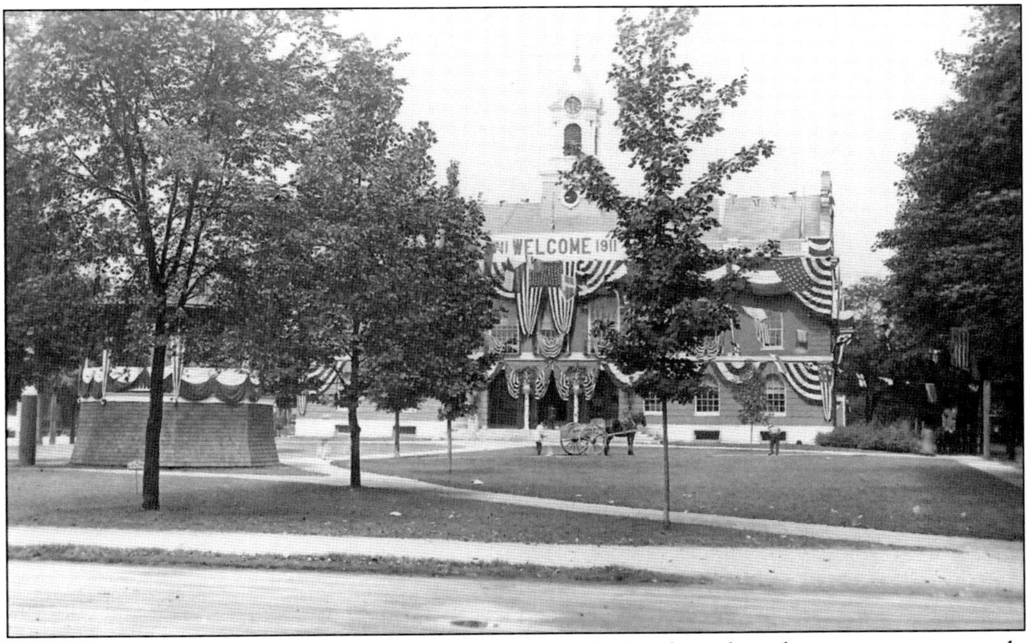

This 1911 photograph shows Needham town hall and the bandstand on the town common gaily dressed up to celebrate the 200th birthday of the town. The high school and other town buildings were also decorated for the bicentennial.

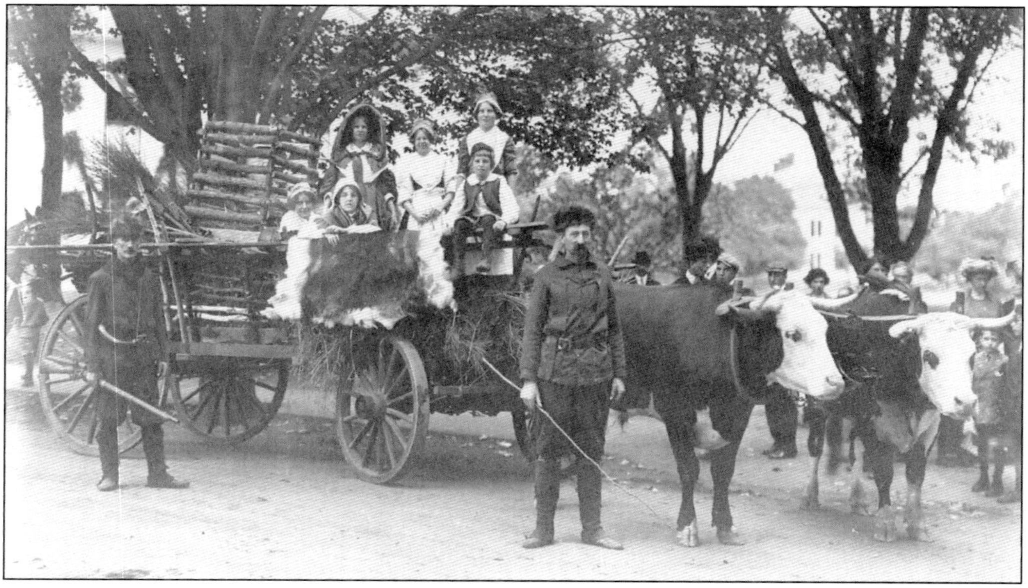

This float depicted the hardy farming families who came from Dedham at the beginning of the 18th century to settle in Needham on land surrounded on three sides by the meanderings of the Charles River.

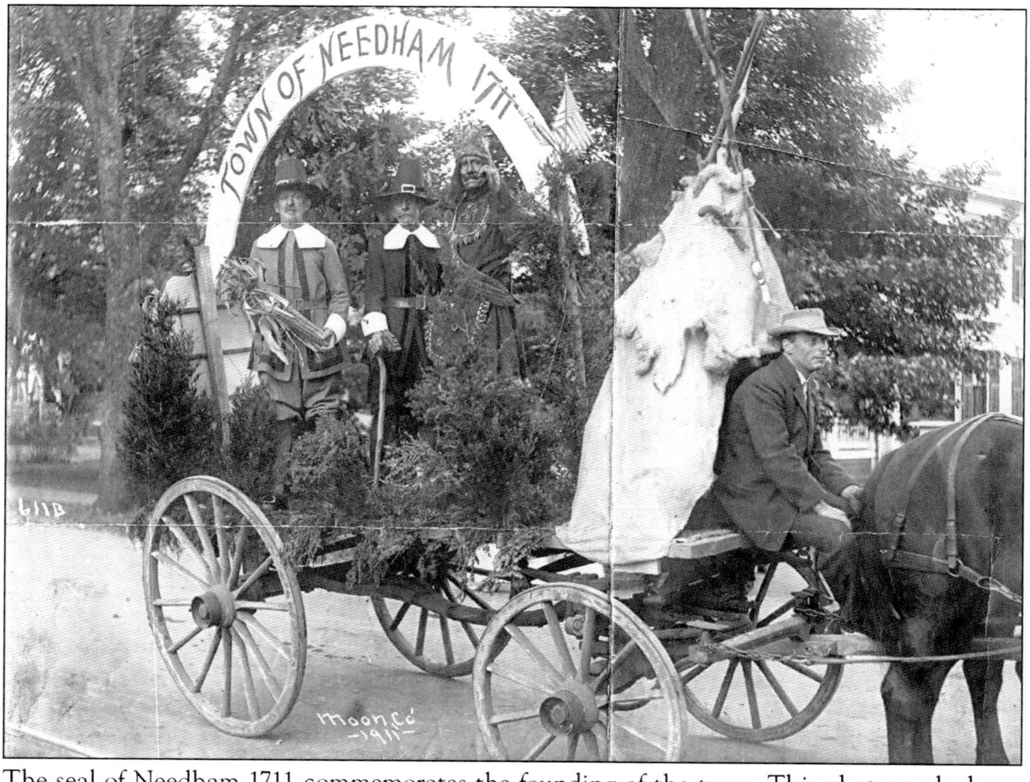

The seal of Needham 1711 commemorates the founding of the town. This photograph shows John and Sumner Mills in pilgrim dress accompanied by George Kingsbury, dressed as Nehoiden the Indian tribal leader, who, in the 1680s, sold them the town's land for £10. The Mills and Kingsbury families are among the oldest in Needham.

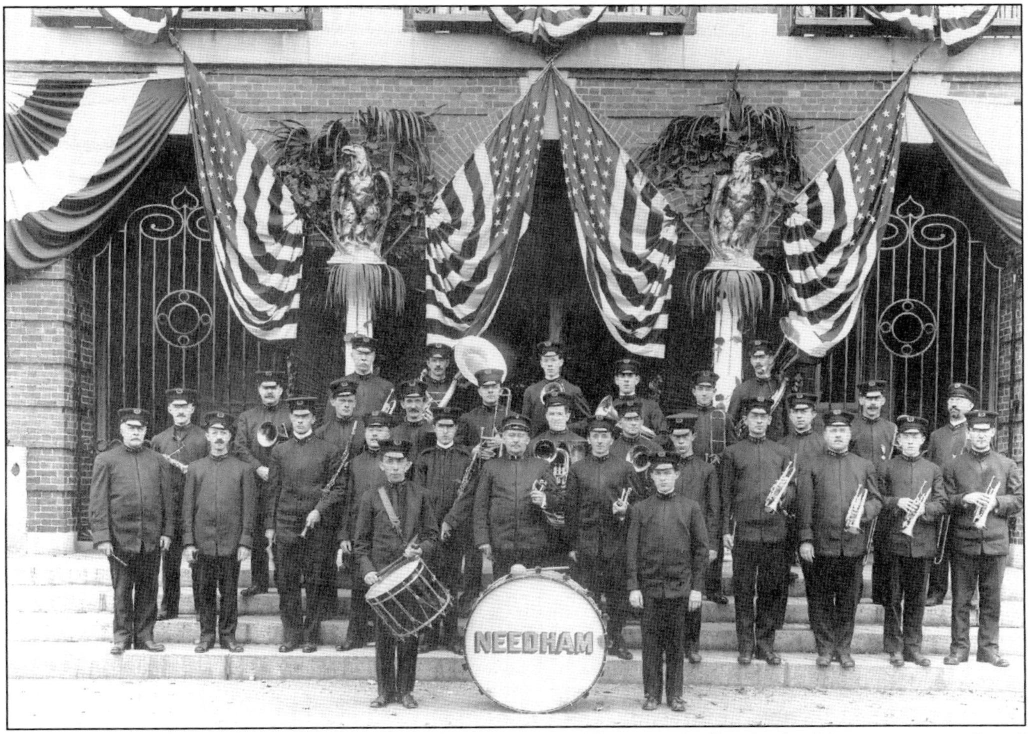

In 1902, the Town of Needham allocated $57,000 to build a town hall. The building was completed in December 1903. The Needham Military Band was formed in 1910 and regularly performed on the bandstand built on the common. Pictured is the band in front of the town hall on September 17, 1911, as part of the bicentennial festivities.

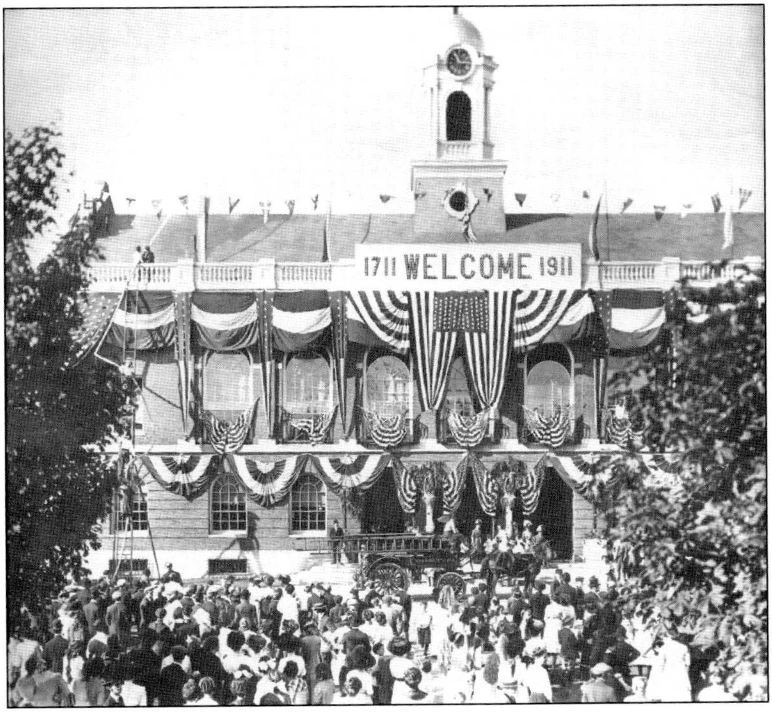

In 1908, Henry Howard Upham was appointed fire chief of Needham. The town maintained four firefighting stations at Great Plain, Highlandville, Upper Falls, and Greendale. Pictured in 1911, the Needham Fire Department displays the latest in firefighting equipment in front of a large crowd at the town hall.

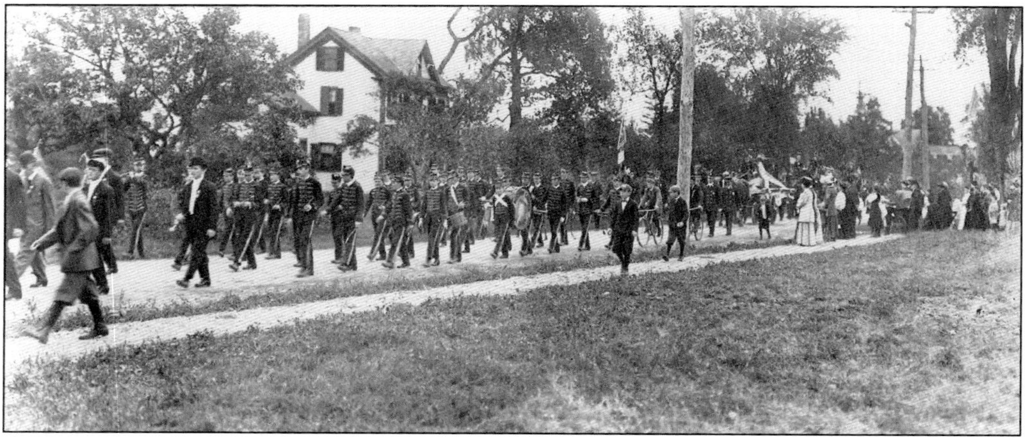

The Needham Military Band, in different uniform, leads the parade along Highland Avenue on Tuesday, September 19, 1911. Behind the band are cyclists and the procession of floats.

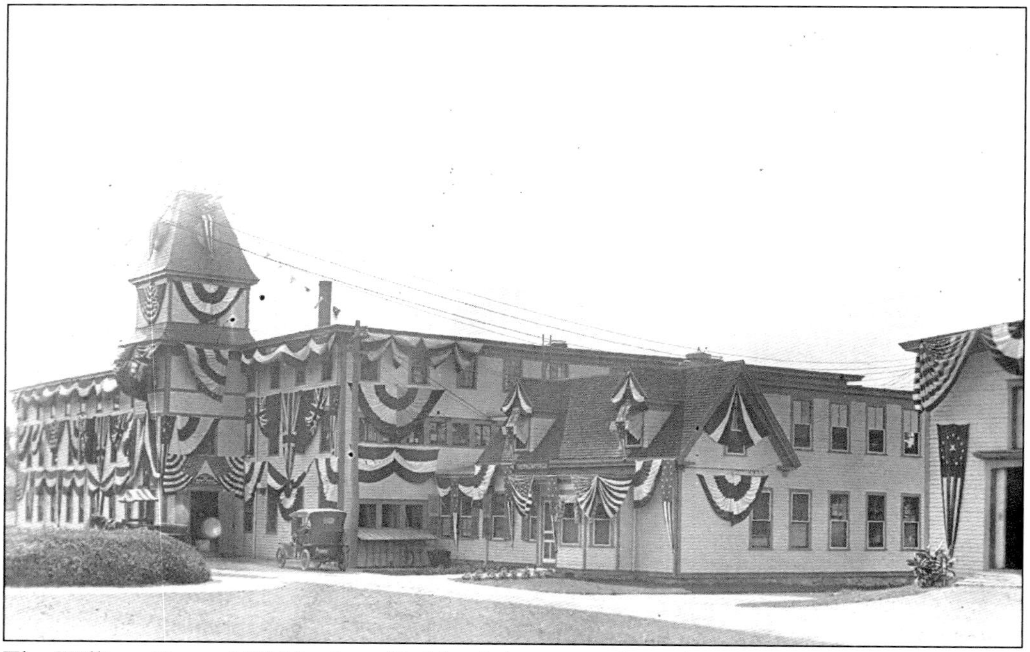

The William Carter Mill No. 1 on Highland Avenue is dressed up for the town's bicentennial celebration. In 1864, Mark and John Lee established a small hosiery mill at this site. Five years later, William Carter joined them as Lee, Carter, and Company. When the brothers retired from the business in 1875, William Carter continued as sole owner, gradually moving from socks and gloves to underwear. In 1911, the William Carter Company made 40 million garments, largely in its Needham plants.

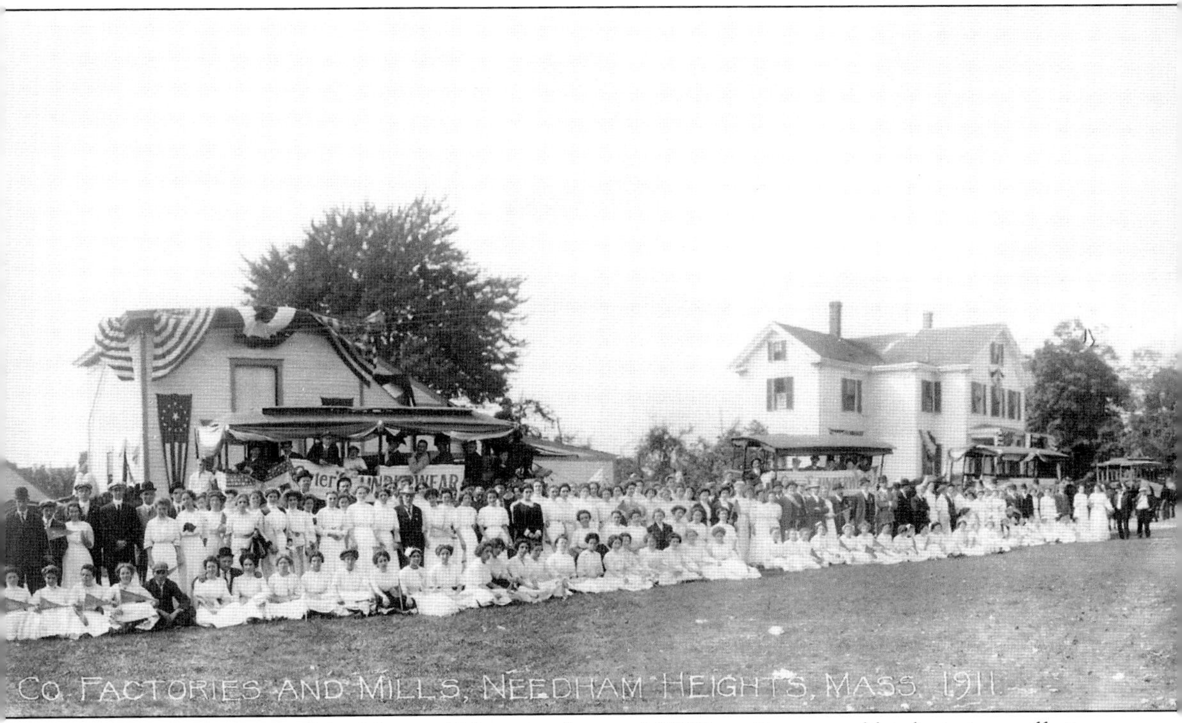

The June 1907 issue of the *National Magazine* featured William Carter and his knitting mills in Needham. Under the title, "A Transplanted Industry—New England Excels Old England," the writer describes William Carter's 50 years in the knitting industry. His success came from making a superior product at a reasonable price and treating his employees well. Publicity from the article as well as increased advertising brought added work to the Needham mills. In the photograph, the large staff of the William Carter Company poses in front of Mill No. 1 in celebration of the 200th birthday of the town of Needham. As befits the formality and order of William Carter, the women employees are dressed in white and the men are in dark suits. Carter treated his workers well by shortening work hours and offering subsidized housing.

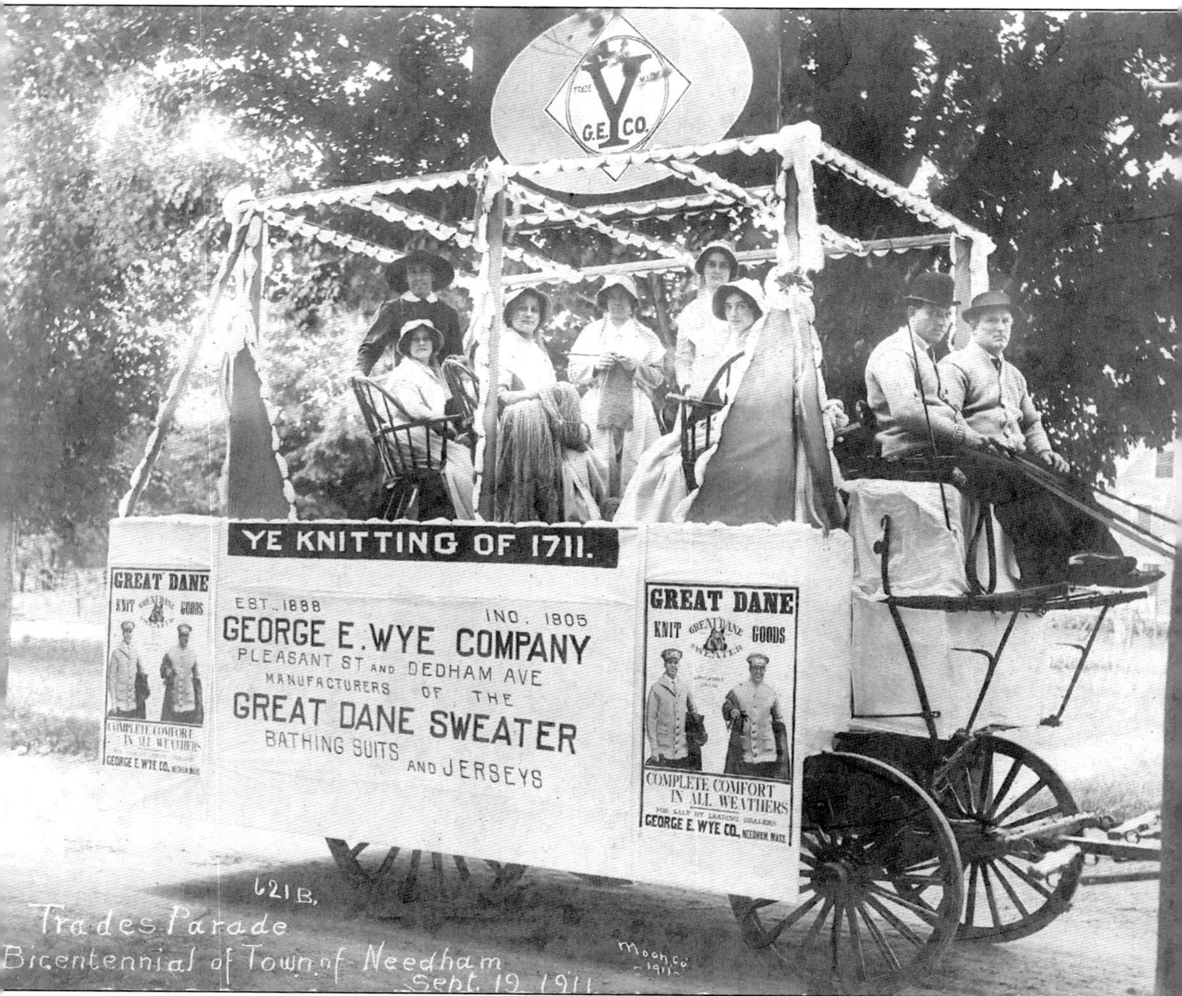

The Trades Parade featured the knitting mills as the leading industry of Needham. The George E. Wye Company were makers of Great Dane knitted garments, in particular sweaters, socks, and bathing suits. The company was located at the corner of Pleasant Street and Dedham Avenue. George Wye garments were sold by fine stores across the nation and promised, "Complete comfort in all weathers." The float, "Ye Knitting of 1711," shows how knitting was done in the old days. George Wye founded his company in 1888 and had it incorporated in 1908.

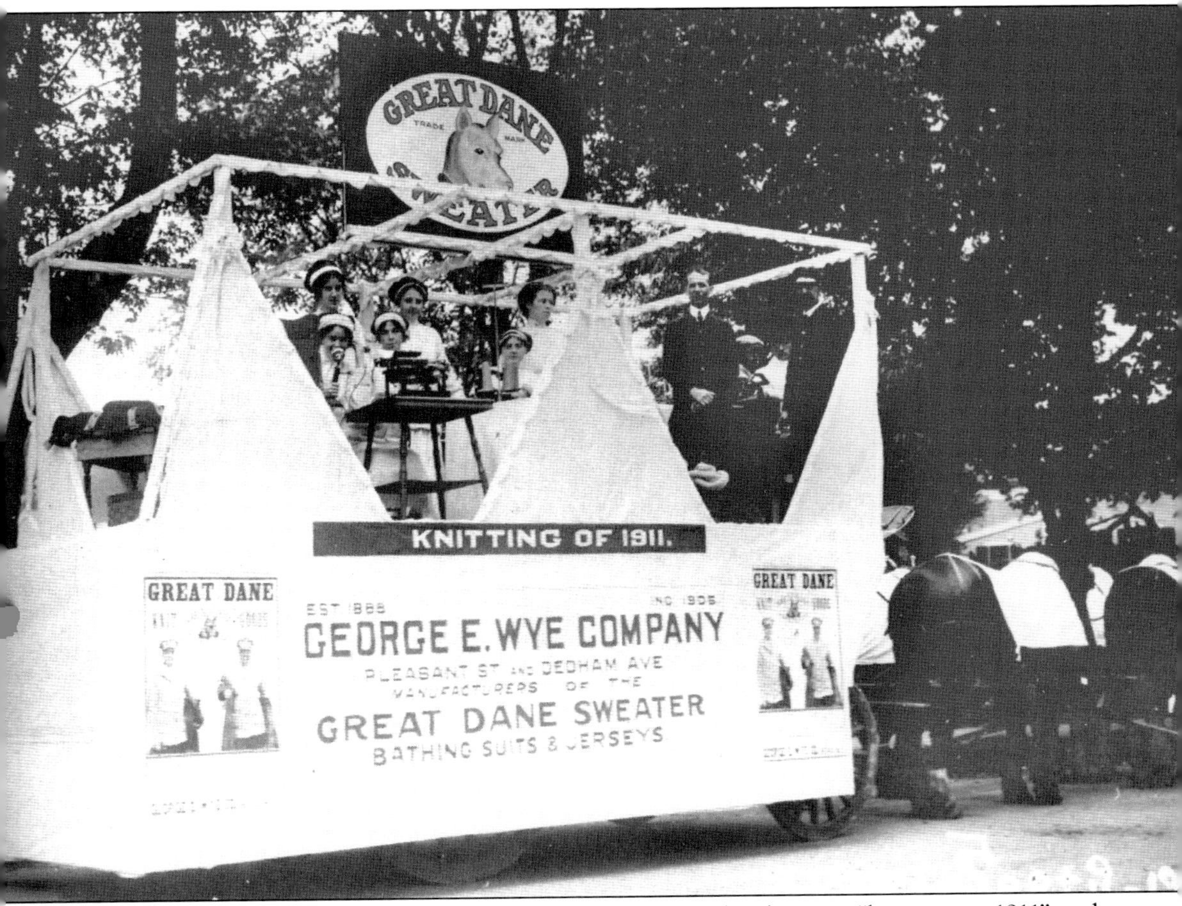

This is the second float of the George E. Wye Company. The theme is "knitting in 1911" and shows the latest in knitting and office equipment. In 1911, Massachusetts was still the dominant textile state, but the South was fast closing in. During each year from 1900 to 1920, an average of 100 knitting mills opened in the United States, with Pennsylvania, North Carolina, South Carolina, and Georgia leading the way. Also, cheap knitted goods were coming in from Great Britain, Germany, and Japan. Small knitting mills, like the George E. Wye Company, were facing intense competition. (Leonard Dawson Collection of the Needham Free Public Library.)

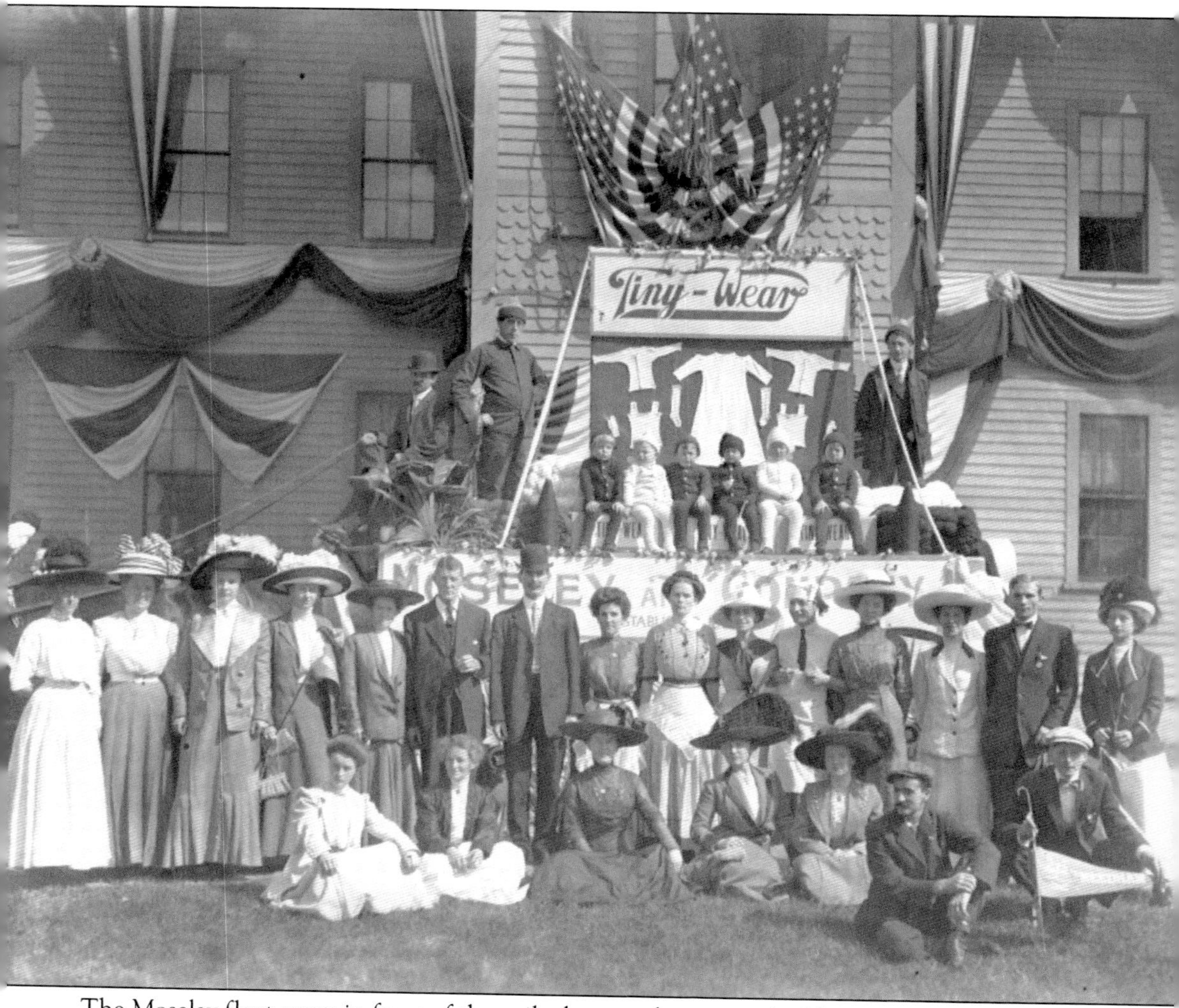

The Moseley float poses in front of the gaily decorated company building on Highland Avenue, Needham Heights. Moseley and Company, established in 1888, featured the Tiny-Wear line of knit caps, leggings, and sweaters. The three children on the left are George, Ruth, and Robert with their father, Samuel Wilson. The three boys on the right are Laurence, Lewis, and Albert, sons of William Jackson. In front of the float, dressed in the latest fashion, are members of the staff of Moseley and Company.

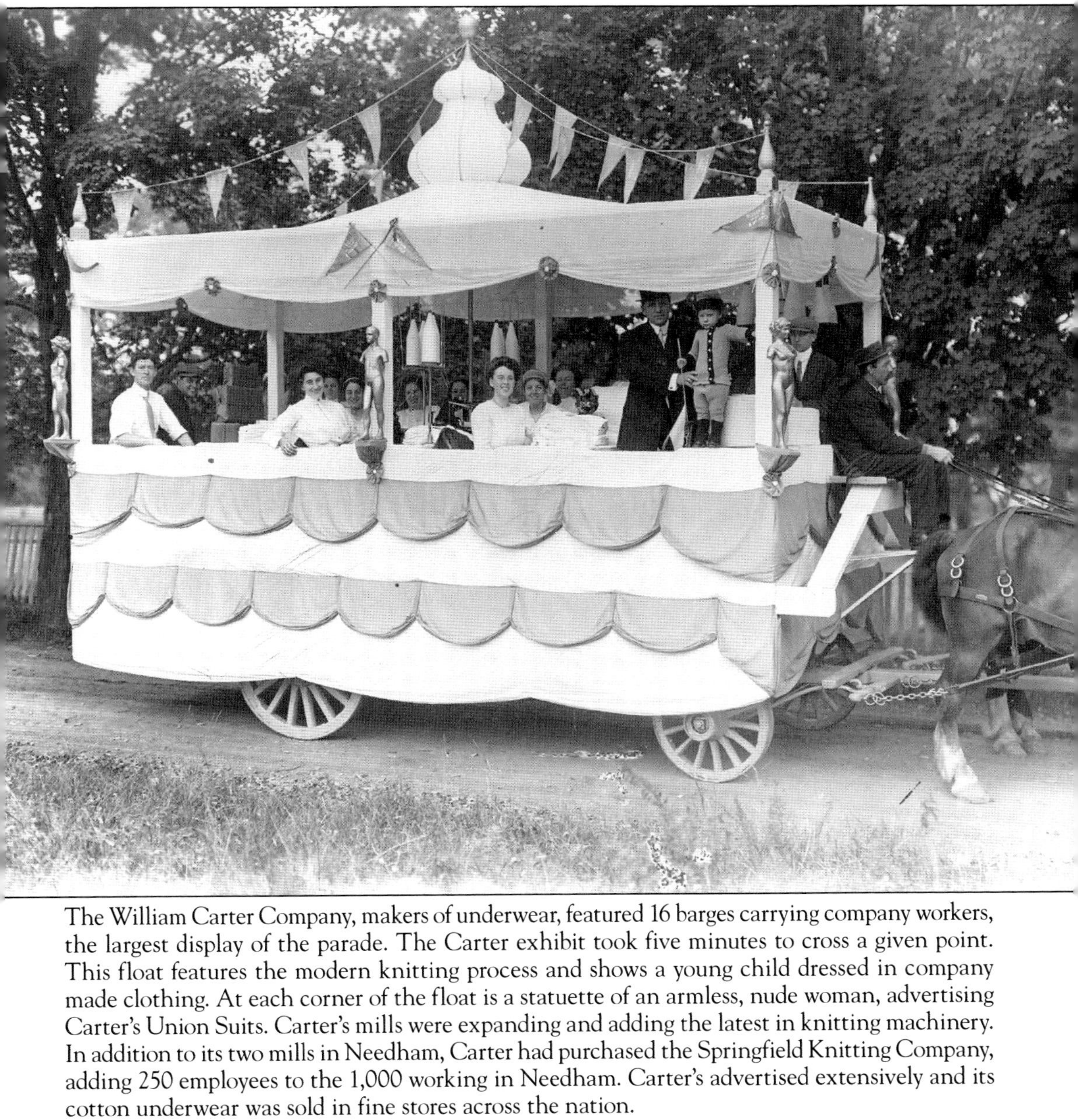

The William Carter Company, makers of underwear, featured 16 barges carrying company workers, the largest display of the parade. The Carter exhibit took five minutes to cross a given point. This float features the modern knitting process and shows a young child dressed in company made clothing. At each corner of the float is a statuette of an armless, nude woman, advertising Carter's Union Suits. Carter's mills were expanding and adding the latest in knitting machinery. In addition to its two mills in Needham, Carter had purchased the Springfield Knitting Company, adding 250 employees to the 1,000 working in Needham. Carter's advertised extensively and its cotton underwear was sold in fine stores across the nation.

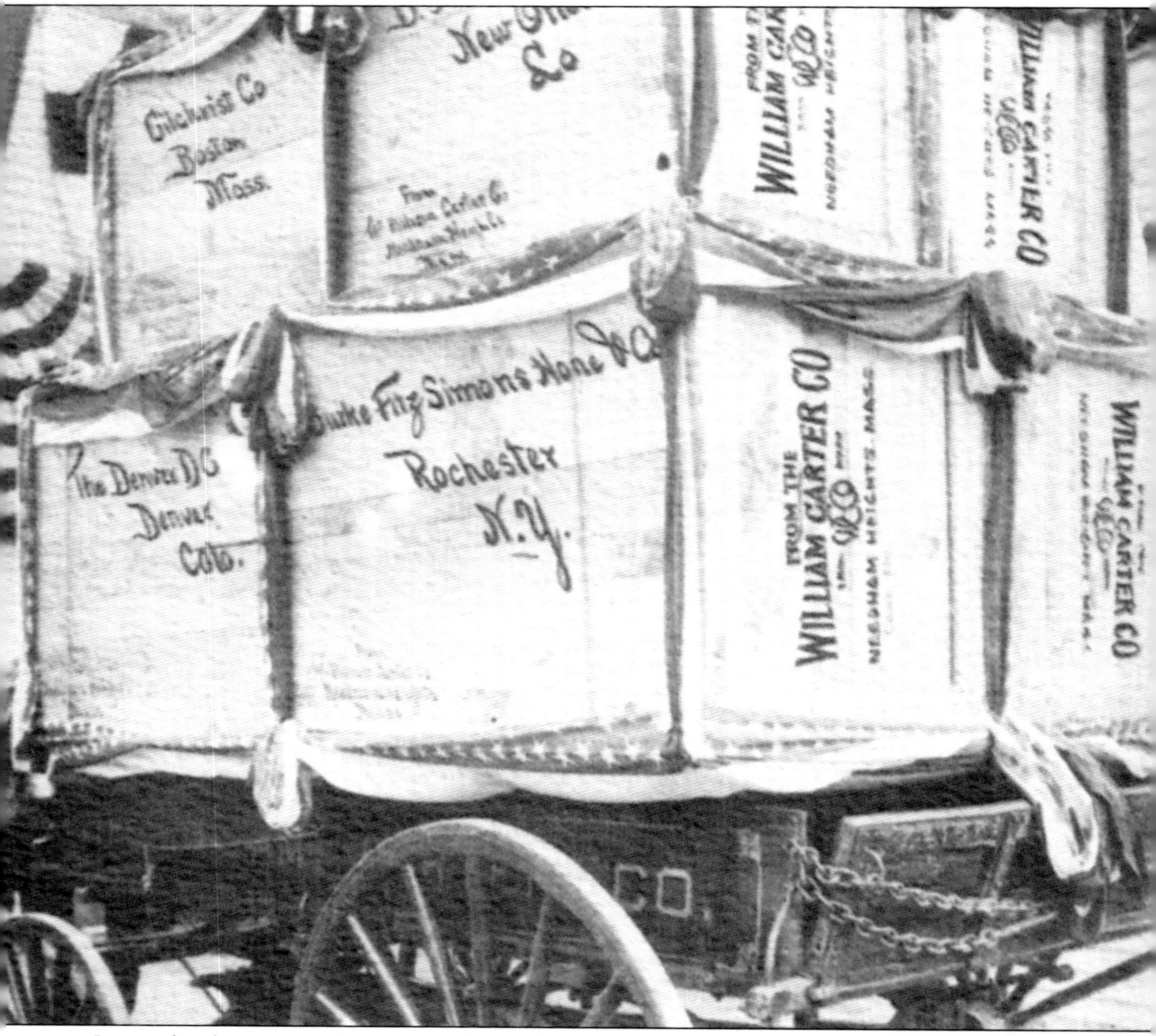

In another bicentennial exhibit of the William Carter Company, the horse wagon is piled high with wooden boxes of Carter's garments ready to be sent off to stores across the nation. Established in the mid-19th century, department stores offered a wide variety of goods under one roof. Using the railroad out of Needham Heights and later its fleet of delivery vans, Carter's shipped bulk orders of its underwear to stores across America. The photograph shows wooden containers of Carter's underwear ready for shipment to Gilchrist & Company, Boston; Burke, FitzSimmons, Hone & Company, Rochester, New York; and the Denver Company, Denver. The William Carter Company was by far the largest industry in Needham.

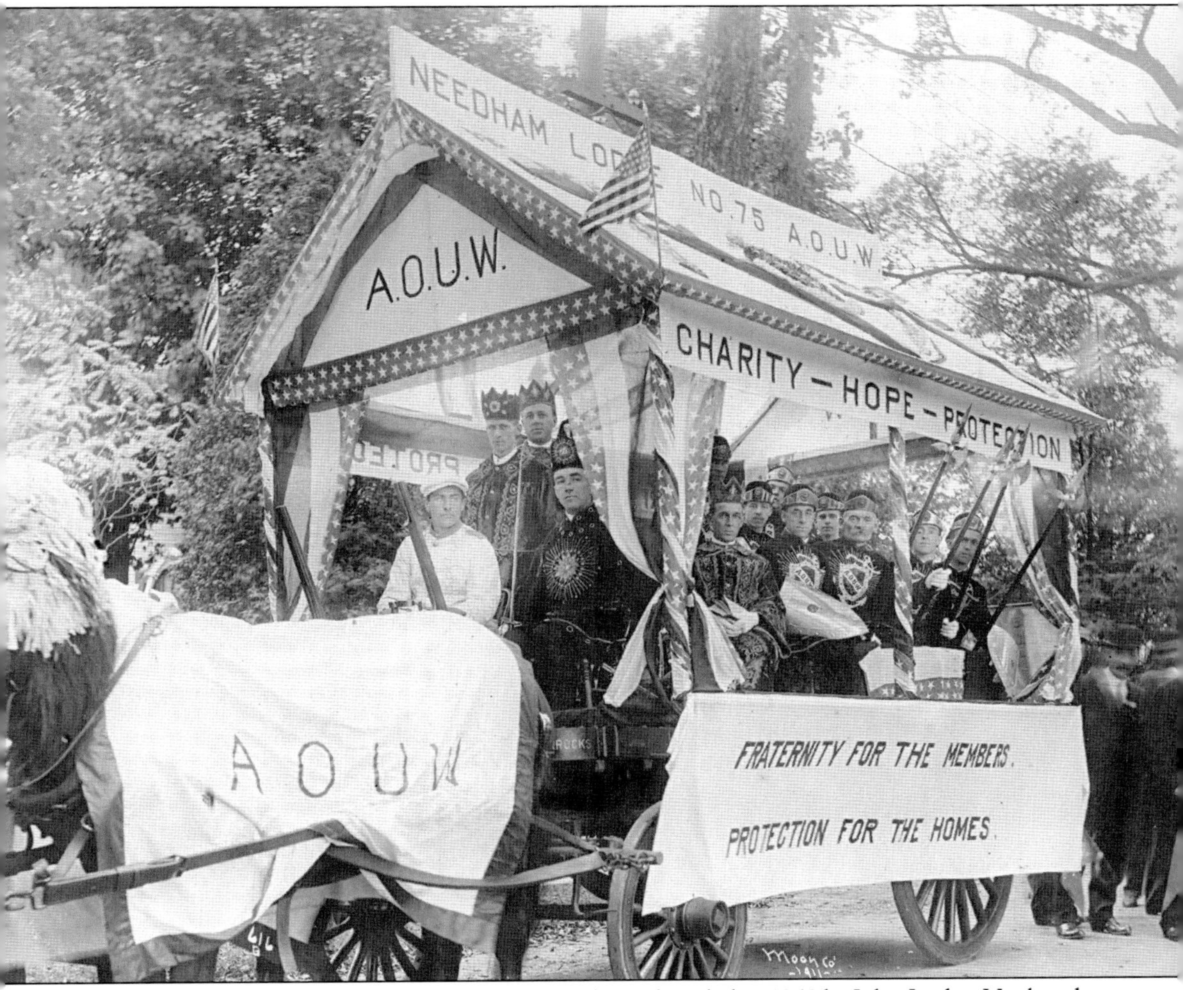

The Ancient Order of Unified Workmen (AOUW) was founded in 1868 by John Jordan Upchurch as a fraternal organization that would provide social and financial help to working people, and to mediate the conflicts between workers and bosses. It was based on the idea that the interests of labor and capital were equal. For an annual payment of $1, a workman was guaranteed that if he died on the job, his dependants would receive $500. In many cities, lodges were formed where members could meet. The Needham Lodge No. 75 was established in 1887, and within 20 years had 200 members, among them knitwear workers. Advocating charity, hope, and protection, the exotically dressed members of the Needham lodge took part in the town's bicentennial parade.

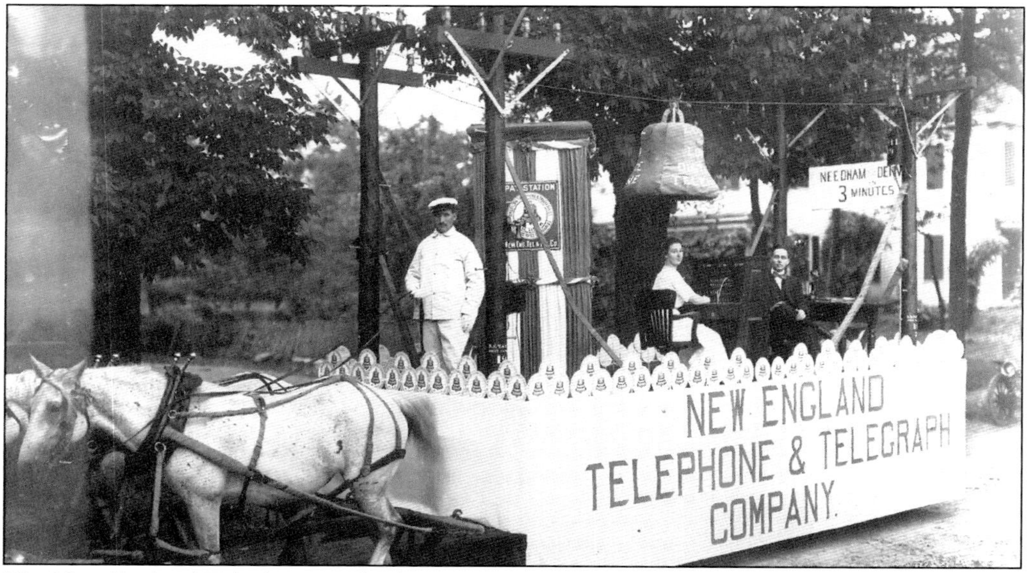

The New England Telephone and Telegraph Company float showed a modern switchboard and promised a telephone connection between Needham and Denver in three minutes. In the 19th century, the telegraph had greatly increased the speed of communication across the nation and around the world. In 1877, the Bell Telephone Company was established with a wire linking Boston to Somerville. By 1880, over 50,000 telephones were in use in the United States. At the 1893 World's Columbian Exposition, Chicago was linked by telephone with New York. By 1911, the New England Telegraph Telephone had greatly extended its grid across the region and beyond. The Needham knitting companies like George Wye, Saxony, and William Carter were linked to the outside world by telephone.

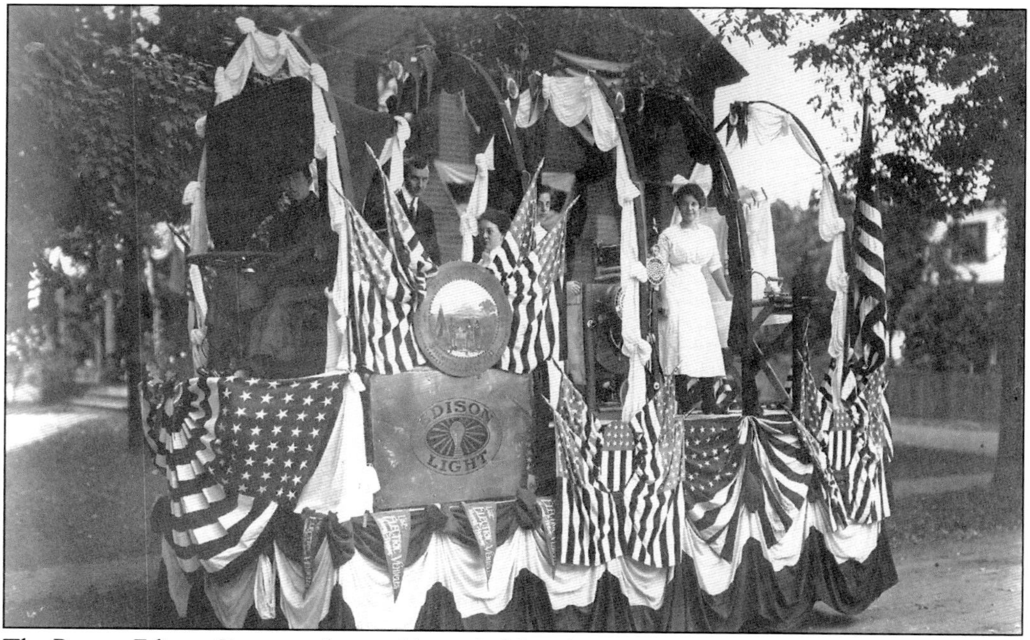

The Boston Edison Company featured household appliances run by electricity. Unlike the horse-drawn floats of the other participants in the bicentennial parade, an electric motor powered the Boston Edison float.

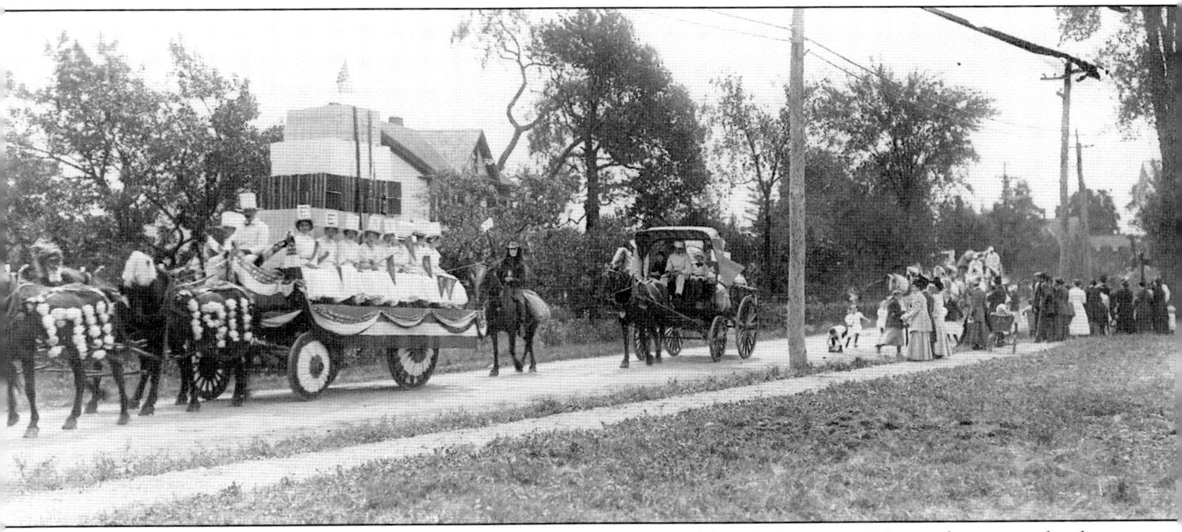

The bicentennial parade makes its way slowly along Highland Avenue. Many distinguished persons, including the president of the United States, the governor of Massachusetts, and the two senators for the state, were invited to take part in the town's 200th birthday celebrations. Through Charles D. Hilles, his secretary, Pres. William H. Taft responded, "he has a tentative engagement in the West and regrets exceedingly that it will not be possible to accept your most attractive invitation. It affords him much pleasure, however, to extend his best wishes for a successful anniversary." The music study class of Needham staged a musical in Bourne Hall, with lyrics by the wife of William G. Moseley.

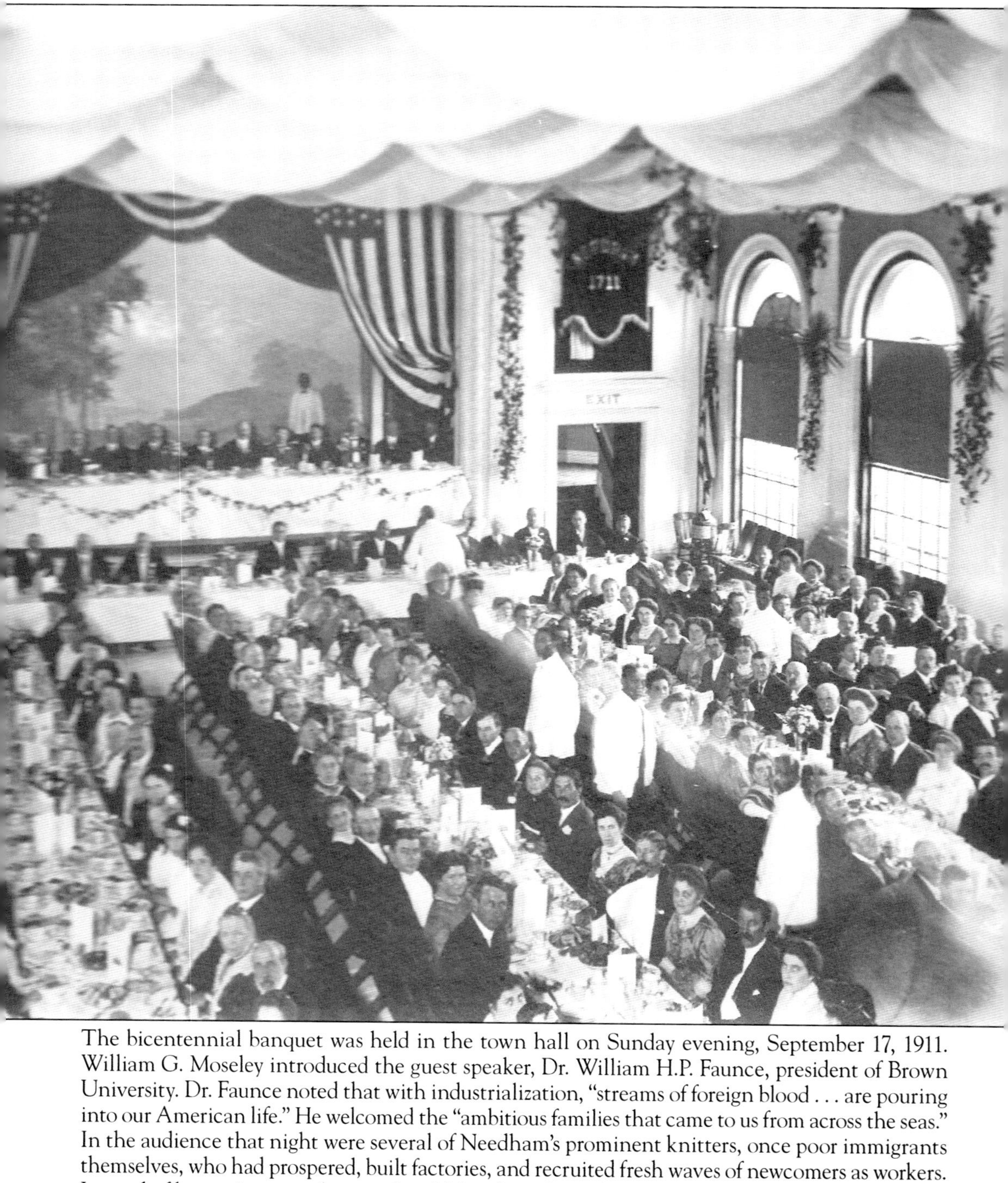

The bicentennial banquet was held in the town hall on Sunday evening, September 17, 1911. William G. Moseley introduced the guest speaker, Dr. William H.P. Faunce, president of Brown University. Dr. Faunce noted that with industrialization, "streams of foreign blood . . . are pouring into our American life." He welcomed the "ambitious families that came to us from across the seas." In the audience that night were several of Needham's prominent knitters, once poor immigrants themselves, who had prospered, built factories, and recruited fresh waves of newcomers as workers. Instead of becoming complacent, the old families of Needham were revitalized by absorbing the successful knitters.

Seven

End of the Needham Knitters

Knitting mills grew into a major American enterprise. By 1890, there were 706 hosiery and knitwear companies across the United States employing 50,000 workers, with some 40 of these companies located in Needham. The 1887 to 1888 Needham Directory listed 90 men as earning their living as knitters. Most continued to work on their own, using the traditional hand and foot operated frame-knitting machines. These small enterprises were gradually absorbed into the larger mills using power machinery.

By 1909, the 1,090 hosiery and underwear companies in the United States employed over 100,000 people. Cotton was replacing wool for a better and more comfortable fit. Because of cheap labor and efficient methods of production in Germany and Japan, imported knitted goods were half as expensive as those made in the United States. William Carter warned in 1909 that soon American industries "will be wiped out and thousands upon thousands of people will be thrown out of employment." By 1915, only 68 knitting mills remained in Massachusetts, of which 11 were in Needham. All used power machinery to knit sweaters, gloves, underwear, socks, and leggings. The smaller mills, such as Moseley, Saxony, Roper, and Wye, went out of business. In 1921, the National Association of Hosiery and Underwear Manufacturers appealed to congress to restrict imports, arguing that, "The scale of wages in Germany, France and England is far below that paid in the American textile industries."

The William Carter Company responded to the challenge by moving production to the South, where labor came cheaper. Carter built knitting mills in Barnesville, Georgia, in 1925; Forsyth, Georgia, in 1946; Senatobia, Mississippi, in 1954; Thomaston, Georgia, in 1956; Centreville, Mississippi, in 1963; and in Leola, Pennsylvania, in 1964. The headquarters of the company, but not the manufacturing, remained in Needham Heights until the 1980s. In 1999, William Carter's mills in the South, which were then manufacturers of infants and children's apparel, shut down because of increased imports.

With the opening of Route 128 and easy access to Boston, the town of Needham largely gave up manufacturing to become a commuter suburb. Needham was able to make a smooth transition from a blue-collar to an affluent white-collar community, where most of its residents traveled elsewhere to their jobs.

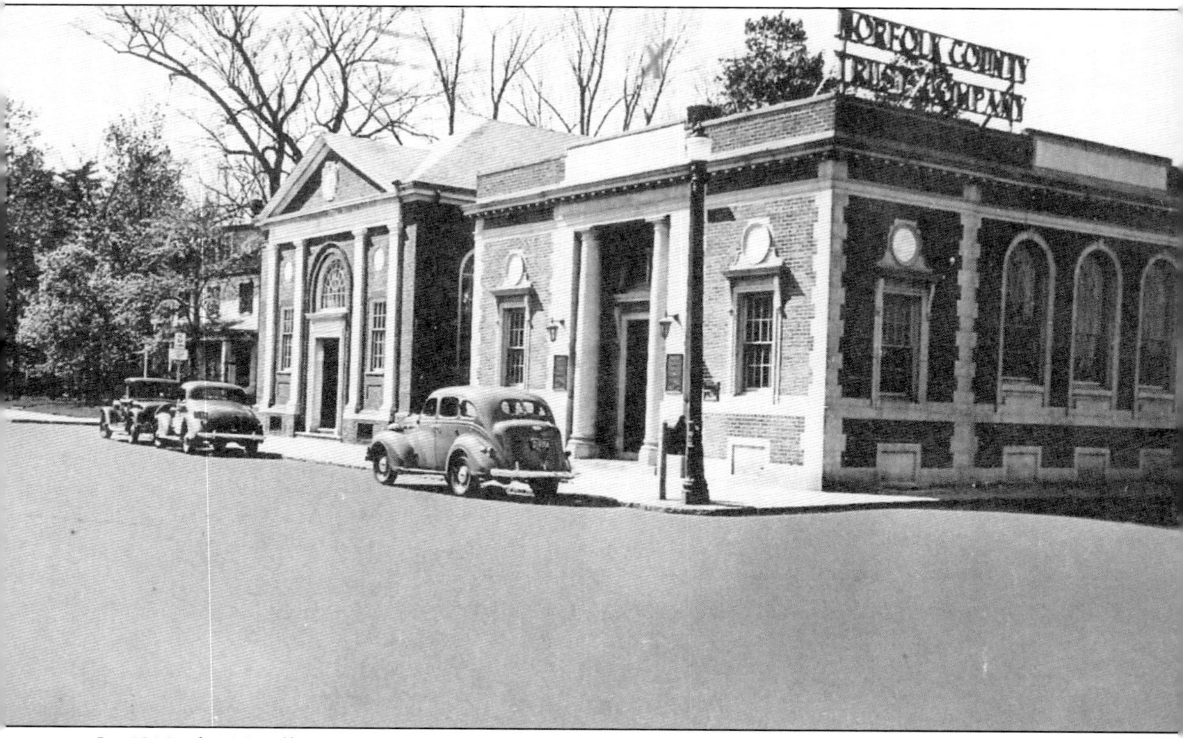

In 1910, the Needham Trust Company was established with a capital stock of $50,000. William Carter was elected president, with William G. Moseley as vice president. Amongst other knitters selected by the board as directors were John Moseley, William H. Carter, and William Wye. In 1934, the Needham Trust merged with six other banks to form the Norfolk County Trust Company, pictured here in 1939.

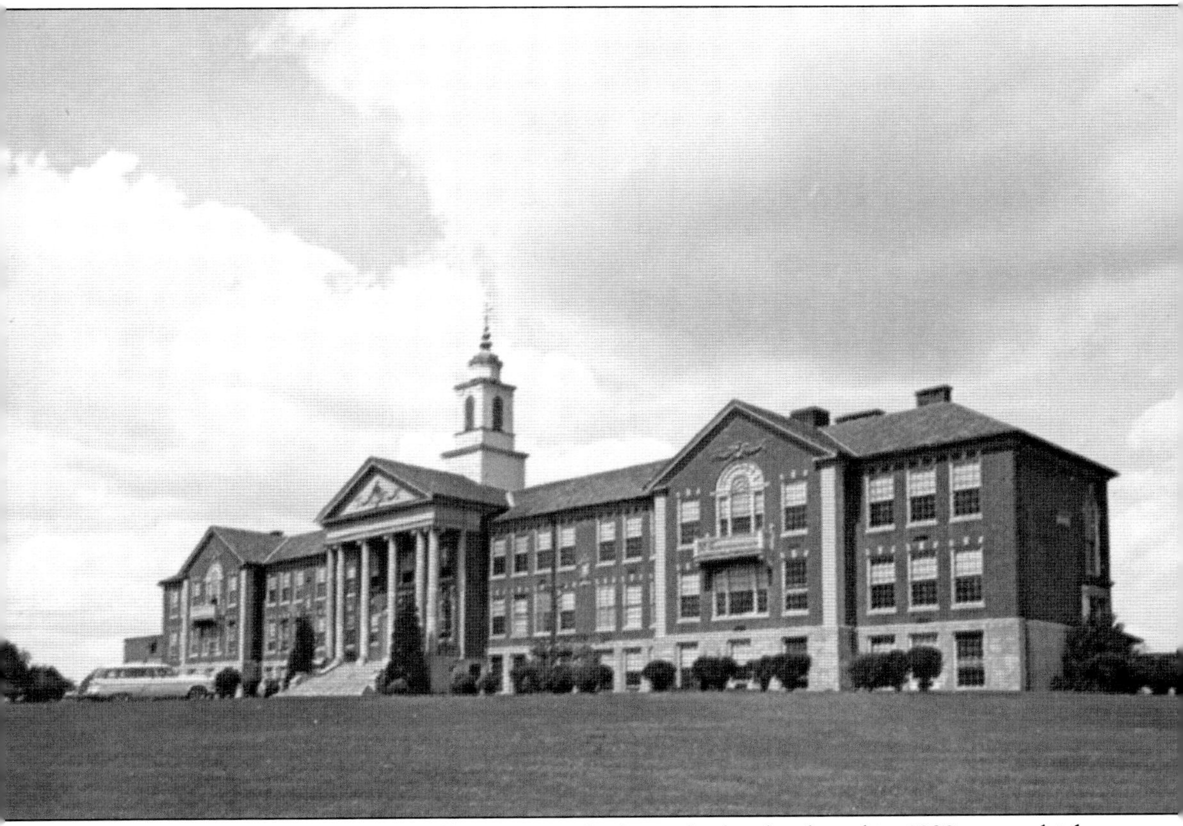

With its population growing, Needham required a larger high school, and in 1930, a new high school was opened. Sited on a hill above Memorial Park, the high school is equidistant between Needham Heights and Needham Center. The school was enlarged in 1955 and again in 1967. These additions were demolished and replaced in 2007 by classrooms and laboratories more suited to the times.

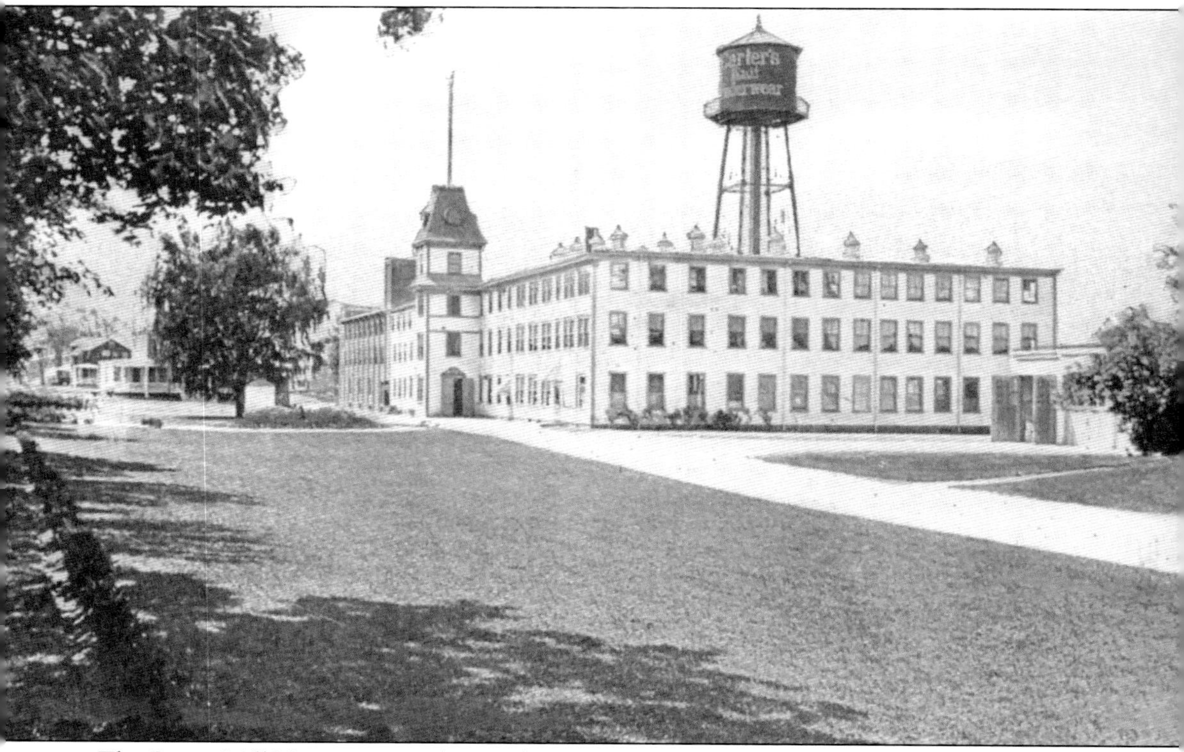

The Carter Mill No. 1 is pictured around 1910, when the manufacture of underwear in Needham was at its height. To meet growing orders for underwear, William Carter and his sons bought the Springfield Knitting Mill in Springfield, Massachusetts. After William Carter died in 1918, his sons expanded manufacturing by buying mills in the South, taking advantage of cotton at its source, and hiring cheaper labor. Carter's was following the pattern of other New England textile mills by relocating manufacturing to the South. William Carter invested heavily in the town of Needham, owning a large acreage of residential land. To the end of his long life, he remained involved in his various enterprises as well as in civic affairs.

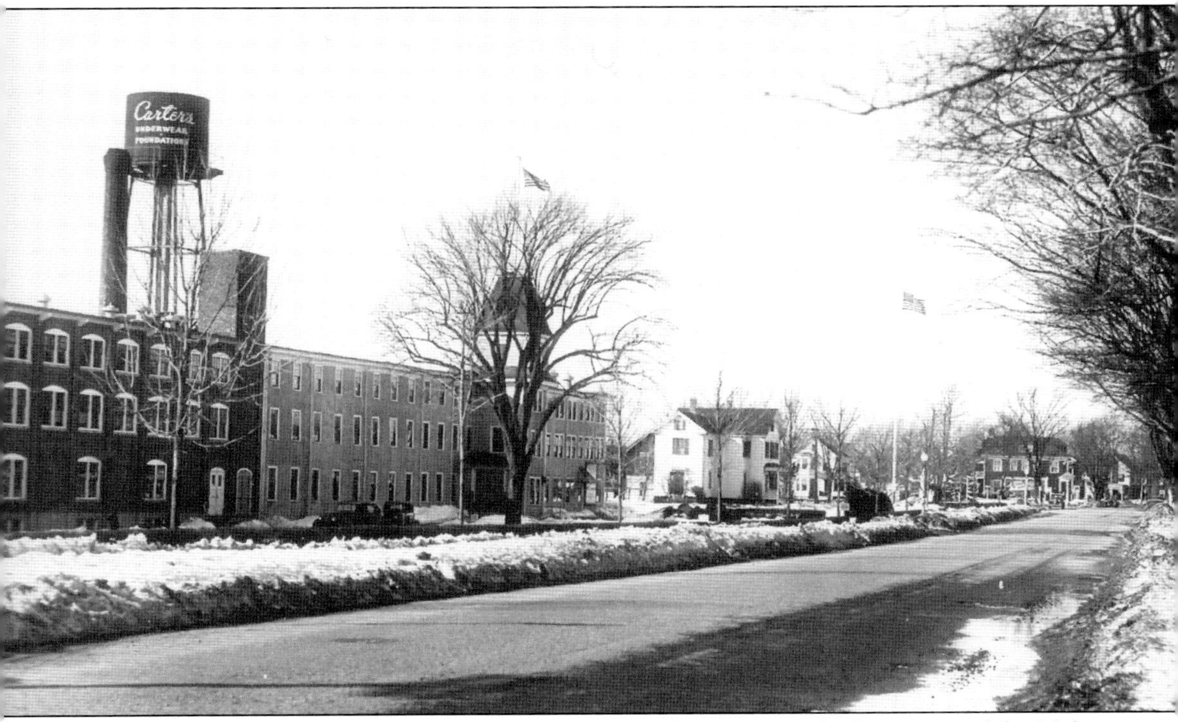

Carter's underwear plant on Highland Avenue is pictured in 1942. At the beginning of the 20th century, Carter's moved from hosiery to underwear. In the 1940s, Carter's shifted production from one-piece Union Suits to more comfortable cotton undershirts and briefs. The Middle English word "trig" can be used as an adjective to denote smart and trim in appearance. Used as a noun, it has the meaning of propping up. Carter's used the word for its new line of boys' and men's briefs, and even tried to gain copyright of the word. Starting in the late 1940s, Carter's heavily advertised its trigs: "Men and boys: Get that he-man look in Carter's Trigs." Instead of cotton, Carter's used DuPont Orlon, an acrylic fiber, for warmth without weight. Carter's Trigs were easy to wash, did not need ironing, and offered freedom of movement without itchiness.

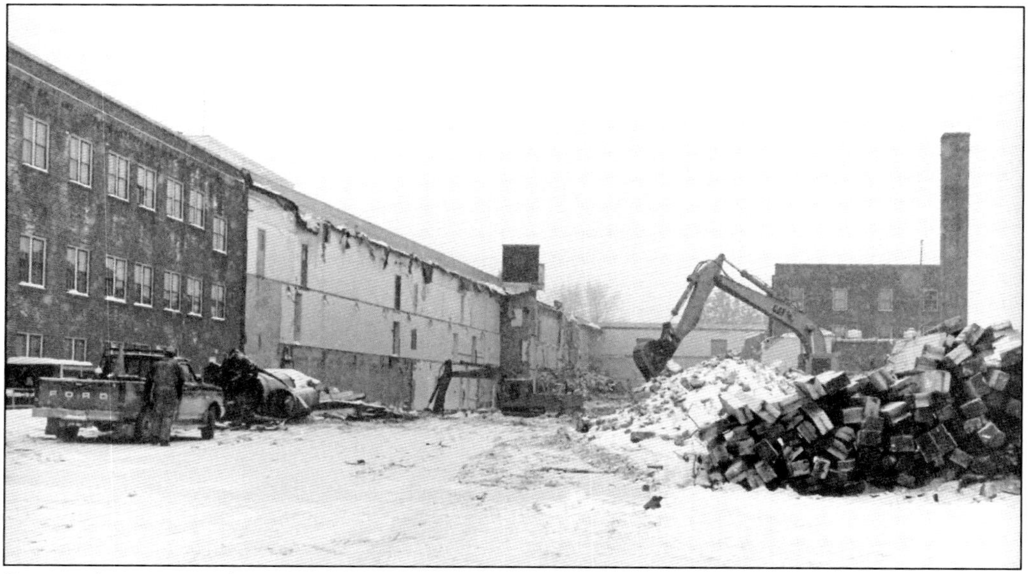

During the nineteenth century, Massachusetts led the nation in textile production. By the 1890s, attracted by low taxes, cheap labor, and low-cost cotton and energy, Massachusetts mills began opening subsidiaries in the South. By the 1950s, the textile industry had left New England and was firmly rooted in the South. Carter's Mill No. 1 on Highland Avenue was demolished in the 1950s and replaced by the administrative headquarters of the company. Calvert's clothing store opened across the street. In 1990, Carter's moved its administrative headquarters out of Needham. (Leonard Dawson Collection of the Needham Free Public Library.)

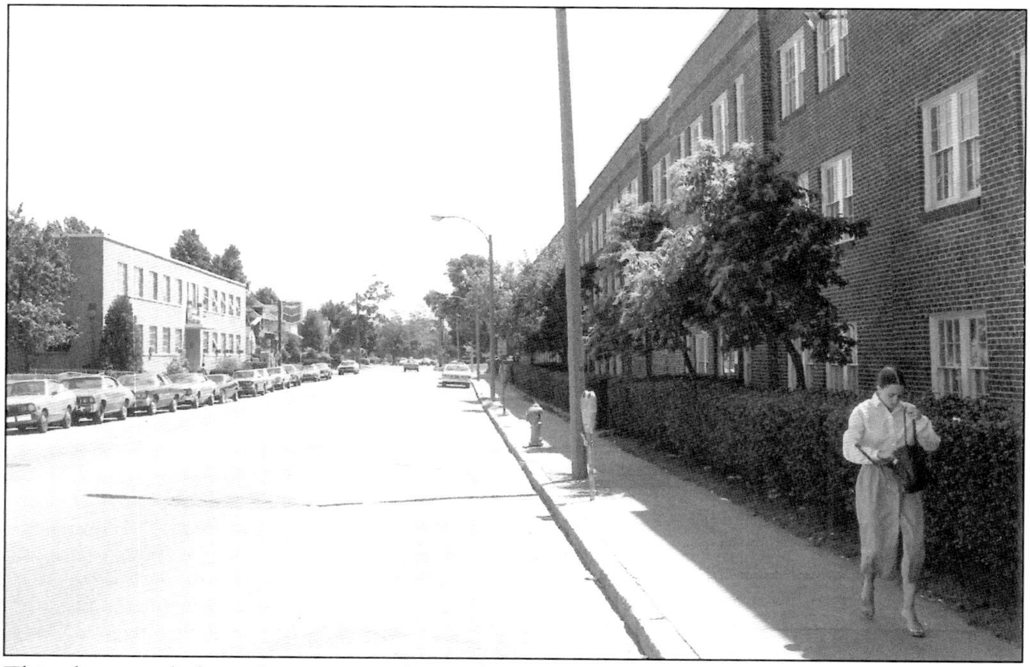

This photograph from the summer of 1979 shows Highland Avenue southbound, with Carter's administrative headquarters on the right. The three-story brick building replaced Carter's Mill No. 1, erected in 1865 with later additions. The building now houses Avery Manor, an assisted living facility.

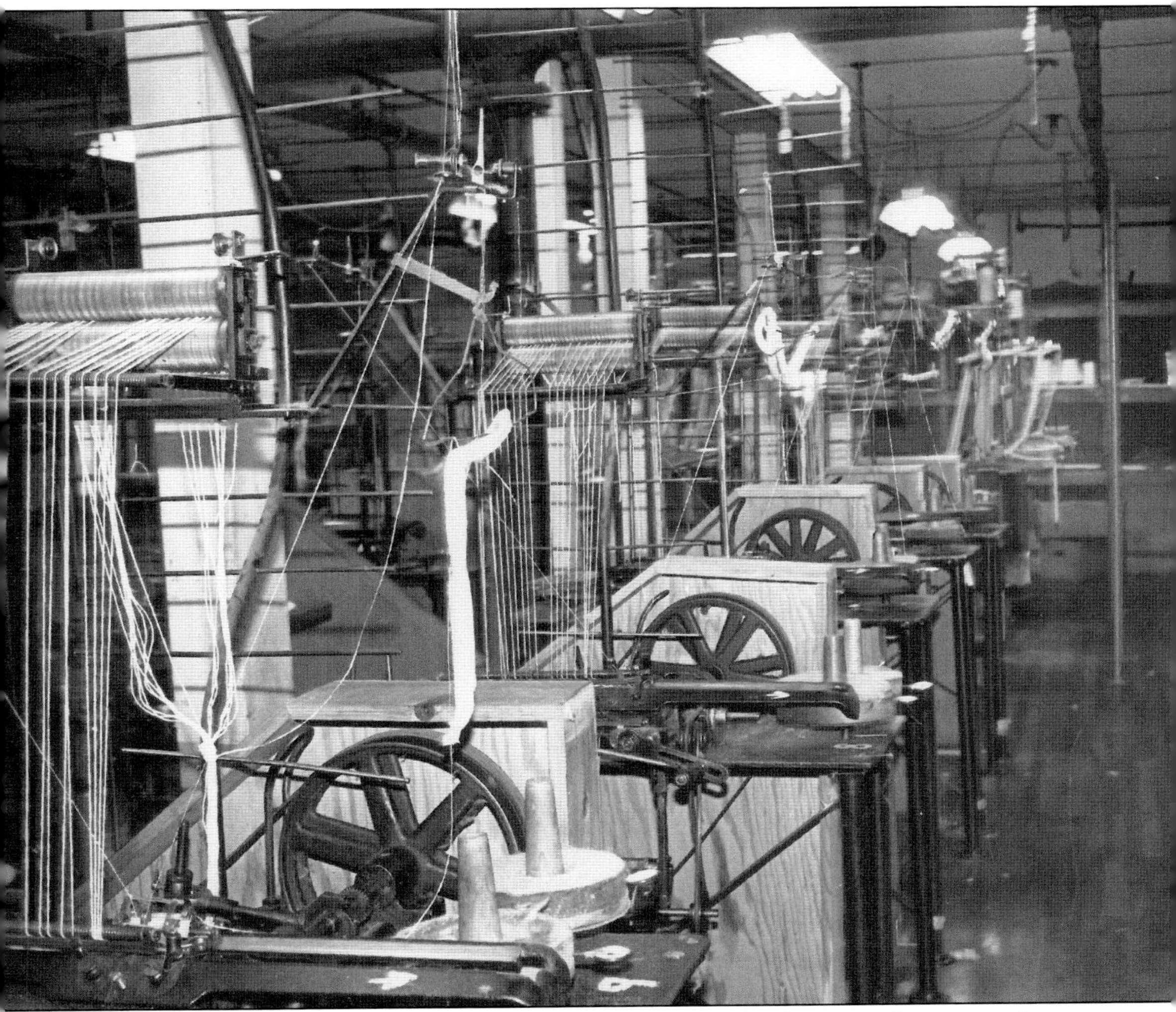

As early as the year 1900, serious problems were emerging in the American knitting industry. Companies were reducing wages and hours of work, and one company reduced average weekly pay from $15 down to $13.50. In New York, 40 knitting companies met to control their output of underwear. Other mills formed a knitting trust. With German goods shut out, World War I was a highly profitable time for the American knitting companies, but the market contracted at the war's end. Mills in New England were closing down while Spartanburg, South Carolina, which was known as the Lowell of the South, was booming. In Needham, a few mills survived well into the 20th century by offering specialized goods. This 1982 photograph of the interior of the Thorpe-Gorse Elastic knitting mill shows old and no longer used knitting machines. This was one of the last knitting mills of Needham, ending over 100 years of commercial knitting in the town. (Leonard Dawson Collection of the Needham Free Public Library.)